# LILA

# Books by Elizabeth Reyes

## Desert Heat

## Defining Love

## Moreno Brothers Series

Forever Mine

Forever Yours

Sweet Sofie

When You Were Mine

Always Been Mine

Romero

Tangled—A Moreno Brothers novella

Making You Mine

## 5th Street Series

Noah

Gio

Hector

Abel

Felix

## Fate Series

Fate

Breaking Brandon

Suspicious Minds

Again

Rage

His to Guard

Uninvited

## Boyle Heights Series

Lila (2017)

# LILA

(Boyle Heights #1)

## Elizabeth Reyes

Lila

Elizabeth Reyes

All Rights Reserved. This book may not be reproduced, scanned, or distributed in any printed or electronic form without permission from the author. Please do not participate in or encourage piracy of copyrighted materials in violation of the author's rights. All characters and storylines are the property of the author and your support and respect is appreciated.

This book is a work of fiction. The characters and events portrayed in this book are fictitious. Any similarity to real persons, living or dead, is coincidental and not intended by the author.

Copyright © 2017 Elizabeth Reyes

Edited by Theresa Wegand

Cover Design by Amanda Simpson of Pixel Mischief Design

# Prologue

## Lila

"Which one?"

Lila scanned the lunchroom full of loud rowdy kids, the one she rarely stepped foot in. She spent her lunch time by herself on the bleachers.

"It was only the one time, Lila," Ali said nervously, already tugging on her arm.

"One time too many." Lila stared out into the crowd, hoping it was someone in the group of Barbie dolls she hated so much. "You let her get away with it one time, and she'll do it even more. Which one?"

"You're gonna get suspended," Ali urged. "Can't you at least wait until after school when we can do this off school grounds?"

"No. I want every one of her fucking little friends to know what they're in for if they ever do that to you again."

Lila turned to her anxious sister. "Now tell me," she said as her fingers fisted at her side. "Which. One?"

Ali's shoulder slumped and she exhaled loudly. "Missy," she finally blurted. "She's on the left with that big group."

Lila started toward them immediately. "Are the assholes that were with her when she pushed you here too?"

"Yeah, most of them anyway."

"Good. Which one's Missy?"

It wasn't the Barbie dolls like Lila had hoped. But knowing this group had been bullying her sister for weeks and Ali hadn't said anything until they hurt her, made Lila hate them just as much. More.

"She's the tall one with the backwards baseball hat."

"The big bitch?"

"Yeah."

Lila scoffed under her breath. Typical big girl who used her size to intimidate others. She was pretend tough. Lila was about to show this broad and all her stupid friends how tough the big bitch *wasn't*.

As soon as they were close enough to Missy's crowd, some turned and snickered when they saw Ali, no doubt still amused by the scrape on her cheek from where she hit the asphalt when Missy shoved her from behind. The instant Lila reached them and stalked right through their crowd to get to Missy the snickering ceased.

Missy smirked when she saw Lila coming toward her. It was a nervous smirk, one Lila knew all too well. Any time one of these wannabe tough girls ever got called out on their shit, they had no choice but to *pretend* to not be scared. Llla could already smell her fear.

She turned around, thinking Ali would be right behind her. But she'd fallen behind as the crowd apparently closed in around Lila and Missy. Lila knew she had to move fast; the growing crowd around them would only get the attention of the dean or someone to break this up *too* soon, and she wanted to make sure they all saw the consequences of messing with her sister.

This wouldn't be the first time she'd be suspended, possibly expelled from school, but it already felt like it'd be the most satisfying.

"C'mere," she said, holding out her hand to Ali.

A few of the girls blocking Ali from getting through, moved out of the way, but one was still blocking her, so Lila shoved her. "Move!"

As soon as Ali was close enough, Lila took her arm and turned to Missy. "You've been bullying my sister and then did this to her."

She pointed at the scrape on Ali's face, which only lit her insides more, like it had when Ali finally admitted how she'd gotten it yesterday.

Missy shrugged. "I don't remember."

"Well, let me help you remember, you fucking bitch!"

Lila's fist nailed Missy right on the nose, getting a thunderous response from the crowd, mostly loud gasps and guys yelling "*damn!*" then cheering. Before Missy could bring her hand up to her already bleeding nose, Lila landed another blow making blood splatter onto the nosey onlookers standing too close, and Missy fell back onto the lunch bench. The moment she was no longer taller than Lila, she went in for her move. Grabbing a handful of Missy's hair to hold her firmly in place, Lila proceeded to pound her face repeatedly.

She'd been right. Hearing and feeling the crush of Missy's nose and then the crackle and slush of her bloodied face with every punch that followed was beyond satisfying. How dare this bitch put her hands on Lila's baby sister?

As expected, the big tough bully never laid a hand on Lila, except to try and block some of her punches. Her attempts at even that were laughable. If Lila had to guess, Missy had never been in a fight in her life.

By the time the narks pulled Lila off Missy, the girl was a bloody, blubbering mess. Even seeing the damage she'd done when they'd contained her flying fists, Lila still threw a few kicks while she was close enough.

She stopped fighting the narks once she was too far to do anymore to Missy and turned to the stunned group of Missy's friends instead. "You see that?" she barked. They all stared at her, wide-eyed. Some held their hands over their mouths. One of them even cried. She knew what she looked like to them at that moment, a raving animal. One of her foster parents had called her that once because it's what she felt like anytime her temper crossed the boiling point.

"Remember that the next time any of you even think of *looking* at my sister the wrong way," Lila barked at the still stunned crowd. As the narks began walking her away, arms twisted and held tightly behind her back, she turned to Missy, who was still crying as a few cafeteria workers tried cleaning her bloodied face. "Shake it off, bitch! Isn't that what you said to my sister yesterday when you shoved her to the ground?"

The very thought made Lila want to pound her some more, and she tried in vain to break free of the narks' hold. That only made them twist her arm farther up. "Enough, Rico!" the dean said. "You're already in enough trouble. Don't force me to expel you too."

It was a slight relief to hear this wouldn't be an automatic expulsion, not that she gave a shit about the school. She and Ali had only been attending this one for a little over a semester, and unlike Ali, who made friends almost immediately, Lila always preferred to keep to herself. Now she knew why they'd lasted this long in one place. Ali had been keeping the bullying from her. It burned her up to know this had been going on for weeks, maybe longer.

The whole way to the dean's office, Lila tried her hardest to stay on her best behavior, which was difficult given the adrenaline still pummeling through her veins. Her biggest incentive by far for not getting expelled again was

Ali. The last time her fists had gotten Lila in trouble at school, she'd been warned Ali wouldn't be coming with her if she had to go to a new school. She hadn't wanted to chance being separated from her sister, so, for months, she'd kept to herself and steered clear of any trouble. This time it just couldn't be helped.

For nearly an hour, she'd sat just outside the dean's office, waiting on him—first while he checked on Missy's condition and talked with her parents in another office and then while he made phone calls in his office to Lila's foster parents and therapist, no doubt. The last time she'd been in trouble with her foster parents was when she'd nearly strangled a middle-school punk from up her street. For weeks, he'd been a dick to the poor young pit bull he dragged around on a leash. He wanted to show off, but he didn't know the first thing about training it, so he'd drag the pup who'd often sit like a stubborn mule and refuse to move. The punk made the mistake of kicking the dog in the head to get him to move, right in front of Lila's house as she sat on the porch. It was all she could take. She jumped her own fence to grab the leash and wrapped it around the idiot's neck.

That probably would've been enough to teach the kid a lesson. Unfortunately, once in a rage like that, it was hard to come down from it and stop. Luckily for the stupid kid, she'd been pulled off him before she did too much damage. And fortunately for her, the boy had been too embarrassed to want to call the cops or report to anyone that a girl had kicked his ass.

But her foster parents had insisted she get back into therapy. After many hours of talking to her therapist, it had since been established she was "very angry." What a joke. She could've told them that from day one and saved them all a ton of money and time.

Finally, the door to the dean's office opened, and he motioned for her to come in. Dean Martinez was a tall muscular man with a wicked glare. He had a penchant for making examples out of smartasses who were stupid enough to talk back to him. But for the most part, the loud hallways literally quieted when they saw him coming. Lila could see herself being a dean someday, putting the fear of God into all the smartass trouble makers, *if* she was any good at school, that is. She wasn't stupid; she just *hated* all the boring shit, and she didn't think she could handle another four years of it, once she finally graduated from high school.

"Close the door behind you and have a seat," he said as he walked around his desk and sat down. "Why are you trying to get kicked out of school, Rico? You have less than a semester to go."

"I'm not," she said; though she was aware her indifference was anything but convincing.

"You know we have a zero tolerance for fighting here."

"And you're supposed to have a zero tolerance for bullying. That bitch—"

"Language!" his deep voice bellowed.

Lila took a deep breath. "She and her friends have been bullying my sister for weeks. Probably longer. That scrape on Ali's cheek is from that—" She paused to take another deep breath as her therapist had taught her to do to calm herself. "That Missy chick and her friends did that to her. You do that to my sister; you answer to me."

Lila looked him straight in the eye, matching his wicked glare. Zero tolerance or not, this man had to understand that, unless he could promise no one would mess with Ali, she couldn't make any promises about her behavior either.

"You're very angry," he said.

For the first time that day, she chuckled, sitting back in her chair. "My therapist tell you that?"

"He didn't have to. I saw what you did to that girl."

"And I'd do it again," she said, sitting up. "I'm all my sister has and I'll be damned if—"

"I get it," Martinez said, holding up his hand. "And trust me. I understand. But doing what you did to that girl is not the answer—"

"Bullshit! If she's gonna fuck with my—"

"Rico! I warned you about the language. I don't care *how* angry you are. You will watch that mouth when you're in my office."

Lila glared at him and nodded, remembering she *did not* want to get expelled.

"Tell me something." He sat back in his seat. "What are you gonna do if one day you beat someone so bad you get thrown in jail? Who's gonna look after your sister then?"

Still staring at him, she swallowed hard. This wasn't the first time she'd been asked this. Most of the times she'd lost it so bad were because someone had messed with her sister. The foster care system had been brutal, and she and her sister had found out real fast the only people they could rely on were each other. Ali had been born with numerous medical issues. She was better now, but those issues had done some permanent damage. Because of her hypothyroidism, she'd always struggled with her slow metabolism.

Coupled with her stunted growth, being short and plump most of her life made her a target for bullying. Even when they were very young, Lila had made sure she was clear to the bullies what they were in for if they chose her sister to pick on. Her therapist and her foster parents were always quick to point out she'd be no help to anyone if she was locked up.

Her rage was only getting worse. She felt it today. The reality was she could've killed Missy, and *that* was the real reason why she'd chosen to give her the beating in school. As incensed as she'd felt yesterday when Ali had gotten home with a swollen and scraped cheek, Lila hadn't trusted herself to beat whoever was responsible somewhere where she might have too much time to inflict her punishment on them. Even if it'd been a guy, she'd been ready to take a bat to his fucking head.

"I'm working on it," she muttered.

"Really?" This time Martinez chuckled. "How's that working out for you?"

Lila rolled her eyes, looking out the window. "I'll double up on my therapy."

"No, I don't think that's gonna work." He sat up, moved his mouse around his desk, and then typed something on his keyboard. "I hear your mother was a fighter. Boxing."

Lila shrugged, glancing back out the window, refusing to show any emotion. This wasn't something she wanted to talk about, and she didn't want to lose her patience. All she wanted was for him to tell her how long she'd be suspended for and how else she'd be paying for today. Detention? Saturday school? Whatever it was, it'd been totally worth it.

"Ever think about fighting? Like in the ring?" He peered at her curiously. "Like your mom did?"

"Nope." She glanced down at her already swelling knuckles.

"Why not?"

"Because it's stupid."

"Oh, *that's* stupid." He chuckled again. "Fighting in a controlled environment with a ref and rules to abide by is stupid. But fighting in the streets or school isn't?"

Lila didn't respond to that. She stared at the knuckles she needed to get home to ice. They were starting to hurt. Only she knew the pain would just be a pleasant reminder of how much more pain Missy was in.

"Why's it stupid?" He raised his brows, confused. "You're good at it. I saw what you did today against that big tough girl and—"

Lila scoffed, finally looking up at him. "Tough? She's not tough. She's nothing but a big bitch who likes bullying weaker and smaller kids because that's what makes her *feel* tough. And that wasn't fighting." Lila pointed to the door.

"That was me kicking her ass because she deserved it, not me against some trained fighter who might actually have a shot at hitting me. Fighting out of necessity *isn't* stupid. Fighting for the sport of it is."

"Is that why you're so angry at your mom?"

Lila glanced away. She was *not* going there today. "Am I suspended?"

"Yes." He turned from his computer screen and faced her. "And, technically, I can expel you. Missy's parents are *pissed* that the cops weren't called. They were talking about pressing charges."

"What about what she did to Ali?"

Martinez nodded, holding up a hand again. "I explained all that and that Ali is not the first one she's bullied. They know this. Based on our zero tolerance for bullying, I could have Missy expelled too."

"Then why don't you? She shouldn't be allowed—"

"Because I made a deal with them," he said before Lila could go on with her rant. "Technically, Ali could press charges against Missy too. She still has the marks from the injuries Missy caused. Dozens of witnesses saw Missy do it and others have come forward with their own complaints about Missy. The damage you did to her today is bad, Lila, and while I think it was excessive, this will probably end her days of bullying. She'll be wearing those scars for a long, *long* time. But I was able to convince her parents that it may be for the good of everyone involved if nobody presses charges and we all let bygones be bygones if we can all agree to no more violence."

Hearing the words "press charges" and the possibility of ending up in jail scared the hell out of Lila. She gulped, staring at her knuckles. "If she stays away from my sister, you have my word I won't touch her again."

"Another part of this agreement and my decision not to expel you is that I'd personally see to it that you deal with all that anger in a positive way. So, all of this comes with one more condition."

"Anything."

"I want you to go down to 5th Street, the boxing gym around the corner—"

"Expel me." Lila jumped to her feet.

"Sit down," he said as she stood there glaring at him. "Do you want me to pull you out of this school and put you into a military-type school like your foster parents are suggesting we do? One where you'll be on lock down and away from your sister until you turn eighteen?"

The hot tears from both anger and fear burned her eyes. "No."

"Then sit down." She did and the dean continued in a much calmer soothing tone. "You won't have to fight anyone. But I really think hitting a punching bag and speed bag, working off some of that anger, would be good for you. It's very therapeutic. It's what I used to do."

She stared at her knuckles again as the suffocating emotion she'd begun to feel about being locked away at some military school—away from and unable to protect Ali until she was eighteen–subsided. The thought of even putting on boxing gloves, something she'd sworn she'd never do, was still unbearable, even if she wouldn't be fighting anyone. But the thought of not being there to look after her sister, who still had three more full years of living in foster care, was worse.

"I'll do it," she whispered.

## Three-1/2 years later

This was just a trial thing. No big deal. Lila would try it, and if it wasn't for her, then she'd be done with it. End of story.

Gio, one of the 5th Street owners and a trainer, had met Lila in the private training room as promised. He'd been trying for months to convince Lila to step into the ring. She'd dropped her guard recently. For years, she trained during the slowest hours of the day at the gym, when she was certain none of the trainers would be there to notice her. She'd seen guys approached some times by trainers impressed by them, and she wanted no part of that. But in recent months, she'd had to change her schedule to accommodate the promotion. She'd gone from juice girl at the juice bar to assistant youth trainer for the special-needs youth group the gym had.

So, Gio approached her recently, saying he'd watched her train on the bags, and said she had a gift, especially when she'd told him she never had any formal training.

"I've been looking to get the women's boxing program a little recognition," he'd said when he first approached her. "We've had a few bouts lined up as undercards for the headlining fights here, but we don't get much of a turnout for them. So far, we haven't had a standout, but I think we might with you. It'd be a great opportunity for you. 5th Street has turned out a lot of worldwide champs. This could be a good career move."

Gio had been the one who gave her the chance with the youth training group. She'd since had a chance to talk to him and had mentioned she wasn't sure what she wanted to do with her future. Fitness modeling was something else she'd considered. In the last three years since she started working at the gym, she'd spent so much time there she knew she had the physique for it, but it just felt like such a long shot.

In the beginning, Lila had turned Gio's suggestion down flat. She'd meant it way back when she'd told Dean Martinez she thought fighting for the sport of it was stupid. And she'd still felt the same when Gio had hit her up a few months ago, not just for the most obvious reason—what happened to her mother. But she just couldn't see herself getting punched in the face for a living; though Gio had made an excellent point.

"With your speed and God-given talent, I seriously doubt anyone will be landing many punches on you."

He also pointed out that, for the most part, she'd be fighting with headgear on. What really had her considering it now was he'd also said it could be a good way to get noticed by fitness-modeling scouts.

"We already have some excellent agents representing a lot of the boxers as well as the models who work out here on a regular basis." Gio had pointed out a few of those models, both female and male. "You're right up there, fitness-wise, with most of them, but you'd be in even higher demand to sponsors wanting you to endorse their clothes or equipment if you also have a boxing title. We're talking big bucks here."

Lila had never been greedy. Having lots of money was never on her list of priorities. But it would be nice to be able to afford to live in a safer neighborhood. Nice to be able to afford to have two reliable cars so she and Ali didn't have to share the not-so-reliable one they shared now. Most of the time, she made Ali take it while Lila opted for the bus or to walk home. She'd had Ali take the self-defense class at 5th Street almost as soon as she'd found out about it years ago, and had made sure she took a refresher class at least once a year since. But Lila still worried about her sister and knew the odds of Lila fighting off a would-be attacker were much better than Ali fighting one off.

More than anything, Lila wanted to be able to help put Ali through school. Her dream was to become a journalist someday, only since they both needed to work, Ali could only afford to go part-time to a community college. Lila had pretty much accepted the road to Ali's degree would be a long one. Her own career would likely consist of staying at 5th Street, maybe becoming a full-time youth instructor.

Then Gio began getting in her ear, and trying the boxing thing didn't sound too bad now. She had to admit that having bigger dreams did excite her a little.

"So, what we need to start with is technique, try to figure out what your strengths and weaknesses are, if any. Then we work on them." Gio jumped into the ring. "Get in here. We'll start with you punching the pads so I can get an idea of your strengths."

Trying to stay calm and not get too nervous about this as she'd knew she'd be, she concentrated on something nice, just like her therapist had always shown her. Something nice. Gio's eyes. They were hard not to get caught up in. They were this beautiful light green.

Lila also did her best to concentrate on the training by focusing on the pads in his hands and the different types of punches he began showing her. Each one she got almost immediately. She'd been doing them, not realizing she was mimicking some of the boxers she'd seen in the gym or that each punch had a name: the jab, a hook, an uppercut, the cross, and the overhand.

Gio stared at her, stunned. "You're left-handed?" She nodded as he continued to peer at her weirdly then put up his left pad. "Give me an uppercut with your right hand." She did and he smiled big. "Now try a right hook. Again . . . again . . . again!"

Each time she did, he got louder and more excited.

He'd promised her their first session would be a private one, so she was puzzled when he had her stop and pulled out his phone then alarmed when she heard what he said into it. "Get in here. You gotta see this. Bring Hector with you."

As soon as he hung up, she was on him. "You said today would be private."

"It's just Noah and Hector," he said quickly. "No one else. You're a natural, Lila. You have a gift. Are you sure you've never boxed before?"

"Never," she said for a moment, thinking of her mom and her grandfather, but she wasn't bringing that up.

"So far you have no weaknesses." He smiled big, those green eyes sparkling. "*Zero*. I'm not sure if I'm just a little too excited for my own good. It's why I want Noah and Hector to watch you and—"

They both turned when the door to the training room opened and Noah and Hector strolled in. Lila had met them a few times but only spoke with either on a few occasions. It felt awkward at the time. But she knew now they all tried to meet and greet every single one of their employees. Even Felix and Abel, the other two much more famous owners, had made it a point to introduce themselves. Before either could say anything, Gio said a word she'd heard before.

"Ambidextrous." That made Noah's and Hector's eyes open wide. "She's just as strong with both hands, and she's got crazy speed. So far, I can't find a weakness."

As awkward and unnerving as it was to stand there listening to Gio gush about her, it was also strangely exciting. She still wasn't sure about this, and the way he was talking sounded like this was a sure thing, given her *gift* and all.

Gio turned to Lila, putting up the pads, and asked her for a combination of punches using both hands. She did and once again he smiled big with excitement. When she was done, he turned to Noah and Hector, who were now peering at her just as Gio had earlier.

"You've never fought?" Noah asked skeptically. "Not even for fun?"

"Boxing, no, but I've been in fights." She glanced away before clarifying. "Brawls. Never using gloves though and . . ." She shrugged with a smirk, remembering the most satisfying and last *real* beat down she'd given anyone—Missy's. "I guess some were fun."

"But you've never been in a ring before?" Hector asked this time.

"First time." She scratched an itch on her forehead with the back of her glove.

"No weaknesses, huh?" Noah asked, sounding doubtful. "Let's see her footwork."

"We haven't gotten to that yet," Gio explained.

Noah got in the ring and went over some basics, bobbing and weaving then blocking and parrying. He, too, seemed impressed by how quickly she caught on.

"Show her how to slip a punch," Hector said, leaning his arms against the top rope of the ring with the same twinkle of excitement in his eyes as Gio.

Noah did, and within minutes, she had that down too. "Get a girl in here." He turned to Hector. "See if Trina's here."

"No." Lila's stomach knotted up. "Gio said this would be private. I don't want anyone knowing I'm doing this yet. This is just a trial thing."

"Sweetheart," Noah said with an incredulous smile. "You're a born boxer. You *have* to do this."

Lila started pulling the strings of her gloves with her teeth as her insides began to ripple. "I said I'd think about it. I'm not sure—'

"Hold on." Noah held his hand up. "Alright, we won't get anyone else in here. But don't take them off yet. I just wanna try something."

"I don't want anyone else in here," she reiterated through her teeth.

"I said I wouldn't get anyone else in here," Noah reassured her. "But I still wanna try something."

She stopped pulling at the strings and let Gio retie them.

"I'd prefer a girl to do this, but if we can't get one, then I guess I can try it. Of course, we won't go full force. This is just a test." He turned to Hector. "Get headgear and a mouthpiece on her."

"Are you serious?" Hector's face contorted. "You can't spar with her, dude."

"I'm not gonna swing for real." Noah rolled his eyes. "I'm not even putting on gloves. It's just a test." He lowered his voice, but Lila still heard him. "*Everyone* has a weakness."

Hector handed the headgear and mouthpiece to Gio, who placed them on Lila. They reminded her of her mother. She'd seen her wearing them in her earlier years, but then later her mother began the fights with no headgear.

"Okay." Noah lifted his fists in front of him in a blocking stance. "You go ahead and swing at me as hard as you want, but block me when I reach around. I'm just looking to touch you and see how fast you are at blocking. I wanna test your reflexes. I'll only go for your headgear, and I'm not punching, but expect a good nudge. Okay?"

Lila nodded, bringing her gloves up in front of her. As soon as he gave her the go-ahead, she tried to punch him, but he blocked it each time then reached around her gloves and touched the side of her headgear. *Hard.* He'd warned her he would, but it still pissed her off. She swung at him again, this time landing one on his chest, and he laughed.

"Good one!" He reached around and she blocked him, but he was fast. He went the other way and got the other side of her headgear this time.

That time it was hard enough to make her head move. She hadn't even had a chance to recover when he pushed the other side of her head, making her lose her balance slightly and see red. She punched at him furiously, making him back away. "Whoa." He held his hands out. "Easy."

Lila spit her mouthpiece out and charged him. "Easy, my fucking ass!" Seeing him smile and then laugh as he easily blocked her punches only infuriated her further. "Asshole!" She continued in vain to try and land more, but he blocked each one.

Feeling someone try to pull her away only made her spin around, and she almost punched Gio but completely missed and nearly lost her balance. If it weren't for the rope she fell on, she would've gone down. There was more laughing, this time from Hector. She turned and glared at him, trying to take off her gloves as she struggled to catch her breath.

"I think we found her weakness," Hector said, smiling big. "Sloppy as shit when you get hot."

"Temper, temper," Noah tsked with a smirk.

Lila turned to Gio. "Get this shit off me."

"Wait up," Gio started to say. "You can't just let—"

"Get 'em off," she said louder.

Noah and Gio exchanged glances and Noah shrugged.

"Misplaced negative energy in the ring is a waste," Hector said as she watched Gio untie her gloves, still breathing hard. "You gotta learn to make it work for you not *against* you. But it's okay. That's part of training."

"I'm done training."

"*What?*" Gio asked, exasperated.

The moment she was free of all the gear she went through the ropes and jumped out of the ring, even as Noah and Gio called out after her. Lila wanted nothing more than to get the hell out of there, but she had a class to supervise in less than an hour. She couldn't afford to lose this job. Already, she'd called one of her bosses an asshole. She needed to get it together, so she went into the employees' ladies' room and splashed her face. Taking long deep breaths with her eyes closed, she concentrated on her happy place: the beach. Aside from the pool at a local park, it was the only place her mother could afford to take them recreationally every summer when they were much younger, and Lila had loved it.

She was just in the beginning stages of calming herself down but still on the testy side, when a girl she'd never seen in the gym and who was clearly a bottle blonde walked into the bathroom. The "employees only" sign on the door couldn't be clearer. They used a cabinet in there to stash some of their things such as extra feminine products and toiletries. Lila had been known to leave her phone in there when she was in a hurry and couldn't make it to her locker. It was supposed to be a safe place, and she was sick of seeing gym members who knew better, or potential members like this chick who wasn't even dressed to work out, walk right in.

"Are you an employee?" she asked bluntly, staring at the girl through the mirror.

"No," Blondie said, lifting her brow. "But I'm here with my boyfriend, the superstar athlete, the one and only—"

"So?" Lila said, lifting and dropping her shoulder, completely unimpressed. "I didn't ask you who you were here with. This is an employees-only restroom. That means employees *only*. You can use the public one by the entrance like everyone else who's *not* an employee."

"I beg your pardon?" The girl's brows lifted as she brought her hand to her chest, looking completely appalled. "First, not only is my boyfriend a huge name in sports, I'm also a guest here for other reasons. I'm a sports journalist who interviews some of the biggest names in sports, including some of the owners of this place. My boyfriend's also the one who told me it was okay for me to use this restroom."

Lila threw her used paper towel in the trash can, clenching her jaw. This wasn't the first time she'd been irritated by the pretentious boxers' girlfriends. Apparently, there was a new one or this was a new girlfriend to one of the regulars. "Maybe you should tell your *boyfriend* that neither journalists nor any of his girlfriends are *employees* of this gym. There's a sign on the door for a reason."

"I think I'll do that right now." Blondie huffed as if that might make Lila feel threatened.

"You do that."

"I will."

With that, the girl and her little attitude marched her ass right out of that bathroom before Lila could tell her what she could do with it.

As irritating as that had been, it made her feel better to see the pampered little bitch, who was likely used to getting her way, have to walk out of there without getting to use the bathroom.

"One of those days, huh?" Stacia asked as they got out of the car.

Lila groaned. "Don't get me started."

Aside from the huge fail in the ring with Noah then her little run-in with the smug journalist in the restroom, she'd also had to deal with a sick kid in her youth-fitness program. She knew a lot of the single moms in the area used the program as more of a babysitting option than anything, but it was still unfair for this mom to drop him off like that, knowing he might be contagious. He threw up twice for fuck's sake.

Lila shared that part of her day with Stacia—that and the incident in the employee bathroom with the blow-hard journalist. But she kept the other part of her day to herself. She wasn't ready to tell *anyone* about that. She wasn't even sure if she really was through with the idea of giving boxing a shot. It was just frustrating as hell that, after all these years of trying, she still couldn't get a handle on her temper.

They stood in line outside the small club where they'd be watching The Ratz perform in a VIP section. They were a band Stacia's fiancé, Derek, had gotten her into. Stacia and Derek had driven out to Vegas just to see them more than once. The Ratz were finally performing here in Los Angeles, and Derek had gone all out and bought VIP tickets. Unfortunately for him and Lila, he was a highway patrolman and had gotten recalled at the last minute. Lila had never been the club type. Unlike most people who couldn't wait to turn twenty-one to be able to go to the twenty-one-and-over clubs, Lila had hit the milestone over five months ago, and this would be her first time at a club.

She'd like to think she'd grown in the almost four years since she'd last been in trouble, that she'd freed herself a little of the angry anti-socialite she'd become, especially after Marcelo's unceremonious departure. Coming to 5th Street really had been a saving grace for Lila. Not only had it helped her deal with her anger issues, it was also her first job. It was where she met Stacia. Aside from Ali, Stacia was now the only other person Lila trusted completely. Marcelo had lost his spot on that list when he decided to leave without so much as a good-bye.

Not only did Stacia help her get her first job, Lila would be eternally grateful to her friend for helping her and Ali get their own place. A little over a year ago, Lila and Ali were still at a low-income, state-assisted building in a rundown, roach-infested apartment in East Los Angeles. Stacia's roommate had moved out suddenly, and she needed a new roommate fast. With Lila's new promotion from juice-bar girl to the youth-program assistant at 5th Street, she could afford the other half of Stacia's rent. She and Ali were finally out of that horrid neighborhood. The Boyle Heights project, where Stacia's apartment was located, wasn't the most glamorous, but it was a step up from her old neighborhood.

There'd been a few incidents since she'd met Stacia almost four years ago, incidents that thankfully had happened outside of the gym. But Stacia had been there and witnessed Lila's infamous temper. Not once had it ever been directed toward Stacia, who'd always been sympathetic to Lila about it. Stacia got that Lila was trying to break free from that destructive behavior and her knee-jerk reactions. Lila was an adult now. Dire consequences could result from just reacting, and she'd already paid for one. While Lila had made great strides in controlling that explosive part of her when it came to certain things annoying her to no end, today's incident with Ms. Bitch was proof that she still had her work cut out for her.

The incident in the ring with Noah was another story. Lila doubted she'd ever be able to refrain from reacting to anyone putting their hands on her. It was why, aside from her personal reasons, she'd never even considered boxing until Gio began insisting. Like with Noah, if anyone ever got physical with her in a negative way, she'd lose her shit in an instant.

"You're gonna have to get rid of that." Stacia pointed at the Big Gulp cup of iced tea Lila was holding. "They won't let you in with it."

Lila glanced around, downing most of the rest because she didn't want to waste it. The only trashcan she spotted was on the other side of the small alley next to the building.

"I'll be back." She started toward the trashcan, still sucking away at her tea.

Just as she took a step across the alley, a car skidded loudly, making her jump back. Even as her heart pounded, Lila cussed under her breath about the tea she spilled on her T-shirt. When she looked up at the car that had come inches from hitting her, the guy behind the wheel mouthed the word *sorry*.

Another guy popped his head out of the moon roof. "You okay, sweetness? Need a little help cleaning up? I got two extra hands here."

It was only then that she realized it was a limo. Lila refrained from throwing her cup at him like she wanted to. Ignoring him, she walked around the front end of the car to the trashcan. The limo pulled out of the alley and stopped as the back window of the limo reached the sidewalk. A guy in the back seat—not the douche in the moon roof—held out napkins to her. "I apologize for my driver, and I'm not even sure what to say about the guy up there." Their eyes met just long enough for her to notice how deep blue his were. Then her own eyes were on that perfect yet familiar smile. "Seriously though, are you okay?"

If it weren't for the fact that she had a major wet spot on her T-shirt, she might not have accepted the napkins. "Thanks. I'm fine." She took the napkins then walked around the limo from behind.

"Are you okay?" Stacia asked as soon as Lila reached her.

Lila nodded, still focused on wiping the tea off her T-shirt. "Yeah, but your shirt might be stained. I spilled my tea on it."

"Who cares about that. I'm just glad that stupid limo driver saw you in time."

Lila shrugged with a frown. "My fault too. I didn't even look up the alley before walking across. It just scared the shit outta me, but other than the wet T-shirt, no harm done."

They finally made it to the door of the club and entered. "Thank you." Stacia smiled big at the doorman who pointed them in the direction of the stairs to the VIP area. Lila's excitable friend turned back to her with a big smile. "Derek said there might even be celebrities in the VIP room. This band is way bigger in Vegas, where they originate from, but they've been expanding and touring different cities now. And while they used to have mostly a cult following, their following is getting much bigger. Just remember." She touched Lila on the arm. "Derek said to try and not be too starry-eyed and definitely don't do anything embarrassing like ask for autographs in the VIP area or what not."

Stacia laughed when Lila gave her *the* look. As if she were the type to get starry-eyed over *anyone*, much less approach them for an autograph. As big as Felix and Abel were, the most she'd done when she first saw them was stare from afar and made sure she did so very discreetly. As exciting as it'd been to see them in person and later meet them, she'd *never* felt starry-eyed.

"Okay, okay." Stacia laughed as they entered the VIP area. "I guess what I'm really saying is don't let *me* do anything stupid."

This time Lila laughed. That made far more sense than her warning Lila. Stacia had to coax her to come to this in the first place. They both knew the only thing she'd be doing tonight was watching the band. Lila didn't even drink.

They walked around for a bit, trying to find two open seats together. They finally found a perfect spot by the railing with a great view of the stage downstairs. Stacia hurried to the small table and set her phone down on it before anyone else could claim it. It was a close call. A couple of other girls had been headed straight to it just before Stacia got there first. As expected, the girls eyed them with a little attitude.

Since Stacia was engaged now and was supposed to have come here tonight with Derek, she'd purposely dressed down tonight. She'd told Lila not to worry about dressing up. This was a laid-back kind of band.

The girls who gave Lila and Stacia a sneer then exchanged smirks were all done up, tits and asses hanging out of their teeny tiny painted on outfits. Stacia was in jeans she'd dressed up with a pair of black boots but wore an old Ratz T-shirt. While Stacia wore far more makeup and did her hair in a more girlie do than Lila ever did, she was nowhere as done up as those girls.

Lila had worn her hair down, something she didn't do often. But the closest she'd ever gotten to being girlie was wearing what Stacia referred to as her sexy low-rise jeans like the ones she'd worn tonight. She'd also worn one of Stacia's T-shirts. Lila wasn't opposed to the tighter than her normal T-shirt or even the lower than her usual V-neck. Stacia insisted if she had the goods she should show them off. Lila had the goods alright, and she wore sports crop tops for working out because they were just more comfortable than a baggy T-shirt. The short T-shirt Stacia had coaxed her into wearing to show off her equally impressive abs made her uncomfortable. Showing off a little skin in the gym was one thing, but Lila refused to be confused for one of those slutty-looking bitches who clearly didn't appreciate Lila and Stacia beating them to the table.

Tugging at the bottom of her T-shirt for the hundredth time, Lila glanced around. "Maybe having that Big Gulp in line wasn't such a good idea. I have to go, bad."

"Well, you're going alone. We'll just take turns. I ain't giving up this table." Stacia frowned, looking down at Lila's hand. "And will you stop trying to tug it down. You're gonna stretch it. It's sexy, not slutty, to show off a little midriff. You look fine. I promise." She pointed behind Lila. "The bathrooms are probably through that hallway over there."

Lila turned to where Stacia was pointing, unable to keep herself from glancing in the direction of the girls she hadn't been aware were still eyeballing them. Yep. They were still at it. Really? Over a table? And *this* was why she didn't drink. She'd grown out of and was beyond the immaturity of needing to address this kind of shit with a stare down like back in her middle and high school days.

She was an adult now. While she'd never been drunk, she'd been around enough drunks in her lifetime to know how stupid and uncharacteristically brave alcohol could make some people. She'd take a few puffs of weed any day over alcohol. That stuff did just the opposite for Lila. It calmed her nice and good. She hadn't done it in ages because she was trying to set an example for her sister and because

5th Street policy was that they reserved the right to randomly test for drug use, especially since she was the assistant in charge of the *youth* program now.

Glancing one last time at the broads, Lila rolled her eyes. If these girls didn't do anything more antagonizing than just give them stupid looks, Lila could be cool.

She stood up, mindful not to keep stretching Stacia's T-shirt. "Okay, I'll be back," she said, tapping the table with her hand. "I just hope there's not a line."

"This is VIP, baby. I'm assuming that means the restroom situation isn't what it normally is at clubs."

Lila could only hope, because she had to go *bad* now. It was almost a joke how hard some of these girls seemed to try to be noticed by all the guys there. Did they not know all they had to do was make eye contact and crack a smile to have these horny assholes following them around all night? Not that Lila had any club experience, but it'd happened more than once at the gym. And it was annoying as shit. It was during the time where she was trying to be friendlier—nicer. A smile was all it had taken. One damn smile.

After a couple of annoying guys followed her around the gym, trying to make small talk and feeding her cheesy lines, she'd gone back to avoiding eye contact at all costs, especially when she was not in the mood to deal with that stuff, which was often. Let them think she was an anti-social bitch. Unlike most of the slutty girls at the gym, working out with full on makeup and barely there workout outfits, Lila wasn't there to find a man.

The same mentality went hand in hand with night clubs. Agreeing to come here tonight so Stacia's VIP tickets wouldn't go to waste was one thing. Lila may've never been to a club, but she'd been to plenty of backyard parties in her day. This didn't seem all too different as far as leering guys who did nothing to make their elevator eyes discreet. From what she could see, this was a meat market too. Everyone here was looking to either get laid or find their soul mate, which was an even bigger joke. She'd watch the show with Stacia, and it'd probably be the last club she'd be stepping into for a while.

Lila cursed under her breath when she saw the line to the ladies' room. "VIP my ass," she muttered as she reached the back of the line.

The door at the end of the hall opened, causing an instant buzz. A few guys in similar black T-shirts walked out. They made their way slowly through the crowded hallways, stopping a few times to take selfies with some of the girls in line for the restroom and chat a bit. Lila watched, refraining from rolling her eyes so openly at the girls swinging their hair over their shoulders with their big fake laughs.

Obviously, these were band members; though Lila didn't recognize a single one. She'd heard their music plenty. Stacia played it enough. But Lila had only ever seen them on her T-shirt where the photos of them weren't that clear and then a few times online. She accidently made eye contact with one of them, and he smiled, pointing at her shirt, then gave her the thumbs-up. Lila smiled but looked away quickly. All eyes were on him and the rest of the group. She *did not* want all those eyes on her too.

The rest of the band members and their entourage continued to make their way slowly through the crowded hallway. Lila could only hope some of the girls in line falling all over themselves to get noticed would follow them out so the line would get shorter.

Things calmed once the band and their entourage were gone. The line had barely moved, and Lila stood there discreetly starting to dance in place because she had to go so bad. Why the hell had she drunk that entire Big Gulp?

As she glanced around, the door at the end of the hallway opened again. This time three other guys, who didn't look anything like band members because they were dressed more refined than the torn jeans and black T-shirts the band members had worn, came out. They were also a lot bigger—like body guards—club security maybe?

Lila's eyes zoomed in on the tallest, biggest of the three. She'd never proclaimed to have a type, but if she had to be honest, she tended to be drawn to big guys, the taller the better. As big as this guy was, he had to be part of the group's or club's security team. All three men stood out, but he was by far the most impressive.

It wasn't until she brought her eyes back up that she noticed he'd caught her ogling him like a piece of meat. What was worse, she was still dancing in place, and he wore a playful smirk now as he took her in from top to bottom. That's when she realized who he was, the guy in the back of the limo.

Beyond annoyed with herself, Lila turned away without so much as a smile in return. Not only had she done the very thing she'd been trying to avoid since she'd walked into the place, she'd been so busy ogling him she didn't notice the line had moved. With a frown, she crossed her arms in front of her still damp T-shirt and moved up to close the big gap between her and the girl in front of her. She also stopped the dancing in place and refused to look anywhere but straight ahead. Aside from his eyes being that odd color of in between blue and gray, the other thing she remembered about seeing him in the backseat of that limo was that there had been girls in the car with them.

Staring straight ahead as the guys in front of him went past her, Lila did her best to not even glance in their direction.

"There's—"

Lila flinched at the unexpected whispered word in her ear. She was even more surprised to turn and see it was *him*. He flashed that perfect smile that for some reason felt genuine. "Sorry, didn't mean to startle you." He leaned in and lowered his voice again, giving her a good whiff of whatever subtle but very pleasant-smelling cologne he was wearing, unlike some of the overpowering ones she'd smelled on a few other guys tonight. "I can get you into a private bathroom in the back room if you really have to go." He pulled away and looked her in the eyes then smiled once again. "I saw the jumbo-sized cup you were drinking from out there. Not sure if you're gonna make the wait."

If Lila's bladder was even the slightest bit less close to bursting, she would've turned him down flat, perfect smile and all. But she had to go *so* bad. Just the thought of being that much closer to relief made the ache in her bladder worse. She wasn't sure who was more surprised at her agreeing so quickly—her or the guy. His eyes went even bigger and seemed to twinkle when she nodded. Almost as if he was afraid she might change her mind, he held his hand out for her.

"I'll meet you out there," he said to one of the guys he'd walked out with.

Desperate didn't even *begin* to describe how she'd begun to feel. It was why she'd done something so unlike her and didn't protest his leading her by the hand to the back room. It wasn't even until she was in the damn bathroom, blissfully relieved to have made it there without wetting herself, that she realized what she'd just done. She'd let a stranger take her into a back room of a club. Now she was perfectly alone with him. A very large stranger—albeit a good-looking one with a genuinely sweet smile—but a stranger nonetheless. Even Stacia would have no idea what happened to her if she got raped and dumped in the back alley.

After washing her hands, she clenched them at her side. This guy might be big, but she'd taken that self-defense class with Ali, even though she didn't think she needed it. Even before taking the class, she'd known exactly where to aim for if need be, but she'd learned a few new tricks in the class too.

"Thank you," she said as she walked out of the bathroom.

The guy had made himself comfortable on the sofa in the room. He'd better think again if he thought she'd be doing the same. He stood up, and now that she wasn't distracted by the torture of an aching bladder, she noticed a few more things about him. For someone with eyes that could go so light blue they were almost gray, his hair was very dark. When he'd first walked out the back door, she pegged him as security because he looked so big, but this close she could see he was slim in all the right places with a very impressive physique, yet big in all the right places as well. He wasn't wearing an ear piece like the guys at the door.

For the second time that night, Lila did something uncharacteristic of herself. She decided to give into her curiosity and just ask. "Are you security for the band?"

The expression on his face was a strange one. It seemed amused with a hint of something else she couldn't quite make out. Surprised or suspicious maybe?

"No." He shook his head. "No, I'm not."

"Oh."

Despite that his smile bordered on the smug side, he didn't come across as your usual arrogant jerk who knew he was hot. Without Lila knowing anything about him, he seemed far more likable. Maybe it was that he took the time to apologize outside about his driver and his friend and even offered napkins. Lila wasn't sure what it was. All she knew was he didn't appear dangerous.

Something about that smug yet friendly smile, coupled with the fact that he wasn't dressed like a wannabe rocker like so many others in attendance, deemed him safe. He seemed a bit older than most of the boys here too—mature—and his attire was far classier with the untucked, buttoned-up long-sleeved shirt he rolled up to his elbows and his crisp dark denim jeans. Not like the holey and faded jeans most of the rocker wannabes wore. His entire presence was far more respectable as he'd sort of proven outside. At least it was what her head had started to convince her of, what she would tell Stacia when she admitted to going into a back room alone with a stranger.

"Well, thank you for letting me use the bathroom in here." She started for the door. "I really appreciate it."

"Can I get your name?" he asked as he also started to the door.

"Lila." Their eyes met, but she glanced away quickly, cursing inwardly at the strangeness in her belly.

"Lila?"

Lila turned to him again because the way he said her name sounded like he was about to ask her something. But he didn't. Instead, she was treated to another smile. "That's different."

She nodded, reminding herself the polite thing to do was to smile back, so she did and then turned back to the door.

"I'm . . . Santino?" he said as they reached the door at the same time.

The odd way he said it had her glancing back at him again. It was almost as if he wasn't sure if that was his name or not.

He cleared his throat then added, "But most people call me Sonny."

She nodded again. "I was gonna say I don't think I've ever heard the name Santino before."

This close to him she could smell the scent of the cologne again. The continued strangeness she felt in her belly annoyed her. She'd *never* been one of *those* girls, the kind to get all stupid over a handsome face and a few polite smiles.

"It's Italian," he elaborated, still sounding a bit unsure with that same strange expression. Lila didn't know what to make of it. "But my mom's Mexican and my dad moved to New York when I was younger. I grew up here in East Los Angeles, so I've always considered myself more Hispanic than Italian."

Still not sure why he was sharing all this, Lila nodded again, giving him the polite smile she'd had to practice in the mirror sometimes. "Well, thank you, Sonny." She opened the door and started out.

Sonny pulled the door open all the way and walked out behind her. The line to the ladies' room was still as long, and all eyes were on them as they walked out into the hallway. The girls in the line were so outrageously obvious about trying to get Sonny's attention, despite Lila walking out with him; it was disgusting.

"It was nice meeting you, Lila," he said as they walked back into the VIP lounge.

A guy in a crowd in a corner, waving their way, got their attention. "Those are my friends." Sonny lifted his hand to acknowledge having seen his friend.

"Oh." Lila nodded, ignoring the glaring girls next to the guy waving Sonny down—the same girls who'd given her and Stacia the stink eye earlier. "I'm over here." She motioned towards Stacia, who was engrossed with her phone. "It was nice meeting you too. And thanks again."

Before he could say anything else because he looked like he might, she rushed away.

"That was fast." Stacia barely glanced up from her phone. "So, I guess I was right about— Oh, shit."

Lila peered at her, a bit concerned because Stacia was still staring at her phone intently. "What's wrong?"

"Derek's dad." She held up her hand because she was still reading. "Derek said he just got the message from his mom saying his dad had been rushed to the ER but she didn't say for what, and he can't get ahold of his mom now, so he's getting worried." She stood up, grabbing her purse from the table. "It's too loud in here. Stay here and save our table. I'm gonna go outside to try his mom and then his sister and the hospital. Maybe I can get some info for him. He said he can't be on the phone too long since he's on duty. I'll try to make this fast."

"No, you do what you gotta do," Lila said firmly, feeling bad for Derek. "Take your time. I'll be fine."

Stacia rushed away as Lila glanced around nervously. The lounge overlooked the standing-room-only area downstairs. The opening band was already playing, and many were dancing along to the music. Lila glanced over the rail and did some people watching. Thank God she had VIP passes. Otherwise, she might be stuck down there in that crowd by herself, waiting for Stacia.

"Is it just you and your friend tonight?" Lila turned, surprised to see Sonny taking the seat across from her.

# 3

Normally, Lila would be irritated by his taking the seat without even asking if she minded. But strangely, she was a bit relieved. Having never been to a club before, being left alone was unnerving, so she welcomed the company, especially because, technically, he wasn't a *total* stranger anymore.

"Yeah." She nodded, glancing away and trying to not get caught up on how big the man's presence was. "It's just me and her, but she had a call she needed to make."

"I'm normally not this forward, I promise," he said with a big smile that once again *felt* genuine. "It's just that I still feel bad about what happened outside, and you walked away so fast earlier I didn't even get a chance to formally apologize."

Lila shook her head before he went on. "You already did outside. There's no need to do it again."

"But there is. That's not the first time that driver's done something reckless. I should fire his ass."

Instantly, Lila felt bad. She knew all about living paycheck to paycheck and counting on every penny of it. "No, don't do that. It was partly my fault. I should've looked up the alley before just crossing blindly."

Sonny smiled, staring at her with that strange twinkle in his eyes that had Lila's belly doing that annoying thing again. "I said I *should*, but I won't. He's the brother of the idiot in the moon roof. I didn't want to admit it at that moment, but the guy in the moon roof is my cousin. They both are. I was hoping you'd throw the cup at him."

"I almost did." Lila laughed softly, shaking her head.

"You should've. That would've been epic."

Lila peered at him for a moment. *Why did it feel like she knew him from somewhere?* She'd thought so when she'd first seen him in the limo, only despite the color of his eyes, he had a very typical Hispanic look to him, something she'd seen a lot in this area. Though she had to admit he was much bigger and hotter than most. She'd begun to think so when she'd gone in that back room with him, but she'd been too nervous and hesitant to really take him in. Now that he was sitting face-to-face with her, she could take him in better and longer. Though she refused to get sucked into that bedroom-eyed gaze he indulged her with when he was listening to her talk.

"You look so familiar."

Snapping out of the gaze, his eyes widened in reaction to the comment; though he seemed to catch himself just as fast and he glanced away.

Lila peered at him for a moment, wondering what to make of it, then went on. "You ever go into 5th Street? The boxing gym?"

Sonny turned back to her, his eyes narrowing. "I've been in there a few times."

He tilted his head with that same strange expression she'd noticed when they were in the back room. Amused suspicion was the only way she could describe it. Only there was something tense about the way his rigid jaw flexed for a moment.

"Why?"

"Because I—"

She caught herself before her dumb ass could tell this guy she barely knew, where she worked. As nice as he seemed so far, even he admitted he was being a little forward. The last thing she needed was for him to start showing up at her work. She still knew nothing about him.

"I, uh . . . go in there occasionally," she said as offhandedly as she could. "You know get free passes sometimes. As big as you are, I can see you must work out. I was thinking maybe that's where I've seen you."

Whatever tension she thought she'd picked up on seemed to wane and he smiled big again. "Could be. I've actually been in there a few times this past month."

"I knew it," she said, feeling triumphant—and a little disappointed. "I must've seen you in there."

She explained about his looking familiar from the moment she'd seen him in the limo but not being able to place his face. Glancing at the door to see if by chance Stacia might be on her way back, Lila was secretly glad Sonny wasn't wearing your typical meathead attire. There might still be a chance he wasn't one. But if he started talking about protein drinks and how much he could lift, she was out of there.

"I've never seen you before today." His comment had her turning back to him as he indulged her with a smoldering-eyed smile. "Because I *know* I'd remember you."

Smiling politely, Lila had to look away. *Calm your ass.* She inwardly chided her suddenly pounding heart. *He's probably said the same thing to other girls a million times.*

As if he read her mind, he chuckled. "That's not a line by the way." She glanced back at him as he shook his head. "I just realized what you must be thinking of me."

This time his smile seemed a little embarrassed as he scratched his temple. But again, it felt sincere. "It's been years since I've gone out and actually tried to hit on anyone. So, I swear to you I really have no game when it comes to that stuff. This is only my second time here. I'm here tonight because my cousins are always raving about this band and I caught them out in Vegas once and liked them. This crowd is a little young for my taste. I really did only come here tonight to hear the band." He paused for a moment, staring into her eyes. "And then I saw you."

He paused again, smiling in that way that had her insides fluttering, making her panic, so she glanced away again. That gaze was just too much for her to continue the eye contact.

"I figured with my luck I wouldn't even see you in here, since there was a good chance you might be down there." He motioned to the crowded first floor. Lila's eyes followed in the direction he was looking, glad for the reason to turn away from him again. "I doubted I'd be able to find you in that mess. When I saw you out in the hallway, I still wasn't sure if that was the only ladies' room in the place, so I figured I better make my move. I can't even remember when's the last time I approached a girl like that." He seemed to think about that for a moment then shook his head. "I'm not sure I *ever* have. Anyway, my point is, if I've come across as a regular at a club, trying to get lucky, I can assure you that couldn't be further from the truth. I'm totally winging it here." He laughed, glancing around nervously. "But I am hoping maybe I can hang with you a little longer. Is your friend gonna be gone long?"

Lila lifted a shoulder, trying to appear less affected—*excited*—by everything he'd just laid on her. With a gulp, she glanced at the door again. "Not sure. It was kind of an emergency call she had to make, so she might be out there for a while."

"Let me buy you a drink then while you wait."

"I don't drink." She turned back to look at him then added, "Plus, I got lucky the first time. I don't wanna risk having to stand in that line again."

"I can take you in the back room at any time tonight." He smirked playfully as Lila felt her face heat. "I mean geez." He laughed this time. "I meant I can take you *into* that back room any time, you know, if you need to go."

Once again it was the damnedest thing. Maybe his trying to apologize again and his little speech had really gone a long way. Either he was really a nice guy or an evil genius because her usual irritable self would've automatically found his suggestive comment annoying, despite his backpedaling. Instead, she smiled, and that alone would've floored Stacia if she'd been there and heard the exchange.

"I'm really not a drinker."

"They have non-alcoholic stuff you can order or you know what?" He glanced back at the corner where all his friends were. "Some of the girls over there ordered piña coladas that pretty much looked like dessert with whipped cream, pineapple slice, cherry, and all. All those fancy drinks can be made without alcohol."

A waitress dropped off drinks over at the next table. One of them was a fancy drink like the ones he'd just described. "If you get a blended one, you can't even drink it fast or you risk brain freeze. So, you probably won't even need to use the ladies' room too soon. Let me buy you one." He pulled his wallet out of his back pocket and stood up.

Lila didn't know much about fancy purses and wallets, but she'd seen enough fake Louis Vuitton handbags and wallets to know his *wasn't* fake. Eyeing his wallet as he opened it, she noticed the big gaudy ring on the fourth finger of his right hand and the Rolex like the ones she'd seen Felix wearing a few times. Lila glanced up at him, getting a better look at his chiseled jaw and how perfectly groomed the man was. He was no security guard and he was right. He looked way too mature for this younger rocker crowd. Maybe he was the band's manager or something.

"I'll get you the drink and keep you company until your friend gets back. It's the least I can do to make up for my driver nearly taking you out. Yes?"

Lila giggled at that last comment. *Giggled!* "I'd hardly say he nearly *took me out,*" she said, clearing her throat and sitting up a little straighter.

What the hell was the matter with her? Because the place was getting crowded fast and she'd hate to be sitting there alone—or worse having to fend off other guys she didn't know *at all*—she surprised herself once again when she agreed with a nod. "Okay, I'll try a virgin piña colada."

Sonny's big, infuriatingly beautiful smile went even bigger. Even more infuriating was what a challenge it was trying not to match it too eagerly. "I'll be back." With that, he rushed off toward the bar.

Lila took in his big muscular physique as he sauntered away. What the hell was going on with her? So, he was good-looking and nice—so far. She was around plenty of good-looking guys with great bodies, daily, down at the gym. Lila knew better than anyone good looks and muscles only went so far. She'd never allowed herself to get caught up with a possible meathead, and she wasn't going to now.

So far Sonny had made a notable enough first impression, but she shouldn't be getting her panties wet over some flirty guy who talked a good talk at a club. No matter what he'd just told her, for all she knew, he was a regular here hooking up with different girls every weekend. For someone who claimed to not be a club regular, he certainly hadn't been shy about approaching her.

The guy could just have his approach down to an art. She had to stay mindful of that and stop letting the pitter patter of her heart get carried away by a smooth-talking guy with a smile that'd begun to make her weak. It's why she'd never been interested in frequenting places like this. She'd have the drink with him and let him keep the seat across from hers occupied so no one else would. Then when Stacia got back, she'd thank him for the drink, politely dismiss him, and be done with it.

Lila pulled her phone out and set it on the table. If Derek's dad's issue turned out to be serious, Stacia might text or call her to tell her they needed to go. She clicked on the several messages she had from Ali.

> I've been blowing minors all night.
>
> Mirrors
>
> MY NOSE! OMG I hate this phone! I'm faking Nyquil and calling it a night, so in case you fall and I don't answer don't sorry.

Lila shook her head with a smirk. Her sister was the queen of auto-correct errors. The girl texted so fast, and often she sent texts out left and right without bothering to check before hitting send. Lila texted back, starting to giggle—for the second time that night. But she caught herself, clearing her throat again as she carefully made sure her text was correct.

> Don't FAKE the Nyquil it's your friend! LOL And don't WORRY I won't be sorry if I call and you're asleep. ;) Kiss, kiss, love my sis! I'll make you soup tomorrow. XOXO

She was still smirking from rereading her text when Sonny made it back to the table with their drinks: her virgin piña colada with all the fixings as he'd described it and a beer for himself. "Not much of a drinker myself." He motioned to his beer. "But I throw a few of these back whenever I go out. Maybe a shot or two here and there."

He pulled out his wallet again and checked something then cussed under his breath. Just as he looked up, the young waitress rushed to him. "Mr.—"

"Sherry, sweetheart." He held his hand up to her and started toward her. "I gave you the wrong card."

"Yes, and I know you, Mr.—"

"Let's, uh . . ." He interrupted the waitress again then turned back to Lila with a strange almost panicky expression. "I'll be right back."

Turning back to the waitress before Lila could even respond, he placed his hand on *Sherry's* shoulder, practically ushering her away. Lila heard him say something about them taking care of it at the bar. Not sure what to make of the odd exchange, Lila shrugged it off. She started to look down at her phone when she noticed one of the bitchy girls who'd been standing with Sonny's crowd earlier make her way toward him. Lila watched curiously as the girl reached him, said something, then laughed hysterically at whatever his response was. It was actually funny to watch. The girl was *ridiculous*. Sonny turned his back to the girl for a second to sign the receipt the waitress handed him at the bar. Then the girl turned to Lila, flipped her off, and mouthed the words, "Fuck off."

Utterly stunned, it had Lila sitting straight up, sending a shockwave of heat up her spine. She had to look around to check if the bitch was really talking to her or someone else. There was no one else it appeared the gesture might've been directed at. No one else seemed to be looking in the girl's direction, and she'd been looking right at Lila when she'd mouthed the words. By the time Lila looked back at her, the girl was back to flirting outrageously with Sonny again.

Sipping her drink slowly, Lila concentrated on remaining calm and collected. She didn't give a rat's ass about this girl and Sonny. She'd just met the guy, and *if* he was a regular here, maybe this was one of his past one-nighters pissed about being ignored tonight—for his newest conquest. But if this ghetto whore had it in her to do what she just had, Lila better just finish her drink and get her ass out of there. She may've come a long way from the hothead she once was, but there was no way she was taking anyone's shit if they got in her face. She promised her sister she'd never get arrested again.

Instead of allowing herself to get worked up, she glanced down at her phone and concentrated on reading her sister's response to her text.

> Ugh, this phone. Yes! Thor chicken soup! Chicken vegetable not noodle. I'm watching my carbs remember? Already in bed. Talk tho hooky tomorrow! Kiss kiss love my sis!

Normally, her sister's messed-up texts would have her smiling again. But once the heat shot up her spine like it had moments ago, it was *really* hard to just snap out of it. She had to though. This slutty club rat was *so* not worth her time and energy.

Bringing her thoughts back to her sister's response, she frowned. Ali's preoccupation with her weight bothered her. Lila was constantly trying to get the girl to embrace her curves. Because of her hypothyroidism, she still struggled with her weight, but it wasn't like she was fat. She was just curvier than most. Being top heavy didn't help either, but Lila assured her most guys wouldn't protest about that. Still she knew Ali was sensitive when it came to her weight.

Glancing back down at her phone again, Lila decided she wouldn't respond to Ali. She knew how fast that Nyquil knocked her out, and she didn't want to risk waking her. But she was beginning to worry about Stacia. She texted her, knowing full well if she was on hold with the hospital or something she likely wouldn't be able to respond. Lila just didn't want Stacia to rush on her account. So, in case she checked her texts in between calls, she'd know Lila was good.

She put together a quick text reminding Stacia to take all the time she needed then wrote another Stacia would be surprised to read. Lila was actually allowing someone to keep her company in the meantime. Hitting send, she glanced up and watched as Sonny and the bitch walked away together to his crowd in the corner. She hadn't even noticed they'd gone back there. Surprised by the slight disappointment that maybe she'd sent that last text too soon, Lila glanced away before Sonny could see she'd seen them. Maybe the whore had made him an offer he just couldn't turn down, and he was done with Lila for the night.

Lila sipped her drink that was surprisingly good and focused on the opening band playing down below. To her surprise, Sonny was back at her table soon after, sans the bitch.

"Sorry about that." He took the seat across from her again. "I totally forgot that credit card I first gave her hasn't even been activated yet."

Not wanting to sound the least bit irritated about his smiling as sweetly at the club rat as he was now smiling at Lila, she peered at him as she sucked on the straw of her drink. She took a deep breath but couldn't help giving into her curiosity. "Is that girl someone you've gone out with?"

Sonny glanced around, and Lila rolled her eyes when it appeared he was going to pretend he didn't know who she was talking about.

*Good-bye.*

It's what her next word to him would be if he played that card. She'd leave her unfinished drink there with the rest of the cast of *Jersey Shore* and walk out to look for Stacia instead. Her friend taking this long couldn't be a good thing anyway. They were probably going to be leaving if something was seriously wrong with Derek's dad.

"I met her last time I was here, and we hung out a little. But I haven't seen or talked to her since."

Lila chuckled, glancing away. She figured as much. He probably fucked the girl and then never called her back. No wonder her pathetic clingy ass was all over him tonight. He just better not get any ideas about what he might be doing with Lila since he had mentioned hoping to *hang out* with her a little longer.

"Something funny?" he asked with a smirk.

Lila shrugged, sitting back and tilting her head as she stirred her drink with her straw. Ironically, she was thankful for the stupid bitch who flipped her off now. She couldn't believe she'd begun to let her guard down with this guy. She'd actually been *nice* just because he seemed different. "Your little friend flipped me off." His smirk went flat and his brows furrowed in a good show of appearing completely shocked.

"Yeah." Lila nodded, glancing back at the girl who was in the very VIP corner with the band members and other groupies. "My guess is you did more than just *hang out* with her, and she's not appreciating my taking her time with you tonight."

"She *flipped* you off?" he asked incredulously. "When was this?"

"When you and her were laughing it up at the bar. Of course, she waited until you turned your back to sign something."

Lila shrugged because she was already over it. She just wanted this guy to know, no matter how perfect his little act had been so far, she hadn't fallen for his BS.

"And you're sure she meant to flip *you* off? I've heard her and her friends refer to each other as whores and bitches."

That made Lila genuinely laugh. "Hey, at least they're not delusional and think more of themselves than they should. Gotta give 'em credit for that much, right?"

"I'm serious, Lila." Sonny sat up a bit, still appearing to be very stunned. "I can't believe she'd do that. Maybe it was meant for one of her friends. You don't know her, do you?"

Lila laughed again. "Hell, no, I'd never associate with someone like her."

Not entirely true but he didn't have to know that. As soon as she was done with her drink, if Stacia wasn't back, she'd be out of there anyway. And sweet-talking Sonny boy here would be nothing but a reminder of why she didn't do clubs.

"I can't believe she did that." Sonny said again, bringing the tip of his beer bottle to his mouth.

This time Lila rolled her eyes right at him. "Really? That kind of behavior from that cock socket surprises you?"

Sonny nearly spit up his beer but managed to not spray it all out. He grabbed a napkin to wipe what *had* dribbled out the corners of his mouth. "Cock socket?" He laughed out loud.

"Sorry if that's offensive to your friend." Lila didn't even try to sound genuine in her apology. "It's just the kind of nickname girls like her exude." She shrugged, taking a quick sip from her straw.

"Wow." He peeled the label off his beer but stared straight at her. "Maybe I *am* clueless. I'm not sure what I'm more stunned by: Barbie flipping you off or the mouth on such an otherwise sweet-looking girl."

"Don't compare me to that piece of shit." Lila glared at him, already holding her glass a little tighter in case she had to throw what was left in it at his face.

He lifted his hand immediately. "Whoa! That's not what I meant. I'm just saying that name you called her . . ." He laughed, shaking his head. "I've heard it before just not coming from such a sweet-looking mouth. It surprised me. That's all."

Lila glanced away, not sure why she even cared what this guy said, but for some stupid reason, she blurted out her response. "Yeah, well, when you grow up around a lot of people using that kind of language, it sort of rubs off."

She shook her head, annoyed that she'd even seen fit to explain this to him. Who the hell was he for her to have to explain why she was the way she was? She started to scoot off her stool, ready to just leave. Coming here was exactly what she'd thought it'd be like, from the catty bitches checking each other out, to the sweet-talking meathead trying to get laid.

"Where you going?"

"To check on my friend."

"But you're coming back, right?"

She was standing now, ready to bolt, only she hesitated and didn't understand why. It made her frown, but she didn't respond or even look at him.

"Look. I'm sorry about Barbie flipping you off, and I'm sorry I compared you to her. That's not what I meant. I was more *appalled* by what she did. Your response was just funny. But both were completely unexpected. It's all I meant. And I take back not believing she would do that. She and her friends are pretty lit. They must've started early. I'm not making excuses for her, but I can see how her drunk ass would do something stupid like that." Lila glanced at him in time to see him turn to her still near full drink on the table. "You haven't finished your drink. Go check on your friend, but please say you'll come back and at least finish this."

Never in her life had Lila felt so inclined to give someone the benefit of the doubt, especially someone she barely knew and still had loads of questions about. It was always the other way around. But there was something so genuinely endearing about him and those sweet familiar eyes.

Exhaling, she nodded. "Unless we have to leave, because like I said the call was kind of an emergency, I'll be back."

He pulled out his phone. "Just in case, because I have the shittiest luck when it comes to this stuff, can I get your number?"

Without thinking, because she was afraid she'd change her mind and the thought of talking to him again was one she might actually look forward to, she rattled off her number. She did it so fast she thought maybe he wouldn't get it, but he smiled as he tapped at his phone screen quickly. "Got it."

*That* smile was the last thing she saw before she turned to walk away. Despite how quickly she'd begun to snap at him, her insides were still doing that thing they hadn't done in too long. It was faint, barely discernible, but it was there: that tiny glimmer of giddiness—hope. Maybe she was normal after all. Maybe she *was* meant to feel the same excitement and happiness other girls felt, and maybe not all guys were horny assholes. Maybe she could allow herself to open up again. Let her walls down. Take a chance.

At that moment, she decided to keep walking. She'd walk out and find Stacia, apologize if she still wanted to stay and watch the show, but tell her she was suddenly not feeling well. Because she wasn't. This scared the hell out of her. How could a guy she'd just met, and knew nothing about—at a meat market *club*—have her almost considering what she hadn't in so long?

So, he had her number. Big deal. If he tried calling or texting, it'd just be a reminder of how close she'd come to being weak. She was at the top of the stairs, ready to make her way down when she heard it. "That's probably because she sucked him dry for that piña colada when she gladly followed him into that back room."

Lila turned to see the same two bitches from earlier sniggering and stupidly still walking toward her.

# 4

"Who the fuck do you think you are?" *Barbie* slurred as she sped up toward Lila. "Walking in here, taking our table and—"

Lila easily grabbed her wrist the moment the bitch lifted her middle finger at Lila's face again.

The shock of how fast Lila had been to block her hand and the strength in her hold had stunned Barbie silent momentarily. Digging deep for the inner strength to remain calm so she could keep her promise to her sister about not getting arrested again, Lila took a deep breath and spoke through her teeth.

"One warning," she said as her grip on Barbie's hand went even more lethal. "Get out of my face or I'll break your fucking hand."

Barbie grimaced in pain already as Lila began twisting slowly. Then Lila saw the drunken stupidity in Barbie's eyes and her stomach plummeted. She thought Lila was bluffing.

"Fuck you, bi—"

The snapping of Barbie's wrist as she'd reached for Lila's face with her other hand, was so loud she heard it even over the bitch's big mouth. It silenced Barbie for a second again before she cried out in agony.

Her friend stared at Barbie in utter disbelief before turning to Lila. "You fucking animal!" She grabbed Lila's hair as Barbie held her hand against her chest and continued to wail in pain.

It didn't take more than a few seconds for Lila to have the upper hand, and she landed blow after blow on the girl's face. It took a little longer than she thought, but she felt the arms of security wrap around her waist and pull her away, as she kicked and landed a foot on bitch number two's shoulder. The girl flopped to the floor as Lila was carried in the air and rushed through the crowd, still cussing and resisting the whole way as they made it to the back door where Sonny had let her in earlier. The moment the door closed behind them, she was put down, and she spun around. "Why the fuck are you—?"

Seeing who it was sucked the air out of her. Sonny stared at her the way she'd been stared at many times in her life. She knew what he was likely thinking of her because she felt like it now. The very thing that girl had called her—a raving animal.

*All* the therapy, *all* the time at the gym beating the bags until she was completely spent had done nothing to free her of the uncontrollable fury she'd dealt with most of her life. Her feeble attempt at grasping any control had been pathetic. Those bitches coming at her the way they had, erupted the volcanic temper she knew now had only been dormant but never gone. She hadn't managed to tame it. And seeing Sonny stare at her the way he was now wasn't helping.

"What?" she asked loudly. "Why the *fuck* are you looking at me like that? They came at me! Those bitches—"

"Come on!" He grabbed her hand and pulled her toward another door at the back of the room.

"Where are you taking me?" She tried to pull her hand away, but just like when he'd carried her, she was no match for his strength.

"I'm getting you out of here. They're calling the cops for sure, and you fucked those girls up bad."

She fought him some more, refusing to just let him pull her out into the alley with him until he turned around, brought his big arm around her waist, and slammed her body against his. It took Lila by such surprise she gasped breathlessly as she stared up at his intense eyes. "If I don't get you out of here *now*, you're gonna be arrested. Is that what you want?"

With her adrenaline still going a mile a minute and now the distraction of having his hard body pressed against hers, she could barely think. Then his words sunk in. There was still the chance she might not be getting arrested. Grudgingly, she gave in, shaking her head, and he dropped his arm from her waist but slipped his hand into hers and tugged her along. He brought his phone out with his other hand as they walked into a stairwell. "Bring the car out back," he said as they rushed down the stairs.

With her adrenaline still pumping hard, everything that happened next was a blur. The fresh air in her face as they walked out the door downstairs gave her a blast of relief she so desperately needed. The limo that had nearly hit her earlier was there a few seconds after they walked out. Sonny opened the back door and rushed her into it.

"My friend will be looking for me," she said, finally snapping out of her stupor, and the panic set in.

"So, call her." Sonny then said something she didn't quite hear to the driver outside of the car, but she did hear the part about him telling him to just drive—anywhere away from the club.

He climbed into the back seat with her, and the driver closed the door and rushed around to the front. "Tell her we'll meet her anywhere she wants, but you can't go back there. You'll be arrested."

It wasn't until she reached in the purse slung over her shoulder and across her body that, somehow, she'd managed to hold onto, she realized her bloodied hand was shaking. She must've hit speaker because Stacia's hello was loud enough for Sonny to hear.

"Stacia," she said in response to hearing her friend's voice. But she was still too shaken up she didn't even think to turn the speaker off.

"Oh, my God, Lila! The place is suddenly flooded with cops, and they're not letting anyone in. Can you get out? I gotta go. Derek's dad had a massive heart attack. He's in surgery right now, but it doesn't look good. I need to be there for Derek."

Sonny's hand on her leg made her flinch, and he lifted it away just as quick. "I can take you home if she needs to leave."

Lila looked up at him, shaking her head, but she was already in a car with him and Stacia sounded so anxious. "I have a ride." The words flew out before she could think it through. "Go ahead and go. Call me and let me know how his dad is."

"Are you sure?" Stacia sounded as surprised as Lila expected her to sound.

"Yes. Don't worry about me. I'll be fine. Go. Be with Derek."

The moment she hung up, she was flooded with that same mixture of shame and utter frustration that she'd felt so often in her past after one of her irrepressible eruptions. All the times when her fury had completely overpowered any sense of composure she might otherwise have, came crashing back at her.

"They said you broke her hand," Sonny said as he finished reading something on his phone screen then set it down on the seat.

He soaked a napkin with water from a water bottle then wiped Lila's bloodied hand. Lila couldn't even look at him. She took a deep breath, staring at her hand as he wiped away the blood gently. "Yeah, well she flipped me off again," Lila said defensively. "This time right in my face."

"Then she had it coming."

That surprised Lila. But she still refused to look at him. As she had her entire life, she swallowed back the frustration that nearly choked her up now. She hated feeling so out of control once she was that angry. This time she'd been ready to explode the moment she realized those two whores were talking about her. She'd been ready to punch the first bitch in the throat before she'd even reached her, so seeing the bitch's finger in her face had just made it too easy. And while it surprised her that she'd managed to at least warn her, it still wasn't good enough.

"No, she didn't," Lila's said bitterly and shook her head, still unable to look up at him. She stared down at her already swelling knuckles instead. "It was stupid of them to come at me the way they did, but what I did wasn't right. They were drunk. I didn't need to break her hand or beat the other one the way I did."

"Shit happens, Lila." She glanced up in time to see the unsympathetic shrug. "You go out and get that stupid drunk; you never know how the night's gonna end. They're lucky it wasn't worse. VIP areas don't usually have a lot of security. They're usually at the door, in this case downstairs, to make sure no one sneaks in. They don't expect many getting out of hand and risk getting thrown out or banned. Those girls are lucky I noticed I missed a digit in your phone number and rushed out to look for you before you left."

Unbelievably, for a moment, a smile almost slipped, but Lila caught herself. Only she still had to ask, as indifferently as she could of course. "You rushed out because of that?"

His intense expression eased up and he smiled. "Well, yeah. If you didn't come back, how else would I have ever gotten in touch with my Cinderella?" He chuckled. "It's how my running after you felt anyway. Like I was that close to losing my chance of getting to know the first girl in a *long* time who'd left that big of an impression on me. Only I didn't even have a glass slipper that might lead me to you."

Despite how sweetly he smiled and how kind he was being or maybe it was *because* of it, Lila couldn't help feeling even more emotional. This was the kind of guy *normal* girls landed. The girlie girls with class who could handle their shit without resorting to violence.

"Hey." He slipped his hand in hers, and she didn't even snap her hand away. "What's wrong? I'd ask if that's the first fight you've ever been in, but I can't imagine it was, given the way those girls got their asses handed to them."

She shook her head, knowing he meant it as a bit of a compliment, but for her, it wasn't, not after all these years of trying to better herself. Lila couldn't even remember the last time she'd felt this emotional—it was maddening. But it was for more than one reason. For one, it terrified her that she'd been close to allowing herself to show any emotion aside from anger, especially to someone she barely knew. While it was mostly frustration he was seeing, even *that* she kept to herself. She could hardly believe she was in a car with a guy she'd just met, not just *tolerating* his fingers intertwining with hers, but liking it.

Her incredible disappointment that she'd lost it again clouded any excitement she might otherwise be feeling. Ironically, what was making her the *most* emotional was that Sonny had seen this ugly side of her and yet he was still there smiling and gazing at her the way he had earlier—before her outburst.

"I just," she whispered, still unwilling to look him directly in the eyes. "Let's just say I can be quick to snap. But I hadn't in a long time, and I guess it pisses me off that I thought I was beyond letting bitch—" She cleared her voice. "*Girls* like that get to me." She glanced up at him, trying not to frown. This was more than she'd ever shared with anyone, especially someone she'd just met. "I'll get over it. I always do. No biggie."

She glanced out the window, not wanting him to see how beyond disgusted with herself she was really feeling.

"You were provoked, Lila." He squeezed her uninjured hand. "If anything, it would've been self-defense. *Two* girls came at you. You just did what you had to—reacted the way most would."

"I have a sister," she said, refusing to look back at him, but reminding herself there was no way he'd understand, and she wasn't about to get into all that with him. "She's younger and I need to set a better example. If I'd gotten arrested tonight, I wouldn't have made it back to her tonight, and she's not even feeling well."

Lila shook her head as the reality sunk in about how bad this really could've been had Sonny not been there to get her out in time.

"Okay, but you said it'd been a long time, right?" His squeezing her hand had her turning to him again, and he smiled sweetly, moving a strand of hair away from her face. "So, you've proven you can do it. This was an unusual circumstance. It's not like you snapped at someone who just cut you off in line at a store or something. You were *attacked*. It could've been anyone tonight. Even someone who's never been in a fight in their life, would've been forced to defend themselves against those two drunk *bitches*. And it's okay to call them that because it's exactly what they are."

Curious, suddenly she peered at him. "You really hung out with one of them?"

He winced. "Yeah, but just there at the club. And by hung out, I mean, once I bought her a drink, she clung to me the rest of the night. When I saw her tonight, I knew she'd likely do the same thing again. Only once I saw you, I knew nothing would stop me from trying to at least talk to you a little longer. Am I assuming too much?" He gazed at her a bit nervously. "You are single, right?"

Lila nodded, her heart going wild with equal parts of thrilling excitement and utter alarm. His relieved and somewhat vulnerable smile eased her, but just a tiny bit. "Does your sister need you home right now or do we have time to drive around? Maybe grab a bite to eat?"

"She's asleep," she heard herself say without thinking. "Took Nyquil and I'm sure will be out until morning." She shook her head quickly, feeling like an idiot. "Not that I don't have to be home until then. I just mean I don't need to be home just yet."

"Cool," he said with another relieved smile. "You hungry? I know this really great steakhouse we can stop at."

Lila shook her head, glancing down at her short T-shirt and jeans, already regretting saying she didn't have to be home yet. "I'm not dressed for a steakhouse or feeling very hungry for that matter. I really do appreciate you saving me from all the trouble I would've been in tonight, but I think I should get home—"

"Lila, I don't usually beg," he said, squeezing her hand again. "In fact, I don't think I ever have, but I'd be willing to if it'd get me a few more minutes with you. I feel completely responsible for what happened tonight. All I want is a chance to make up for it a little. I'll be a perfect gentleman, scouts honor."

He held up his three middle fingers, and for the first time since they'd made their escape, Lila smiled.

"I really was a boy scout," Sonny said, tilting his head with a smirk. "Well, only for a year until I discovered . . ." He brought his fist to his mouth, clearing his throat for a second. "I discovered sports, but I really did take it seriously. How 'bout we just grab some coffee? Although a burger sounds even better, but that's up to you."

"A cheeseburger actually does sound good." The words flew out of her mouth without thought again as they'd been doing all night.

This was *not* being cautious like she always said she'd be if she ever considered opening her heart again. What was she thinking? She didn't even know this guy. Hell, she was in a car with *two* complete strangers. If she went missing, no one would have a clue whom she was with, not even Stacia.

"Great," he said, and that smile alone was enough to have her feeling somewhat okay about this. "Any place in particular?"

"Jim's," she said immediately, "on First Street in Boyle Heights."

*Now* she was using her head. The Jim's on First Street was in her *barrio*. If she stayed close to home, at least she had a chance to make a run for it if she had to.

"*Ooh.*" He nodded with a smile. "I haven't been there in a while, but I do remember their burgers being the best." He directed his driver, whom Lila noticed wasn't the same guy who'd been driving earlier, then turned back to her. "Is it okay if we just go through the drive-thru. I don't think they have parking that'll accommodate a car this long."

Glancing up front at the driver, Lila then turned to Sonny curiously. "*Why* are you in a limo?"

His smile waned a bit; then he shrugged. "Just playing it safe. I don't get together with my cousins too often. They're a little younger than I am, so I thought it'd be fun to get a limo. No drinking and driving. This is really the driver. Earlier, my cousin just took the wheel for fun. That reminds me . . ." He pulled his phone out of his pocket. "I gotta let them know where I am and when I'll be back."

It suddenly dawned on her and she felt bad. "You're gonna miss the concert," she said, watching him text. "You don't have to drive me around, Sonny. Just take me home and you can go—"

"Are you kidding me?" He looked up from his phone. "I can catch their show any time. Who knows when, if ever, you'll give me a chance to hang out with you again?"

Again, her insides went a little crazy. This was no different from when she was angry. Despite her better judgment warning her to calm her too excitable heart, Lila was beginning to feel incapable of controlling this either. She gulped as he finished up his text and sent it. He was so different from any of the guys she'd ever gone out with. That was for sure. So much more sophisticated and put together. Even his phone looked more expensive than normal, and as perfectly groomed as his nails were, there was something so ruggedly masculine about him.

She didn't want him to think she was one of *those* girls, the type that put so much weight on monetary things. Even though it was unlikely given his overall appearance, Lila could already tell it wouldn't matter to her if he was a janitor. The thrill she was feeling just knowing he was interested in her would still be the same. She was just curious now.

"What is it you do for a living?"

That same expression she'd seen on him more than once tonight was back, the strange one she hadn't been able to make out and still couldn't. He stared at her for a moment then glanced out the window. "A lot of stuff. Advertising, investing, but I've done some modeling." He turned to her with that same odd expression. "You said I looked familiar earlier; that might be why. I've been in a few magazines here and there."

"Really?" This didn't surprise Lila. The guy had the body and looks to model. "Maybe that's it."

She should've guessed as much. Lila shopped downtown all the time, and she'd seen enough of the fake Armani shirts to recognize the logo on his expensive-looking shirt. Just like his Louis Vuitton wallet, if she had to bet, this was one hundred percent authentic.

Before she could ask exactly what he modeled, his eyes were on her lips, making her breathing hitch. Then he smiled, gazing into her eyes. "So, tell me why's a beautiful girl like you single? I was blown away the moment I laid eyes on you and you're different." She felt her brows jump; then he quickly added, "In a good way."

Lila smiled nervously, incapable of holding the eye contact too long, and glanced away. "Thank you," she said softly then shrugged, willing her hammering heart to calm down. "I guess I just haven't been open to relationships for a while." She turned back to see him apparently waiting for her to go on. "Long story, so I won't bore you with the details, but I had a bad experience and haven't been in a hurry to relive anything even remotely similar."

"Got it," he said with a nod. "But you wouldn't be boring me if you wanna share. I'm actually curious now what I'm up against." He gave her a sheepish smile. "Not to jump ahead of myself or anything, but I do like to be prepared. You seem like someone I'd definitely like to get to know better. Knowing what I should steer clear from doing or saying to make sure you're not reminded of your bad experience might help me down the line. Something tells me I may eventually want to change your mind about relationships."

Lila's insides went a little crazy, and she smiled but had to glance away from his intense gaze. They reached Jim's and pulled into the drive-thru. Both ordered the same thing—cheeseburger specials—except Sonny made his a double. Sonny directed the driver, for whom he also ordered a special, to drive them to Hollenbeck Park. "What do you know about Hollenbeck Park?" Lila asked curiously as she munched on one of her fries.

To her relief, they got off the subject of her bad experience before he could ask more about it. Instead, he told her about growing up in the area, but his work had him traveling a lot. "I've been gone for years, only coming home to visit temporarily, but I think I'll be home more often now."

"Home? Do you still live in this area?"

"Not in Boyle Heights." He smiled, shaking his head. "But I do have family that still lives in the area, and my mom lives in Los Angeles but a little farther out this way. I love this area though. I have so many memories here. Love coming back here, and I'm glad my work has brought me back. I'll be out here more often than I have in the past few years."

"Yeah, I can't imagine ever leaving," she said, looking out the window at the waterfalls in the park's lake. "But I wouldn't mind living somewhere a little safer."

She'd keep to herself about having lived in low-income housing all her life. No way was she getting that chummy. But she did tell him how her neighborhood could get rough, what with the gangbangers and such. He'd been gazing at her again. He wasn't even eating his food; he was so busy hanging on her every word. "I worry about my sister. Ali's not like me."

That made him smile. "And what does that mean?"

Lila lifted and dropped a shoulder, taking a swig of her soda. "Unlike me, she's never been in fights. Growing up, I made sure no one messed with her, and the ones that did . . ." She shook her head, slipping a fry in her mouth, then continued when she was done chewing. "The ones that did, never did again once I took care of them."

"Tough girl, huh?"

"I've never been tough for the sake of being tough," she explained, not happy that the conversation had gone there. "Like tonight, I just did what I had to. But I was never a bully. I hated fucki—"

Catching herself, she cleared her throat. This was probably the only thing she didn't like about talking to Sonny. She'd only known him a few hours, and already she felt beneath him. Despite his showing an interest in her, she might blow any chance she might have with a decent guy like him because of her tendencies to act and speak like a ghetto rat.

"I hated bullies." She took a frustrated bite of her cheeseburger to keep her foul mouth full for a while.

"I did too." Sonny finally took a bite of his own cheeseburger, and they ate silently for a few minutes until he wiped his mouth. "So, you wanna tell me about your bad experience or is this too soon?"

*Too soon?* She wasn't even sure what that meant, but it made her as uneasy as it strangely excited her. Only hell no, she wasn't about to get into this. "I'd rather not."

"That bad?"

Lila glanced up at him, once again surprised she wasn't more annoyed by his intrusiveness as she'd normally be. "There's just some things I don't like talking about."

"Fair enough, but can I at least ask how long it's been?"

Taking another sip of her soda, Lila took a deep breath. Okay, maybe this guy could annoy her. Good to know. Maybe he didn't have superpowers like she'd begun to think. "You always ask so many questions of someone you hardly know?"

"I said I wanted to get to know you."

The amused tone was a little annoying too. Was he being a smartass now? "Yeah, well, when someone says they'd rather not talk about something, maybe you should just take the hint and drop it."

"My bad. Maybe it *is* too soon."

They went back to eating silently until she heard him mutter, "*Shit.*"

Lila glanced up to see him holding the ketchup pack to his burger, only instead of it squirting onto the burger, it squirted clear across his fancy shirt.

"Never fucking fails," he said, putting his burger down and grabbing a napkin.

She refrained from laughing like she wanted to, but then he tried wiping it off and only made it worse. When he let his head fall, pressing his lips together, she couldn't help laughing.

Jerking his head back up, he turned to her, and for the first time that night, he looked annoyed. "Are you laughing at me? This is a brand-new shirt."

That made Lila laugh even more. She covered her mouth with her napkin before she spit anything up.

"I have to have my shirts specially made because of my size, you know? It's not cheap either."

Lila couldn't stop laughing now, especially when she saw him further smear it when he tried wiping again.

"Here," she said after wetting a napkin with a water bottle. She reached over and did it herself, ignoring what touching his hard chest did to her. "You're supposed to dab," she said, refusing to look up and meet his eyes, but with her heart suddenly pounding she was done laughing. "Sorry I laughed," she said when she'd cleaned him off as best as she could.

She finally looked up at him, and he was smiling now. "No worries. Sorry I pushed about your ex."

Leaning back in her seat, Lila wiped her mouth because she was done eating. She was stuffed. "It's been two years." She looked up at him from the corner of her eyes. "He was a shitty boyfriend, who broke things off in an even shittier way, but I'm over it. Haven't seen or talked to him in years, and I couldn't care less about him now."

Sonny crumpled the paper to his now gone cheeseburger and put it in the bag their food had come in, then wiped his mouth. "You don't care about him anymore, but he's the reason why you've sworn off relationships all this time?"

Lila shrugged, feeling a little foolish, but it was the truth. She was long over him. "I didn't say I swore off relationships because of him. He's just the reason I haven't been eager to put myself out there again. Until a few months ago, I hadn't even seen or talked him in years."

"Where'd you see him a few months ago?"

"His sister and Ali are best friends. I picked up Ali at her house and he happened to be outside." She rolled her eyes. "If it'd been up to me, I would've driven away when he started toward my car, but I was still waiting on Ali. It was a short conversation and I wasn't very pleasant.'

That had Sonny smirking as if he knew exactly what she meant. "What's this guy's name?"

Narrowing her eyes, Lila lifted a brow. "Marcelo. But I'm done talking about him."

"For now," he said a little too smugly then pointed at her fries. "Are you done with those?"

Lila handed them to him, ignoring his *for now* comment. "Yes, I'm stuffed. You want them?"

"No, but the ducks will." He opened his door. "Let's go for a walk."

# 5

# Sonny

Technically, he still hadn't lied, not about his name or what he did for a living. He was just being vague—cautious. And he had a good reason. So far, it appeared she genuinely had no idea who he was. Tonight had been a hell of a night for Lila, and he was just trying to keep it from getting *too* overwhelming.

He'd come clean soon enough, just not yet. He'd almost decided not to suggest they go for a walk, but it was dark enough now that he wouldn't be recognized. Most of the people in the park now were young couples too into each other to notice anyone else strolling the park anyway.

It was just hard to believe he was here again after all these years with a girl he'd just met. Except given everything that'd happened tonight, he felt more connected to her faster than he'd ever felt to any girl he'd met in *years*. This was not a night he'd be forgetting any time soon.

He already knew Lila was not someone he'd be forgetting anytime soon, if *ever*, not just because of how blown away he'd been by everything about her so far, but because he really couldn't help but feel responsible for Barbie going at her the way she had. Maybe he'd done a little more with Barbie than he'd admitted—or rather Barbie had done more to him—that had her feeling a little more entitled than she should. But there just wasn't a good way to put that out there, not without the conversation getting a little awkward. And he valued his nut sack too much to chance offending Lila.

Besides, he didn't see the point. It wasn't like he anticipated seeing Barbie again, especially after tonight. His cousin texted him that Barbie and her friend were demanding his phone number so they could track his *girlfriend* down and have her arrested.

Barbie knew as much as he'd told his cousin. Lila went out the back and was so upset she'd immediately left with her friend. She'd wanted nothing to do with him, blaming him for having been attacked, so he didn't even get her number. Lila—he hadn't even given his cousin her name—was gone. Those stupid bitches would just have to deal with the consequences of messing with the wrong girl.

Already he knew he'd be dealing with phone calls from the police, but he wasn't worried about it. His lawyers could deal with them. Truth was he stopped a brawl at a bar between two girls he barely knew and had nothing to do with Barbie or her friend's injuries. There were dozens of witnesses who could attest to that. Those girls had nothing on him and his mysterious Cinderella that *almost* got away, which reminded him of something.

He handed the fries to Lila as they got closer to the lake with the ducks. She took them after sticking a piece of gum in her mouth and offering him one. He took it, unwrapping it quickly and sticking it in his mouth, but pulled his phone out just as quick. "Before I forget, because I'll be kicking myself if I do . . ."

After he rattled off the number he had for her, she let him know which digit was missing. Lila threw a few fries out to the ducks, which promptly crowded around them, then turned to him. "So where *do* you live now?"

"Not too far." He glanced back down at his phone where he was still fixing her contact info. "About twenty-five minutes from here."

Done with her contact info, he glanced up at her. She was staring at him a little weirdly. Okay maybe that was *too* vague. "In Los Feliz," he clarified.

Lila nodded, tossing more fries out at the ducks. "I've heard of it, but never been."

"How's your hand doing?" He brought the attention to her still red knuckles, to change the subject.

Lila held her hand up to examine it then opened and closed her fist. "It'll be sore for a few days, but I'll be fine."

"How'd you learn how to land those kinds of punches?"

Like earlier, when he'd called her a tough girl, she almost frowned. Note taken. She wasn't proud of being street tough with a wicked right hook. He'd already made a note earlier not to get on her bad side, especially after he'd picked her up and felt her hard body. Honest to God he couldn't think of anything sexier than a girl who clearly worked hard on her body and knew how to stand up for herself. And holy shit, did she ever.

"With my childhood, it was sort of a requirement. But I'd rather not talk about that right now either. I'm still pissed I broke my streak of being able to keep my cool."

"Fair enough."

They started a slow stroll along the side of the lake, and he decided to get back to a subject he was even more curious about anyway. "So how old is your sister?"

"Eighteen." Like earlier, when she spoke of her sister, her face instantly brightened. "She's a journalism major.

Investigative journalist specifically. But it'll be a while before she gets her degree because she has to go through community college first and then transfer. She did get a few grants, but they weren't enough."

Sonny couldn't remember the last time he smiled this much. Lila was something else. In the short time he'd known her, he'd already seen such extremes in her personality. She came across as sweet when she smiled the way she did speaking of her sister and when she'd laughed so wholeheartedly. But he'd seen the other side now too, the side that had already begun to turn on him more than once tonight. He liked knowing Lila wouldn't be the kind of girl where he'd have to dig deep to find out what was bothering her. Nope. If anything, she'd be letting him know loud and clear if he ever did or said anything to piss her off.

But he was curious about one more thing, and since he was still catching Lila's smirk every time she glanced down at the ketchup stain, he decided to take his chances and ask. Since it did happen to be about Ali, a topic that always brightened her eyes, he figured his chances were good she might not snap.

"So, Ali is still very much in touch with your ex's sister, right? Does that mean you still stay in touch with his family?"

"No, it doesn't," she said immediately as they reached the bridge that went across the lake. "I mean I still talk to Jenny when she comes over. She never did me wrong and she's a sweetheart, but I don't stay in touch with his mom or anything like that. I never go *into* Jenny's apartment either."

They reached the top of the bridge and stopped to look over at the water. He decided to let it go because he wouldn't be a hypocrite. He was still very much in contact with the family of the only girl he'd ever considered himself to be serious about.

But there was one last thing he had to ask and, technically, it wasn't about her ex. "So, you said it's been almost two years that you've been hesitant about relationships. Has it been that long since you've allowed anyone in for something less?"

The change in the serene expression she'd worn since she'd mentioned her sister was instantly replaced with a fiery one. Sonny held his hand up just as quickly. "Back up. That's not what I meant."

"Is that why you're driving me around?"

"No!" he said adamantly because she was already backing away. "I'm just wondering if I'll get a knee to the groin if I try to kiss you tonight." Lila stared at him for a moment, searching his eyes, but said nothing. "I swear to you I normally wouldn't ask a girl if I could kiss her. I'd just sort of ease into it, but I'm not looking to get decked here." Finally, she smirked and he could breathe a little easier. "Is even kissing something you haven't allowed in that long too? Because I'm not stupid, Lila. I wouldn't dream of pushing for anything more this soon. I just thought the bridge of Hollenbeck Park, a place I hold so near and dear to my heart, would be the perfect place for us to have our first kiss."

Lila leaned against the bridge again, still smirking, and gazed out into the water. "It has been that long since I've allowed even that much." She was quiet for a moment, but he dared not say anything until she answered the entire question. "But I guess you're right," she said, turning to him with a sweet smile. "This *would* be a perfect place for a first kiss."

*Thank you, Jesus.* He'd been waiting all night.

"But," she said, lifting a hand up and a sweet, yet dangerous-looking eyebrow. "If I let you kiss me, doesn't mean I'm ready for anything more, even a relationship. I always said if I ever did allow for one I'd make it absolutely clear I'd *need* to take things very slow. So, I don't want you calling me a tease—"

"Are you kidding me?" Sonny said with a laugh. "You think I'm an idiot? I won't be calling you anything but beautiful. Not just because it's the truth, but like I said earlier, I'm not looking for a knee to the groin. I heard you loud and clear, Lila. If slow is what you want and need, then slow is what you'll get. Already, I can tell it'll be totally worth the wait."

Without waiting for her to change her mind, he took a step forward, cradled her beautiful face in his hands, and kissed her lips softly. Mindful of her body language that at the moment didn't seem to be protesting, he kissed her again. He pulled away to look in her eyes. They seemed strangely startled, but she didn't pull away. So, he went in a little deeper the second time.

Zero resistance.

Even as he pressed his body against hers gently, she didn't push or pull away. She kissed him back just as eagerly as he did now. Not since he'd been a teen had he felt this much excitement over kissing a girl. Tracing her lips with his tongue, he finally pulled away and gazed into her eyes, breathing deeply as his heart pounded in his chest.

"Wow," she said as if reading his mind.

"Wow is right." He smiled. "I don't know about you, but I heard music."

Lila laughed, glancing in the direction of the couple over by a picnic table with a radio playing. "I'm hearing it too."

She let him kiss her again and again and again . . . and Sonny couldn't even remember the last time he felt *all* this over just kissing. They held hands all the way back to the car. They were supposed to drive around town, taking in all the scenic areas of Los Angeles. While they did at first, with Lila letting him know this was her first ever ride in a limo, they spent the next several hours, making out like teenagers, giggling and chatting about light stuff. He'd get around to asking her about heavier subjects like her childhood because he was very curious now about *everything* about her. But he'd respect her not wanting to talk about that stuff this soon.

By the time he dropped her off, something had changed. Instead of eyeing him suspiciously and even annoyingly at times as she had in the beginning of the evening, she gazed at him in a way he hoped meant she was feeling for him what he'd so quickly begun to feel for her. He wished he could cancel all his plans for the next several weeks so he could stay here and get to know her better in person.

Unfortunately, he couldn't. He had too many things he needed to do before finally settling in, in Los Angeles. But at least he knew once he did he'd be there for a while. But he would make something abundantly clear before he was gone.

"I hope you know this isn't a onetime deal for me." He leaned his forehead against hers and that brightened those beautiful eyes of hers. "I just have to be out of town for the next several weeks or so. But you'll definitely be hearing from me. When's the best time for me to call?"

"Evenings are best, but I can text or email anytime of the day."

That made him smile. She didn't want to wait all day to hear from him either. "Good to know." He took out his phone and keyed in her email address. "Check your phone often. You'll be hearing from me every chance I get."

He kissed her good and long, trying not to imagine what he'd imagined the whole night: if the rest of her firm body tasted as good as her mouth did.

# **6**

# **Lila**

Not since the first night she'd slept with Marcelo had Lila been so incapable of sleeping. But with him, she'd been worried. They'd been reckless. Marcelo had assured her if he pulled out they'd be okay, even though Lila knew how irresponsibly *stupid* that was. They'd also been in the backseat of a car like she'd been last night when she made out with Sonny. Only it was hardly an elegant and spacious limo. They'd parked deep into Griffith Park in his mom's tiny Nissan Versa. Lila wasn't even sure how they managed to fit in the backseat, but fit they did. They were supposed to have just made out like all the other times they'd gone up there, except things got carried away.

Unlike Sonny, who she could feel almost come undone last night but respectfully refrained from pushing for more, Marcelo had *begged* just like he had all the previous times. Her dumb ass had finally given in, and for the entire night and all the others until she'd gotten her period that month, she hadn't gotten a single good night's sleep. Now she'd been tossing and turning since four in the morning when she woke and remembered what she'd done last night.

This time there was no chance she could be pregnant, but for some reason, she felt even more worried that she'd made a terrible mistake. Not that she couldn't just take it back. No one was forcing her to continue anything with him. At this point, she wasn't even sure when to expect to hear back from Sonny—when to start worrying if she *didn't*. But *that's* what worried her most. Lila had enough going on in her life, enough to worry about: getting Ali through college and deciding if she was really going to go through with getting back in the ring. The last thing she needed to be worrying about was her heart being crushed again.

Everything she'd disregarded last night, as the thought of Sonny kissing her eclipsed her better judgment, was now screaming at her. She still knew so little about him. For all she knew, he could be married or have a girlfriend. Unlike him, she stupidly never even thought to ask him. Worst of all, he was actually into girls like *Barbie*, at least enough to *hang out* with her. Lila slapped her forehead with a groan.

*God,* she was an idiot. The man had *hung out* with the last girl he met at that club, whatever the fuck that meant. But judging from Barbie's whorish qualities, Lila could only imagine how much more he'd done with her. Then he admitted to not having seen or talked to her since. Lila had very likely been his flavor of the night this time.

Frustrated, Lila sat up, pulling her legs off the side of the bed. Why couldn't she just be normal? It wasn't like she'd slept with the guy. Even *that* would've been normal in this day and age. The guy was hotter than shit and his kisses . . . She closed her eyes, smiling just from the memory. Lila may not have been kissed since Marcelo, but she'd been kissed *before* him and by Marcelo many times. *Nothing* in her experience had come close to Sonny's kisses. Just imagining how good he was at other things had her entire body heating. Last night she'd been on *fire*.

She was only glad now that she hadn't given into her body's urges. She didn't do one-nighters because the guy would have to be pretty fucking perfect for her to even consider it and that only meant one thing: feelings would inevitably be involved. That only led to heartache and hurt feelings, which led to anger. And the entire day yesterday was a staunch reminder of how far she was from a real grasp on dealing with her anger issues.

Pathetically far.

Shaking her head, she stood up, taking a deep breath. Lila didn't even want to check her phone or emails. Already the bubbling in her stomach from the possibility of hearing from him again was out of control. That meant each time she checked her phone for texts or emails and *didn't* have any she'd be even more pissed about giving into those kisses last night.

It was only eight and Ali was still sleeping soundly. The fact that she hadn't coughed all night as she had the night before was a relief. It meant she was getting better. Still, Lila walked to the kitchen and checked the chicken she'd taken out of the freezer last night when she'd gotten home. Ali loved her chicken soup, which was one of the few things Lila was good at cooking.

Hearing her phone ring in the other room had her insides going crazy. Without sprinting the way she wanted, she rushed back to her room, not just because of who it might be, but because she didn't want it to wake Ali.

To her disappointment, it was Stacia who hadn't come home last night. "How's Derek's dad?" Lila whispered, hurrying out of her and Ali's bedroom and closing the door behind her.

"Better, but they had a hell of a scare."

Stacia explained about the emergency open heart surgery he'd had to have and how he was going to need more surgery. She said VIP night at the Ratz concert just wasn't meant to be. Then she asked the magic question. "I felt so bad about leaving you last night. How'd you get home?"

"I met a guy," Lila said, trying not to make too much of it.

"You *did*? Who?"

Once again, her friend sounded as surprised as Lila had expected her to. Not once in the past two *years* had she just *met a guy*, especially one she'd allow to take her home the same night she met him. "The guy in the backseat of that limo that almost hit me before we walked in. He came over to apologize when he saw me sitting alone and turned out to be a pretty nice guy."

Lila chewed her lip and decided to keep the rest to herself, including having gone in the back room with him when she still didn't even know his name. She'd already decided she'd keep the fight—if you could even call Barbie's and her friend's ass kicking that—to herself too. She didn't need to relive it, and she certainly didn't want any pity from her friend or Ali if she never heard back from Sonny.

"So, you got a ride home in a limo?"

"Yeah." She smiled, setting up the coffee machine. "It was pretty cool actually."

"So how was the show?"

Lila froze. A good liar she was *not* and she knew Stacia well already. If Lila said it was good, Stacia would follow up with questions about which songs they played.

"I didn't stay to watch it," she admitted. "It just felt weird being there alone, even if that guy was talking to me. You know me. I'm not comfortable hanging with anyone I don't know, so when he offered to take me home at any time, I asked if he could before the show even started."

"Oh well." Stacia sighed. "I guess this time it just wasn't meant to be for *any* of us to watch it."

Stacia explained she'd be gone most of the day and might come home just to pick up another change of clothes.

But she wanted to be with Derek since his dad wasn't completely out of the woods yet.

Lila glanced at the clock. She had an afternoon shift today at the gym, so she'd have time to make her sister her soup before she left. She only hoped today she wouldn't blow it again if Gio asked her to get in the ring.

After getting off the phone and pouring herself a cup of coffee, she gave into checking her texts. None. With a deep breath, she checked all the other notifications at the top of her phone screen. The enormous smile on her face when she saw the email from Sonny was ridiculous, but it couldn't be helped. It went even bigger when she saw she had *several* from him. The notification sound for her emails was always turned off since she rarely got any important ones. She'd be changing that now for sure. Maybe if it'd been turned on she would've been smiling a lot earlier today. She clicked on the first one sent just after seven that morning. Even that made her smile.

**To: Lila**
**From: Sonny**
**Re: Will it freak you out if . . .?**

I say I miss kissing you already?
S

Lila smiled even bigger at what the one-sentence email did to her insides, despite how much all this terrified her. She clicked on the next one, trying to focus on the positive. What had gone from a bad day yesterday to what could've turned into a disastrous evening with her sitting in a jail cell all night, ended in such an unexpected and *glorious* way. She clicked on the next one and read it.

**To: Lila**
**From: Sonny**
**Re: I have less than an hour to get to the airport and . . .**

I can't tell you how incredibly tempted I am to drive to your place instead of going straight there for one last kiss.
S

Glancing at the time on that one, almost an hour ago, Lila frowned, pissed about her email notifications being turned off now. It took her a minute to figure out how to turn the sound on, but she did before checking the next email. This one was much longer.

**To: Lila**
**From: Sonny**
**Re: I can't stop thinking about you or last night . . .**

The fact that you're probably still sound asleep is a testament to how bad I must have it because I've been up since before four just thinking about you. And not because I have a flight at eight either. I still feel bad about what happened with Barbie, but is it bad that I'm sort of glad it happened? Not that you were attacked but that it led to me getting you all to myself for the rest of the evening. Hell, I almost blew it for a minute there when I programmed the wrong number in my phone, but because of Barbie, the night ended the way it did. I almost feel like paying for her medical bills just to show my appreciation.
S

Even as she smirked, she couldn't help but feel the slightest bit irritated just reading that bitch's name. Lila responded to that one before reading the next one.

**To: Sonny**
**From: Lila**
**Re: I can't stop thinking about you or last night . . .**

Don't you dare pay a dime of her medical bills. The more I think about it now, the more I'm sure she had it coming. If not a broken wrist in some other way. You were right last

night. Troublemaking drunks like her and her friend are playing Russian roulette when they decide to get *that* stupid drunk in public. I'm not done reading your other emails, but I had to respond to this one first!
L

Smiling and feeling a giddiness she'd never felt, she hit send. This was so much better than talking to him. Lila had been able to go back and undo the F-bomb when referring to Barbie's fucking medical bills and replace words like "cunts" with "drunks." As disappointing as it was to know it'd be weeks before she'd see him again, it was a relief to know she at least had that much time for getting to know him better before having to talk face-to-face again. She just might have a chance of making a slightly better—less abrasive—impression on him this way. She clicked on his next email.

**To: Lila**
**From: Sonny**
**Re: I'm at the airport now and getting a little worried . . .**

I hope I'm not getting blown off. I gotta tell you this really is a first for me, Lila. I've never met a girl I've hounded this early on after meeting her. I've never hounded a girl, period. I've never NOT been able to stop thinking of someone like this. This is insane! I really, *really* hope I hear back from you SOON.
S

Lila's face was going to start hurting if she didn't stop smiling so big. Reading the subject line of the last one made her feel bad, but she still couldn't stop smiling.

**To: Lila**
**From: Sonny**
**Re: I guess I'll just have to wait. =(**

About to take off, so I should turn this thing off. I'll keep my fingers crossed I'll hear from you once we're up where I can turn this back on. Don't make fun of me for all these emails either. I do feel a little pathetic for being so anxious to hear back from you, but I don't even care! Alright, gotta go before they throw me off the plane.
S

Giggling now as she'd done so much last night, Lila covered her mouth. If her sister heard her, she'd be worried. This was *so* not like her. Even worse, she might get an inkling of what Lila had been up to last night. She'd ask questions, and Lila might be forced to tell her about losing her shit like she did.

Lila stopped giggling but bit her bottom lip, still smiling big as she scrolled back to his first email about missing her kisses already, and began responding to each of his emails, feeling that weirdness in her belly that up until last night had been so foreign to her.

**To: Sonny**
**From: Lila**
**Re: Will if freak you out if . . .**

It does freak me out a little but only because I'm missing them too. This *is* crazy.
L


**To: Sonny**
**From: Lila**
**Re: I have less than an hour to get to the airport and . . .**
Sucks that I missed this. It would've been nice to start off my day with more of your kisses.
L

She stared at the email before sending it. *Gads!* Was she really doing this? Flirting? Why not? She'd already done so much more with him than she'd done with any guy in years. But this was *so* unlike her. She'd even practically said she'd missed him after spending just one evening with him. But as insane as it seemed, it was the truth. He said it first.

*Be spontaneous for once in your life, Lila.*

He seemed nice enough, and here *he* was calling himself pathetic for being so anxious about hearing back from her. She chewed her lip a bit and then just sent it and scrolled to the next one. She'd already responded to that one, so she skipped it and went on to the next.

**To: Sonny**
**From: Lila**
**Re: I'm at the airport now and getting a little worried . . .**

Well, I'll be responding to all your emails now. My notification sound for emails was off, but it's on now. Why emails btw? Most people text. I hate to admit it, but I've been thinking of you nonstop too. This is a first for me too, but at least I don't feel so nervous anymore, knowing you're feeling the same. Off to respond to your last email!
L


**To: Sonny**
**From: Lila**
**Re: I guess I'll just have to wait. =(**

"I do feel a little pathetic for being so anxious to hear back from you, but I don't even care!" This made me laugh. I'd make fun of you for being so anxious, but now it's my turn to wait for your response. I'm not even sure what's happening here yet, but I'll leave it at that. I'm not as openly brave as you. I'll plead the fifth for now on what I'm feeling just reading your emails. All I'll admit is *maybe* I can hardly wait to hear from you again.
L

She sent the last email, thinking about how this really was a first for her too. With Marcelo, she remembered feeling excited but at the same time a negative anxiousness whenever he called or texted her. His temper wasn't the greatest either, and a lot of times, he was high and accusatory. She winced now as she walked back into the kitchen at the way she'd allowed Marcelo to treat her and for so long. But in hindsight, it was all she knew. She'd never been treated by any guy with such respect and the kindness Sonny had shown her already.

After placing the chicken in a bowl with warm water so it'd further thaw out, she started cutting up the veggies for the soup. Halfway through making it, her sister walked into the kitchen. Lila smiled when she saw how much better Ali looked than she had yesterday.

"Better?"

Ali nodded. "Yes, much better than yesterday." She went straight to the fridge and pulled out the orange juice. "Thank God because I have finals this week. I can't let this flu mess with my studying."

"I'm working on your soup now," Lila said with a smile. "It always makes you feel better.'"

Ali thanked her and said she'd hug her but she didn't want to pass her *cooties*. She asked about the concert, and Lila told her about missing it and getting a ride home but didn't elaborate much. She knew the only reason her sister didn't grill her about Sonny, who Lila had simply referred to as a nice guy who offered to get her home, was because she was still not a hundred percent well. Ali told her a little about her evening yesterday, trying to study but getting nowhere because she couldn't stop sneezing and blowing her nose. Then she started out of the kitchen. "I'm jumping in the shower."

"Take a long one," Lila said just as her phone dinged.

Her heart was instantly aflutter with thoughts of Sonny. Glad that her sister was out of the kitchen, Lila smiled big again when she saw it *was* from him and it was a long one.

**To: Lila**
**From: Sonny**
**Re: =D !!!**

I'll respond to all your emails in this one, make it easier for us both. I was kidding about paying for Barbie's medical bills. My attorneys wouldn't let me even if I wasn't. So, don't worry. Oh, guess what? Turns out she's on probation. She's not even supposed to be drinking. The guys said last night she ducked out and didn't even give the cops a statement. Nobody's gonna be pressing charges. So, consider yourself completely off the hook. I can text, but I prefer to use my iPad. It's why I'm emailing, but if you prefer, I can text you. You have no idea how just seeing your emails had me smiling like a crazy person. So, reading that you're missing the kissing too, feeling what I'm feeling and not quite understanding what's happening either, just made my YEAR. I won't be in Los Angeles for another few weeks, but I HAVE to see you before that. Let's make a FaceTime date. I'm in meetings most of the day, but I'll be back in my hotel by seven my time tonight. That's about four your time. Let me know what time works for you.
S

Well, so much for buying time to work on her potty mouth before talking to him in person. But at least it seemed most of their communicating would be via emails.

And so, it began. Lila told him how she wouldn't be home until seven her time too, and he said he'd wait up as late as he had to. They made a date for seven that night, which again had her insides doing that crazy thing she'd been so unfamiliar with until last night. But the emails didn't stop for the rest of the day. He said he'd be in meetings but could sneak a few emails here and there, only they were far more than a few. The whole day they went back and forth, even while Lila had been at work. By the middle of the day, Sonny was already feeling comfortable enough with her to take the flirting a bit further. But more surprising was that Lila was going along with it.

**To: Lila**
**From: Sonny**
**Re: =D !!!**

Not to be creepy, I really am curious. What are you wearing?
S

**To: Sonny**
**From Lila**
**Re: =D !!!**

A black tank and gray pants. What are you wearing, creeper?
L

**To: Lila**
**From: Sonny**
**Re: =D !!!**

LOL! Trust me. If I wanted to be creepy, I could get *really* creepy. But I'll hold off on that just yet. I'm in meetings for the next few days, so monkey suits, ties, the works. What kind of pants?
S

Lila could only imagine how amazing he must look in a suit. As usual, she compared how she'd normally feel about any guy asking what she was wearing then admitting he could get really creepy and following up for more detail with how she felt about Sonny doing it. Of course, she didn't feel annoyed in the least. She actually giggled and decided she was curious now. She, too, wanted a visual.

**To: Sonny**
**From: Lila**
**Re: =D !!!**

I'm at work now, so they're spandex capri pants. What color is your suit, shirt, and tie? I can only imagine what you must look like in it.
L

His response took a little longer than his previous ones, and when Lila opened it, she knew why. Her jaw dropped open when she saw the photo he attached, a selfie he took in a bathroom mirror. He wore a charcoal gray suit, with a white shirt and burgundy tie. As expected, he was *breathtaking*. Lila gulped, staring at it, barely able to believe this man seemed so interested in her. *Why* was a man who looked like this, single? Obviously, he made very good money because she could see the Rolex on the hand holding the phone he used to take the photo. It was a silver one this time, not black like the one he'd worn last night.

It made her nervous. Maybe he *wasn't* single. Maybe this was why he seemed as excited about this as she was beginning to feel, because he was being sneaky. Surely a man with his looks and money could have *any* woman he wanted. Last night was a perfect example of it. Those drunk bitches were willing to fight for him.

Feeling a little uneasy suddenly, Lila read the email the photo was attached to.

**To: Lila**
**From: Sonny**
**Re: =D !!!**

Spandex pants at work? What do you do? And quid pro quo, beautiful. Now I'll need a photo of those spandex pants. I felt

that hard body of yours last night. I don't want to imagine what you must look like in them. I *need* to see for myself now.
S

    Lila glanced around nervously, feeling her face warm. She remembered the full-length mirror in the employee bathroom. She'd been on her phone way too much now when she was supposed to be helping supervise all these kids.
    Pulling a strand of hair behind her ear, she walked over to Bianca, who was working with a group of kids. "I need to use the ladies' room. Will you be okay alone?"
    "Sure, go ahead." Bianca smiled, barely looking up.
    Lila's insides roiled as she walked off in a hurry. Why hadn't she given it more thought? Was it really possible that Sonny was single? He'd asked her about her status, and stupidly she still hadn't asked him about his. Of course, the way he was acting, their making out last night and all his emails today, she could only assume. But should she?
    She walked into the employee bathroom and sent off an email first without the photo. As stupid as she felt, she had to ask now. He was also noticeably older than she was. He even made that comment last night about the crowd being a bit young for him at the club when Lila was just barely old enough to be there. It'd make sense if he was a married man at his age.

**To: Sonny**
**From: Lila**
**Re: =D !!!**

I know this is going to sound stupid for me to be asking *now*. But I never asked you last night even though you asked me. You are single, right?
L

Lila started to pose for the photo in front of the full-length mirror while she waited for a response. She finally took one she was happy with when her phone dinged again.

**To: Lila**
**From: Sonny**
**Re: =D !!!**

I don't think it's stupid, but I am curious. WHY the question now? And I'm still waiting on that photo.
S

Just like that, Lila was furious with herself. She'd talked with him all night last night, gone back and forth with him all day today, and not once had she thought to ask the pertinent questions. He mentioned the time difference between them was three hours away, and she hadn't even bothered asking where he was. She'd been so sucked into their silly banter already she wasn't thinking straight—using her head. Was this his way of avoiding the question?

She tapped away at her phone furiously for more than one reason. For one, she was already being stupid about this, letting his charm blind her as she'd known she was susceptible to being and why she'd avoided relationships for so long. And two, she'd known the guy for less than two days and already she felt hurt. "Two fucking days," she muttered as she tapped away on her phone screen then sent it.

**To: Sonny**
**From: Lila**
**Re: =D !!!**

Answer the question or this is the last response you'll get from me. And while you're at it, how old are you and where are you today?
L

Lila huffed, feeling like a complete idiot. He was probably laughing at her now for not asking these questions sooner. To her relief, his response was instant.

**To: Lila**
**From: Sonny**
**Re: =D !!!**

I'm absolutely single. I'm twenty-nine and I'm in New York today and tomorrow. Wednesday, I'm in Miami for a few days.

Letting out a sigh of relief, Lila closed her eyes. She needed to calm her ass. How in the world would this ever work out? How could she possibly have a normal relationship with *any* guy if she was going to be so quick to think the worst and then, of course, that would ignite her ugly temper? She cursed Marcelo for making it so she only ever expected the worst—disappointment. Just because Marcelo had been nothing but one let down after another didn't mean every guy she met would be the same. Least of all, someone who was clearly so different from Marcelo. Taking a deep breath, she began to think of what to respond, but her phone dinged again with another email from him.

**To: Lila**
**From: Sonny**
**Re: =D !!!**

That photo please and answer my questions. What do *you* do? And why the questions now?
S

Lila wondered what kind of meetings he was in that he had so much time to be emailing. Even she was going to have to tell him she needed to put her phone away for a while. She tapped her phone, answering the questions and hit send.

**To: Sonny
From: Lila
Re: =D !!!**

I'm an assistant trainer in a community youth program. And it just dawned on me that I hadn't asked about your relationship status, your age, or where you were today. I gotta put my phone away now. I *am* at work and I've slacked off too much already. I don't want them to say anything to me.

She hit send then glanced in the mirror. "Give yourself some credit, damn it," she whispered.

Just because he was good-looking and had money didn't mean he was completely out of her league. She was just grateful for the ability to edit her emails, and she knew that was why she had an inkling of unworthiness. Sonny was obviously a sophisticated man and she was, well . . . Unrefined would be an understatement.

Lila started to the door when her phone rang. Instantly, her heart thudded when she saw it was him. Gulping, she hit the answer button. "Hello?"

"Is everything okay?"

Jesus, what hearing that deep voice did to her. "Yes," she said, swallowing hard. "Everything's fine."

"You didn't send the photo and that email before the last one you sent was"—he paused then continued— "a little snippy. I honestly was just curious why you'd ask now."

Lila shook her head, bringing her hand to her forehead. The fact that she was speaking to the gorgeous man in that photo made her insides go crazy *again*. "I just," she said, feeling stupid now. "I just got to thinking and wondered why a clearly successful guy your age is still single."

"So, you thought maybe I wasn't?"

"Something like that."

Lila squeezed her eyes shut as a fog of shame settled over her. She'd let her insecurities get the best of her.

"Well, I can assure you I am. And how busy my career has kept me is *why* I'm single. It's why I've been blowing up your phone since this morning. After spending just one evening with you, I decided I'm not letting my career ruin something that hasn't excited me this much in *years*."

Feeling her heart swell, Lila stared at her own smiling face in the mirror. "Oh." She laughed softly, feeling dumb because it was the only response she could think of.

"I can't wait to talk to you tonight and see you." Just like everything else he'd been saying to her from the moment he first apologized yesterday, he sounded sincere.

"I can't wait to see you either."

"I don't wanna get you in trouble, so I'll let you go and stop blowing up your phone until you say I can. But I'll be waiting for that photo. Bye, Lila."

"Bye, Sonny."

# 7

Ali had work and then said she'd be stopping by Jenny's for a while to do homework with her. Stacia was over at Derek's again and would likely be there the rest of the week. It made Lila wonder how much longer it'd be before Stacia moved out indefinitely—another reason to consider the boxing gig Gio was offering and the possible sponsor money she'd get from it. They'd be needing the extra cash for sure if Stacia moved out. For now, Lila was just glad she had the place to herself so she could talk to Sonny in peace. She'd made out with the guy last night, spoken so easily with him in between making out, and exchanged emails with him all day, so why the hell was she so damn nervous now?

It was nervous excitement, she decided. Sonny told her to call whenever she was ready and she finally was. She set up the call and waited for it to go through. He answered almost immediately.

"Hey." He smiled beautifully.

"Hey," she said back, her insides doing that crazy thing even just thinking about him brought on now.

"I never realized what an anxious person I am." He chuckled, looking down at the corner of the screen. "It's what? Five after seven there? I was beginning to worry you'd changed your mind about this."

Lila smiled, taking him in and wishing she had a bigger screen. Unlike the photo he'd sent earlier that day, his attire was far more relaxed now. He wore a sleeveless white cotton T-shirt that showed off the muscle Lila had felt last night as they made out. She saw plenty of muscle in the gym all day, but this was Sonny, so the thought of those muscles touching her again excited her to no end.

"You're beautiful, Lila." The statement was so out of the blue it caught her completely off guard. "I haven't been able to stop looking at the photo you sent me all day."

"Thank you," Lila said softly.

Marcelo had always called her hot or sexy, but she couldn't remember ever hearing him call her beautiful. Such a trivial thing, but it made her inhale deeply.

"We're gonna have to make that a daily thing until I get back to Los Angeles."

Lila nodded. No way would she pass up getting another photo of him in a suit and tie. "And when is that?" she asked, glad she finally remembered to ask such a significant question.

"Well," he said with a frown. "Longer than I thought. This stuff was set up months ago, so I can't reschedule any of it. Before last night, I hadn't even bothered looking at my schedule that closely. Off the top of my head, I just knew it'd be weeks, but now that I'm anxious to get back there, I examined it a little closer, and it'll be at least a month before I'm back."

A very small part of Lila was relieved to hear it. Just knowing she'd be face-to-face with him again through her computer was nerve-wracking enough. She could only imagine what it'd be like when the time came and she knew she'd be seeing him again in person. But a bigger part of her was so overwhelmed with the disappointment of knowing it'd be that long until she did she had to refrain from pouting. And just like the giggling she'd done yesterday, she *never* pouted. Seeing that beautiful smile made Lila yearn for more of his kisses.

"Is this the norm for you?" she asked. "Traveling so much? I know last night you said you'd be home now more than you had been in the past."

"It depends on the time of year. But I'll be home more often now than I have been in the past. After this trip, I should be home for a while."

That made Lila smile. "Good."

He indulged her with another one of his sweet smiles. "I'm looking forward to it too."

He told her about some business ventures he was considering in Los Angeles that would keep him there more often. But he didn't elaborate and Lila was glad for it. Somehow, she got that Sonny's level of sophistication was far beyond hers. She was afraid he might get into something that was way over her head and she might ask stupid questions. Or worse, she'd sit there staring at him blankly without a thing to say about it. She'd just keep her inquiries into the details of his job to a minimum.

"So, you live with your sister and your roommate, the one who had to leave last night?"

"Yes." She nodded then was glad she thought to ask. "Who do you live with?"

"Alone mostly."

Lila raised a brow. "Mostly?"

He smiled. "Sometimes my mom will come stay with me for a while. Again, depending on the time of the year, like in the spring when I'm in Arizona."

"Why Arizona?"

Sonny sat up a little straighter and cleared his throat. "Different jobs take me to different places. I'm in Arizona every March."

As he sat back a bit, Lila saw it. "I thought you said you were in your hotel room?"

"I am."

"You have a piano in your hotel room?"

Sonny turned to look at the piano behind him then turned back to the screen. "Yeah, this room happens to have one."

Lila stared at the screen, feeling the same nerves she'd felt earlier. The only hotel rooms she'd ever been in were the cheap motels Marcelo had sprung for a few times so they could have sex somewhere other than the cramped back seat of his mother's car. Those rooms barely had room for a bed and a TV. Sonny looked to be sitting in a home with a grand piano behind him.

She'd planned on waiting a little longer to ask, but she had to know now, and she had told him all about Marcelo. "You said your career has kept you from having relationships, but you have to have had some."

"I have. Just nothing significant."

Glad she'd asked, Lila pushed for more. "I told you a little about mine. When's the last time *you* were in one?"

He thought about it for a moment. "Well, that depends on what you consider a relationship. I've never even been in love, so I'm not sure if the ones I've been in really count as relationships. The last time I dated someone exclusively was maybe a few months ago. That lasted several months, and not once did I ever feel the craziness I'm *already* feeling for you."

That made Lila smile and set off the butterflies in her belly—something so unlike her. "If it was several months, then I say it still counts as a relationship. Maybe you didn't feel for her, but I'm sure she felt for you."

"Why is that?"

"How could she not?"

That made him laugh. "I'm flattered, but just remember I'm doing my best to impress you. I'm far from perfect; though I'm not stupid enough to point out my flaws. I'm sure you'll see them soon enough."

Lila found that hard to believe, but she supposed it was true. So far, he did seem perfect. *Too* perfect. He went on to mention that the next month wouldn't be all work and no play. Parts of his traveling in the next month were for pleasure, but again, things he'd planned months ago, like the trip he had to make to San Diego this weekend. Next weekend was a Vegas trip. "I've never been to Vegas."

His eyes widened. "You wanna go? I'll fly you out and meet you there?"

"No." She shook her head, floored by the invitation to spend the *weekend* with him. "I couldn't. I mean I can't. I have work and my sister to think about. I was just thinking out loud."

She thought about it for a moment then frowned, wondering why she even mentioned it. She'd never been to New York either. Vegas just seemed more doable since it was only a few hours away. It still made her nervous how enormously different their worlds were. She'd never been *anywhere*. The farthest she'd ever been was three hours up north when her mom had taken them to the quaint little Danish-themed town of Solvang. They'd stopped at some of the beaches along the way, but that was as lavish as her travels got.

She'd keep that to herself. Like the supposed flaws Sonny was keeping to himself, he'd eventually know just how different they were. He had to already. He knew about her biggest weakness, and he did drop her off and got to see the rundown projects she lived in. She already knew it was a far cry from wherever he lived. The suite he sat in now was probably bigger than her apartment.

"You got me excited for a minute there," he said with a poignant smile. "But now that I know, I'll make it a goal of mine to take you there someday. I've been there more times than I can count."

Lila made the mistake of asking him where else he'd traveled. He thought about it, but instead of naming off where he'd traveled, he named off some of the countries he'd never been to but planned on going to and the ones he had no desire to ever visit. It seemed it was easier doing that than naming off all the places he *had* been. But that led to his question. "Where've you been?"

Feeling like kicking herself, she blurted out the answer anyway. "Solvang."

"Oh, wow, I haven't been there in years," he said, all bright-eyed. "But it is one of my favorites."

He told her more about his travels, about a few of his other favorite domestic cities, and what he liked so much about them. By the time he finished telling her about it and answering all her questions, it was well past nine, which meant it was past midnight where he was. Even after admitting he had an early meeting, he kept insisting on talking just a little longer.

While it made Lila giddy to think he really enjoyed talking to her that much, she insisted he needed to get to sleep and they finally hung up. It wasn't until she'd been sitting there rehashing the whole conversation with him in her head that she realized Ali still wasn't home yet.

Instantly worried, she picked up her phone, still on the charger since the battery had begun to die hours earlier, and hit speed dial. When she didn't answer, she texted Ali to call her back then tried again. This time it went straight to voicemail.

"You're kidding me," she said, staring down at her phone then bringing it to her ear. "*Allison—*"

She stopped when she heard a beep and glanced down to see the text that popped up.

Can't talk. On my way home.

Lila assumed her sister was driving but was still irritated that she hadn't called to let her know she'd be late. She never got home this late. Then Lila thought maybe Ali *had* called and Lila had missed it because she'd been so consumed with Sonny. Feeling guilty, she checked her call log. None. Well, at least that wasn't the case, so she was back to being irritated. Ali had never been rebellious or anything. She was a good kid, but she knew how much Lila worried. So, this was a little inconsiderate; though Lila reminded herself she hadn't even noticed her sister was this late until she'd gotten off the phone with Sonny.

She was going to have to be more mindful of how already Sonny could so easily distract her even from the most important thing in her life. Lila cleared up the kitchen, feeling like she was walking on air the whole time until Ali got home.

"What happened?" Lila asked as soon as Ali walked in.

"We were following a lead on a story we think could make the front page of the school paper if we can break it."

Ali explained about the lead they got by listening to the police scanner on their phones, about a possible drug deal in progress on campus. "There have been rumors that the drugs are being sold on campus now. Like in the classrooms even. So, we drove down there and, after much searching, found nothing."

"I don't think I like you searching for trouble, Ali."

"We're just trying to break this story. Some say it might even be one of the professors doing the selling."

"No way." Lila stared at her sister's bright eyes.

"Yes way," her sister said excitedly. "Another rumor is that it's one of the night-school teachers, so this made sense when we heard it."

She still wore the thick glasses and was short compared to most other eighteen-year-olds, but she'd grown into her own. Her temper didn't even come close to Lila's, but she could still be quite the spitfire when she felt passionate enough about something. And she was very passionate about her journalism. She and Jenny, being the newbies in the college's journalism program, got stuck with all the crap stories no one ever read. So, Lila knew it was important to her to try and crack the big on-campus story. Still, Lila warned her again to not go looking for trouble.

Ali promised she wouldn't then said she was taking a shower. Lila walked back in her room where her phone was still plugged to the charger and smiled when she saw the notification light blinking. She tapped in her security code and smiled even bigger when she saw she had an email from Sonny.

**To: Lila
From: Sonny
Re: I can't sleep!**

I know it's not your problem, but I thought you might wanna know in case you're willing to continue to entertain me with your beautiful face. I knew I should've insisted more that I didn't have to hang up. I could've been talking to you all this time.
S

Lila laughed, searching her phone for a cute photo of herself. She hated the way she came out in most of them, but she only saved the ones she liked. She refused to be one of those stupid girls and send him anything too provocative. She found a recent one Bianca had taken of her at work with adorable little Miranda. She was tiny and had Downs Syndrome, but she had the biggest smile that could brighten up the entire gym. Just looking at the picture now made Lila smile. Lila was in her spandex work clothes in it too. The red tank and black pants she wore were a flattering way to show off her curves without it being provocative. She attached the photo to the email and sent it.

**To: Sonny
From: Lila
Re: I can't sleep!**

This is all you get. That's my little friend Miranda from the youth program. Isn't she just adorable? You need to sleep! I *will not* be to blame for you slamming your forehead onto your desk tomorrow. FWIW, it made me sad today to hear you won't be back until next month. What have you done to me?
L

    She almost deleted the last two sentences. Again, this was so not like her. Not even with Marcelo did she ever get so cutesy. She barely knew this guy, but talking to him tonight hadn't felt that way at all. She still hadn't even told anyone about him and wasn't sure she would for a while, until she was sure about it. So why the hell was she considering saying *this* to him?
    "Because he's been completely open about his feelings," she whispered with a smile and hit send, feeling her heart wallop.
    Putting the phone down, she walked away to start changing for bed. This was craziness. She could feel her insides doing summersaults. Her phone pinged, and she took a deep breath, walking back toward the phone. Her heart beat a mile a minute as she picked it up.

**To: Lila
From: Sonny
Re: I can't sleep!**

I hate to say it, but I almost didn't notice there was anyone else in the photo. Beautiful picture but that's just not fair to leave me with those final thoughts. I may have to cut this trip short yet.
S

"Oh, Jesus," she whispered, letting out the breath she'd been holding, then started to respond.

How in the world would *she* get any sleep tonight? She responded quickly, but this should be the last one. He needed to go to bed, and she was serious when she said she didn't want to be to blame for anything that might happen to him tomorrow due to his lack of sleep.

**To: Sonny**
**From: Lila**
**Re: I can't sleep!**

You NEED to go to sleep and don't tease me like that. I'm going to bed now and so should you. I look forward to chatting with you again tomorrow. Sweet dreams.
L

She sent it just as her sister walked into her room with her head in a towel and squinting because she wasn't wearing her glasses. For once, Lila was glad for her sister's bad eyesight because she'd been smiling so unlike her from ear to ear. She wasn't ready to discuss this just yet. It still terrified her how fast and easily she was letting her walls down for this guy. If she told anyone, it would just make it more real. The way it stood now, if by chance she was being too hasty about this, too carelessly allowing herself to fall this fast, she might still be able to pretend it hadn't been real.

"I heard they're doing some kind of work-release program down at 5th Street. Is that true?"

Lila frowned. "I heard something about it too. Supposedly, they're gonna be really stringent about who they let in. I personally don't like it."

"Why?"

"Because there are kids on the premises now. These are ex-cons we're talking about."

"That's probably why they're being so stringent, Lila, but everyone deserves a second chance."

"I guess." Lila smiled when she heard the ding on her phone, but she didn't dare check it with Ali still in the room.

"You think maybe you can get me an interview with one of the owners? I think it'd make a good local news story. It might also help relieve any other locals feeling like you if I can get the specifics on just how stringent they'll be."

Remembering she still needed to talk to Gio about the possibility of getting back in the ring, she said she would. Ali was in her room a little while longer, telling Lila about the pompous editor of the paper at school. As much as it irritated her to hear about it, she was glad she'd made enough progress with her temper that her sister wasn't afraid to share these kinds of things with her anymore as she was once.

"He's just so arrogant." Ali huffed. "But I'll spare you the details. It's not just me he's like that with. He's full of himself all around. Even the professor gets annoyed with him."

"You don't have to spare me anything, Ali." Lila lifted her pinky for her sister to intertwine hers with. "Remember we can tell each other *anything*. I promise I won't go down there and kick his ass."

Ali laughed but put out her pinky, and they did their sister love thing. "I know, but it's nothing big. The bad thing is he's so damn good-looking. He just needs a paper bag to put over his personality."

Lila laughed. "Where are your glasses?" she asked as her sister continued to squint.

"In the bathroom. I just need to make these lazy eyes work a few hours out of the day without those horrid bottle-cap glasses."

Frowning, Lila hugged her sister. "We'll get you contacts soon. I'm saving, I promise, because I may be getting another promotion."

"Really?"

Lila wouldn't dare mention fighting until it was a sure thing, but she nodded. "Yeah, some positions are opening up at the gym, and one of the owners mentioned it to me, so we'll see."

"Cool." As usual, Ali smiled, big and proud. "But don't worry about it if it doesn't happen. I'm used to those stupid glasses. It's no big deal." She started out of the bedroom. "I'm getting cereal before I hit the hay. You want some?"

"No, I'm good. Thanks."

The moment Ali was out of the room, Lila rushed to her phone still plugged to the charger and read the email from Sonny.

**To: Lila
From: Sonny
Re: I can't sleep!**

At the risk of getting decked the next time I see you, I'll just say, trust me, you'll know when I'm teasing . . . and you're gonna *love* it. Good night, beautiful. I'm three hours ahead of you, so expect to wake to emails. I'm sure I'll wake thinking of you first thing.
S

How in the world was she supposed to sleep after reading that? But, thankfully, having been up since four that morning thinking of *him*, she knocked out quickly.

# 8

The next several days were much like the first day after meeting Sonny. She'd wake, smiling big when she saw his emails, then walk around on a cloud the rest of the day, sneaking in responses to the emails he sent her all day. Then they'd chat at night on FaceTime, until Friday when she got out of the shower in the evening after a long day at work because she'd trained.

She'd spoken to Gio a few days prior, and, of course, he was all for trying again. As nervous as it'd made her, she'd started training at the beginning of the week, and it made her even more nervous that she was liking it. Though she made Gio promise her he wouldn't get the other guys involved until she was sure she'd be going through with this. She wouldn't be telling anyone about it until then too. Not Ali. Not even Sonny.

Expecting to settle down into a FaceTime chat with Sonny, she got a text from him instead.

> Where are you?

Lila checked the time, wondering if maybe he hadn't sent it in error. It'd been sent just ten minutes prior. But it wasn't seven yet, their usual FaceTime "date" time, so he couldn't be wondering why she wasn't online yet. Still in her bathrobe, she responded, letting him know she was home, and waited. Not a minute later, she got another text.

> Can I see you?

That confused her. Was he talking about FaceTime? It made her heart speed up, thinking he might mean in person, but he'd already explained he'd be on the road for weeks. So, she responded, telling him she could log on earlier since Ali wouldn't be home tonight. She was spending the night at Jenny's. They were still trying to crack the case at her college, but she'd promised she wouldn't be chasing any trouble, just doing lots of research online. Her phone beeped again, and as usual, Lila's heart and belly did what was the norm now when he sent her anything.

> So, you're alone?

Not sure if she should be alarmed or excited, she responded that she was, and his response was to ask if he could see her again. This time she responded, asking him where? Then her doorbell rang.

"No way," she whispered, glancing up and toward the front room.

Feeling her heart nearly pummel through her chest, she didn't even care that she was still in her bathrobe, wore no makeup, and her hair was wet. She rushed out to the front door and peeked out the front peep hole. It was him.

In. All. His. Fucking. Glory.

He stood just outside her door, holding flowers, looking more handsome and even bigger than she remembered. Lila did something she *never* thought she'd do for as long as she *lived.* She squealed like a school girl. Muffling the unexpected and ridiculous sound coming from her mouth, she opened the door. The moment it flew open, she was in his arms and then kissing him as ravenously as he kissed her.

He felt, smelled, and tasted as *amazing* as she remembered. "Oh, my God," she said breathlessly when they finally came up for air and remembered she was still completely naked under her bathrobe.

They moved into her apartment and closed the door; then he spun her around against her front door. Despite her body being on fire already just like the night she first made out with this man, she was mindful that, technically, she still didn't know this man all that well. She'd just let a guy she'd known under a week into her apartment where he could have his way with her if he pleased, and there'd be no one to stop him. But, Jesus, not even *she'd* be willing to.

In spite of how unbelievable it felt to be in his arms again, a part of her couldn't help but feel nervous. Since when was she *this* girl? It'd been just over a week since she'd met him, and here she was falling all over herself for him. But then there was no denying what he did to her. His mouth devoured hers with the same desperate desire and enthusiasm she was feeling. "Why?" She shook her head, pulling back to look in his eyes. "*How* are you here?"

"I'm passing through," he said even as his big hands ran up and down the outside of her robe, feeling her up, and God damn it, she allowed it again. Every nerve ending in her body was alive and begging her to encourage more. "I have to be in San Diego tomorrow morning," he explained breathlessly as he licked her lips. "My flight should've gone straight there tonight, but I got a connecter just to stop here for a couple of hours because I *had* to see you."

He sucked her lips then moved down her chin and neck. *What the hell was she doing?* If she let him open her robe, she'd be his. There was no way she'd have the will to put a stop to this. She wanted him *so* bad at that moment.

"I have thirty minutes, babe," he said, moving down her neck, and she let him open the top part of her robe.

Thirty minutes? This was *torture,* but at the same time, the voice in her head was screaming this was for the best and Lila somehow found the strength to bring a hand between them even as his mouth moved downward and took her nipple in his mouth.

*Jesus Christ!*

"Tell me to stop," he said breathlessly even as he continued to suck, "if this is too much. I swear I was just hoping to see you for a few minutes."

Lila had to dig deep to find every single ounce of strength in her not to wrap her legs around him and *beg* him to fuck her, right there against the door.

"Don't stop," she said breathlessly, loving his hands and mouth on her breasts. It almost hurt to add the next part, but she had to. "But we can't do more."

It was in that instant that he moved to her other breast and her robe fell open entirely.

"Fucking hell!" He groaned, bringing his hand behind her even as he continued to suck her tits and both hands grabbed her naked ass. "I swear to you, Lila," he said against her breasts, "this was *not* what I had in mind when I thought I'd stop by between flights." Just as Lila began to feel ashamed over her reaction to him, he added, "But *fuck* if I'm not glad I did now. Already this stop is so much better than I envisioned it all day when I decided I'd surprise you. I won't stop thinking about this until I see you again."

Her entire naked body was exposed to him now, and he did nothing but suck her breasts and squeeze her ass. Marcelo would've totally begged if not *demanded* more. Hell, most men would. Yet as hard as she could feel Sonny was against his pants, he didn't push for any further.

It was frenzied. It was wild. It was such a fucking turn on. It was beyond any torture Lila could imagine not to do anymore, and still when the time came, he ended it, as much as her entire body burned for more.

"I gotta go." His words were pained. "My plane leaves in just a half hour, but I had to stop and see you." His hands moved up from her body to her face and cupped it. "Lila." He shook his head, staring into her eyes. "What the fuck?"

She laughed, only because she knew exactly what he was feeling and didn't know how to explain it either. Yet it scared the hell out of her. He hugged her tight, and she loved feeling his hard body against hers, knowing it was still completely exposed and shamefully, if he wanted it, she'd be more than willing. Hell, she was so close—too close—to giving into the temptation and begging him to stay.

"Tomorrow," he said, kissing her again and trailing his fingers down her naked body and stopping just inches away from her hot, wet, and already throbbing *need*. "Tomorrow night will you show me online what might someday be mine?" He stopped and gazed in her eyes with a cautious expression. "Please?"

"Yes!" God, she'd never felt so weak. She was this close to showing him now. "Yes, I will."

Moving her feet off something she'd been stepping on, it was only then that she realized the flowers he'd brought for her were smashed beneath their feet. "The flowers!" She looked down. "Oh, my God, they were so beautiful. "She glanced up again when he cupped her face. "And I've never had anyone bring me flowers."

His face brightened. "Really? So, I'm your first?"

Lila nodded, drowning in his eyes and not wanting to pull her naked body away from him. "Yeah, you're my first."

At least in the sending flowers department he was. "Good to know, baby girl." He sucked her tongue. His lips then went back down to her breasts, making her feel like a puddle as he pulled away. "I hate to go, but I have to, or I won't make it on time to my good friends' kids' Baptism tomorrow. And I'm the godfather; otherwise, so help me God, I'd stay here all night and suck parts of you that would still keep me from doing more than you're allowing. But trust me, I'll still die a happy man if my life ended after this."

Lila smiled, even if she did hate that he had to leave. It was her only opportunity to pretend she wouldn't let him take her right then and there. "You'll email me first thing in the morning?" she asked even as she shamelessly quivered from the sensation of his lips on her lips. "Even with the Baptism going on?"

He finished suckling then came up and kissed her so long and deep it made her even wetter. "Baby!" he said breathlessly as he pulled away from her lips, "I'll email you during the ceremony. You're all I'll be thinking about anyway."

That made her laugh against his lips. He kissed her deep again then pulled away and gazed in her eyes with that strange but almost annoyed expression. "How the hell am I supposed to get through the next few weeks with this on my mind?"

Lila's heart pounded, her mind still struggling to understand her *unbelievable* reaction to seeing him tonight. "Surprise me again?"

Sonny smiled, nodding as he cradled her face sweetly, then kissed her again softly, tenderly, and oh so deeply Lila felt her heart swell, until he finally pulled away with an agonized groan. Then he was gone.

She stood there, her back against the door, still breathless and very tingly—so tingly she was tempted to alleviate the tortured state Sonny had left her in. But she didn't. Instead, she closed her eyes, smiling and trying to push away the sudden fear in her heart. As much as she'd been trying to deny it all week, that it was way too soon to be falling for him the way she could feel herself falling, after tonight, there was no way she could possibly deny it.

Lila was no saint, but she knew there was no way she would've ever allowed a guy to do so much this soon—see her completely naked and suck her breasts—unless she'd been utterly crazy about him. She could argue all she wanted that, technically, she didn't let him do more, but she knew damn well the only reason for that was that he couldn't stay longer. She'd been so ready to let him, and it scared the life out of her.

---

Sonny had kept his promise that weekend about emailing and calling every chance he could. Unfortunately, she'd yet to keep her promise to him about showing her what he'd asked. She just hadn't had a moment when she was someplace she could do it in private. Doing it at work was out of the question, and Ali had been home all week at the same time Lila had.

She was actually glad Sonny hadn't been pushing for it. In fact, she'd been the one to bring it up each time that she wasn't alone, and he knew what that meant.

A few other things had changed since, after the night of his visit, this had suddenly become very real. Ali knew about him now. As much as Lila had tried to make less of it than it really was, Sonny had sent her flowers several times now. There was no hiding the fact that she was pretty much in a relationship. Ali was excited for her. But the reality of this now was still a bit overwhelming.

Their emails, texts, and even FaceTime conversations had taken on a more sexual tone after that first quick stop he'd made at her place. In a matter of just a few weeks, her life seemed to be spiraling with changes. She'd since agreed to train again and had been doing so for weeks now; although she still wasn't telling anyone about *that* yet.

So far, it'd been just that, nothing but training on the bags and her footwork. The weeks had flown with a couple of more surprise visits Sonny had made that had all been as quick and dirty as the first. If they'd been even slightly longer, she would've given him much more than just the heavy petting and letting him have his way with her breasts. It still scared her almost breathless to think she was this close to being in an all-out sexual relationship with a man she now knew she was crazy about.

Then it happened. Just like his surprise visits, it was fast and dirty, yet at the same time as thrilling as it was terrifying. After getting off the phone with Ali, who'd called to let her know she was going to be a little late, Lila got ready.

She answered Sonny's FaceTime call, wearing her robe—and nothing else. He seemed surprised at first; then it appeared to dawn on him. "What's under the robe?"

Lila's heart thundered, but she could already feel how instantly wet she'd gotten just thinking about what she was about to do. "Nothing," she said, feeling her face warm.

Sonny sat up straighter on the sofa. Sinking her teeth onto her bottom lip, she started to undo the tie on her robe because she knew she was pressed for time. Lila had moved her nightstand a bit so she could position her laptop on it while she sat on the edge of her bed.

"My sister and her friend had a taco truck craving, so she called to say she'd be a little late," Lila explained, still unable to believe she was doing this.

But then this was what Sonny had been doing to her since day one, bringing out the side of her she hadn't even been aware existed. "She's only stopping to grab something to eat; then she's taking Jen back to her place and heading home. So, she won't be too long. I don't have too much time, sorry."

"Don't be sorry," Sonny said quickly, his eyes already taking her in completely. "Just make it fast."

# LILA

As she let the robe open slowly, Sonny groaned. "Swear to God you're gonna make me jump on a fucking plane right now."

Lila laughed nervously as she let the robe fall off her shoulders, then scooted back on the bed. "I've never done anything like this, Sonny," she admitted, feeling stupid that she hadn't exactly planned anything—just stripped out of her clothes and grabbed her bathrobe the moment she'd gotten off the phone with Ali. "I'm not even sure what you want me to do."

"Oh, I'll tell you," Sonny said without missing a beat. "Scoot farther back onto the bed and lie back."

Swallowing hard as her heart thudded wildly, she did as she was told but was glad he'd be taking the reins because she really had no idea what she was doing. "Get some pillows under your head so your head is up. I wanna be able to see your face while you do this."

*Do this?* It dawned on her suddenly he wasn't expecting her to just *show* him what might be his someday. She'd stupidly visualized giving him an intimate peek of her nethers. Now, she realized, he was expecting so much more.

Grabbing the pillows, feeling a strange thrill in her belly she never would've imagined feeling over this new-development, she placed them under her head and stared at the screen.

"Now bend your knees so they're both up." Slowly she slid her legs up so her knees were now blocking her view. "Spread 'em, babe, all the way so I can see your face too." Very slowly she spread her knees apart until she could see the aroused smile on his face. "Beautiful, but spread more and get those fingers ready, Lila."

Gulping, she spread wider, surprised by how aroused she was suddenly feeling too.

"Perfect," he said once she was spread eagle. "Okay, I'd move through this slowly, but no way am I risking running out of time. Lick your fingers for me and reach down and touch yourself."

He was probably too far for him to see it, but Lila didn't need to lick her fingers. She already knew she was wet enough. Seeing that expression on his face had done it to her.

"Stop right there," he said when she touched her tender clit. "See that right there?" Lila nodded. "I'm claiming that. Go lower." She did until her fingers were at her entrance. "Slide 'em in, both of them."

She did slowly, and seeing him close his eyes in reaction with a groan made her smile. Before he could tell her what to do next, she easily slid them as deep as possible then pulled them out and licked them.

"Oh fuck," he said, adjusting what she was sure was the massive erection she'd only gotten to feel over his clothes so far.

Then she had a thought. "Let's do this together," she said, sitting up on her elbow. "I wanna see you."

He jumped off the sofa, and Lila almost laughed that she hadn't had to ask twice. "Hold on," she heard him say even though he was out of the screen now.

A few minutes later, Sonny sat back on his sofa with what looked like a bottle of lotion and a towel. "I'm probably gonna rip through my pants anyway if I don't undo this," he said, unbuttoning his pants and pulling his zipper down.

Lila's eyes were glued to the screen now. "You can't use the towel until you're done," Lila said almost in a trance. "I wanna see when you come."

"Whatever you say, but keep going, sweetheart. Let's not run out of time."

The size of his cock shouldn't have surprised her when he pulled it out. She'd felt it enough over his pants now to have a general idea of what she'd be in for, but it still did. It sprung right out and it was huge.

"Jesus," she whispered as she brought her fingers back down because, just like all the times they'd made out so far, she was on fire again.

Aware that Ali would be home soon, she moved things along because she'd need to finish now. Watching him stroke himself only aroused her further. She'd had sex with Marcelo and even sent him faceless photos of her breasts, but this was a first for her. As long as she'd been with Marcelo, she never would've trusted him enough to send him a photo of her breasts that included her face, much less give him a video chat he could easily record of her playing with herself that included her entire body.

This might be the stupidest thing she'd ever done, but at the moment she didn't care. Lila still didn't understand the spell-like influence Sonny had on her. But she trusted this man like she'd never trusted anyone aside from Ali.

Sonny's breathing was getting heavier as he stroked a little faster. Lila moaned softly as she felt the buildup of what she already knew would be an intense orgasm.

"That's it, baby. Come for me. I wanna see it."

Sliding her fingers in and out of her dripping folds, she worked her clit with two fingers until she was moaning and trying not to make the ugly orgasm faces she'd seen in movies. But she'd been right; she came so intensely her entire body trembled.

"Fuck yeah," Sonny said with a groan and once again her eyes were glued to the screen.

Even as she lay there, still feeling the effects of the amazing orgasm, she watched in trance-like fixation as his semen shot out again and again, until he finally fell back onto the sofa.

"As far as I'm concerned," he said, trying to catch his breath. "We've technically had sex. I own that shit now. It's mine, and as soon as I'm home again, I'll make it official."

Lila smiled. No way could she say she wasn't ready anymore now, not after this. "Never in my life have I been so willing to do everything I've done with you so far, Sonny. So, I can hardly wait for you to get home now."

She let her head fall back onto her pillows, feeling her heart still beating wildly. It surprised her that, even as she came down from the incredible orgasm, she didn't feel even the tiniest bit of regret. Another first for her. What the hell had this man done to her?

⭐

The week before his much-anticipated return on Sunday was also the first week she'd finally be getting back in the ring to do some real sparring. Gio had set it up so she'd be sparring with another girl in private that Thursday. Except for Felix, who wasn't around as much as the others, all the owners would be watching. Even Abel, who stayed as busy as Felix traveling all over, was going to be there. Gio had assured her that, aside from them and the girl she'd be sparring with, no one else would be in the private training room.

She finished up at the youth center then headed toward the training room, her insides as nervous as the first time. But she had to get this over with. If Stacia really moved out, Lila needed to get a bigger cash flow coming in. Gio had already explained about the upcoming fight in a few weeks—how if he could get her trained enough, she might be able to make her debut in a two-to-three round friendly bout before the undercards, just so she could get a feel for the rush of being in the ring in front of an audience. But he said, depending on how well she did and how much attention they could garner, they might be able to line up a paying gig in as soon as a few months. And he had a feeling she was going to get a lot of attention.

"I'm telling you, you're a natural," he'd said yesterday while he coached her on the speed bag. "I've yet to see *any* of the other girls I've been training for months now come close to your strength and speed. It's why it's been a struggle to get any real excitement for the women's boxing program. You may be the very thing this program needs. I know *I'm* excited."

Seeing the genuine excitement in those amazing green eyes of his should've had her excited too. Instead, it made her even more nervous. She still planned on keeping this to herself until she was *absolutely* certain she'd be committing to this.

On her way to the private training room, she saw Gio and remembered to ask what she'd forgotten to for weeks. Ali hadn't brought it up since the first time, so until this morning when she reminded her, it'd been the last thing on her mind. So, she pulled him aside before she'd forget again. "My sister asked me to ask you about something and I keep forgetting." Gio nodded, willing her to go ahead. "That work-release program I've heard rumors about. She's heard them too."

"It's not a rumor," he said with a smile. "It's really happening. Nellie's just about done getting it together, and we should start getting the first ones in the program in here soon. Some will be women." He pointed at her as that brightened his eyes. "Some, like you, have had enough experience on the street fighting, but are now interested in getting some real training in the sport. This is good news for us. Might actually find a contender among them."

That only unnerved her further. Not only would she be doing what she said she'd never do, but she might be doing it with an ex-convict. Great. But she did her best to try and look a little excited about it.

"My sister wanted to know if maybe she could come in here and get an interview with whoever will be running the work-release program for her paper—"

"I have the exclusive on that." The female voice came from behind Lila.

Lila turned to see Ms. Bitch, the one she hadn't allowed in the employee bathroom the day of the concert, staring at her blankly. She then turned to Gio. "Right, Gio? I get all the 5th Street exclusives."

Lila felt that same familiar heat she always did whenever someone repulsed her the way this girl did.

"I didn't know your sister was a reporter?"

Lila kept her cool and turned to Gio, ignoring Ms. Bitch. "She's not yet. This would be for her college newspaper. She's still a student."

"Oh, well, if it's for a school paper, that's fine." He turned to Ms. Bitch. "That's not the same. She's not a competing paper or anything."

"But I'd still like to run mine first just the same." She turned to Lila. "When does your sister anticipate running her story?"

Lila didn't even respond. Instead, she kept her eyes on Gio. "I'll talk to you about this later. See you in a bit."

She promptly walked away. *Fuck* her. Lila didn't need to answer to her. If Gio or any of the other owners said it was okay, then Ali could get in here and do her interview whenever the hell she wanted. That bitch better not even think about trying to stop her.

As promised, the only ones in the room were Noah and Abel when she walked in. Gio and Hector weren't there yet. Not even the girl she'd be sparring with was there.

"The other guys and—" Noah stopped to think about it. "I think Gio said it's Michele you'll be sparring with. They'll all be in here soon too. I'll start wrapping your hands."

"So, you've been training with Gio," Abel asked, crossing his big arms in front of him. "I've been hearing good things."

"It's only been a few weeks." She held out her hand for Noah to wrap and felt the inevitable anxiety creep up her spine and neck. "I still haven't decided for sure if I wanna do this."

Noah stopped wrapping her hand and looked up at her, brows pinched. "You haven't?"

"Well, not entirely," she said honestly. "You remember what happened last time I got in the ring."

Noah's hardened expression softened, and he even smirked. "Yeah, I was just telling Abel about that. We just gotta work on that short fuse, but something tells me none of these girls will connect enough to piss you off. In fact, I was gonna tell *you* to go easy on Michele today. She may've been training longer than you, but I've watched you this week with Gio, and I can already tell you have a lethal left hook. If you hit just as hard with both hands, they don't stand a chance."

Hector and Gio sauntered in just as Noah was finishing up wrapping her hands. Gio took over helping her get her gloves and headgear on. Then he went over some last-minute pointers while Noah geared up Michele. The girl was about as tall as Lila. Except for her blond cornrows, she had an innocent look about her. Lila almost felt sorry for her, so she'd keep Noah's request to go easy on her in mind.

They got in the ring with Gio coaching them. "We're not trying to land big hits here. Just see if you can land any at all. This is Lila's first time, Michele, so little jabs. Take turns practicing trying to land while the other practices blocking or bobbing and weaving out of the way. Michele, you try landing first, and, Lila, stay cool if she does. She shouldn't be landing anything too hard anyway."

They started and Lila practiced her footwork as well, taking in a deep breath as she blocked Michele's first jab with her right arm. It wasn't as soft as she was expecting, given Gio's little speech, but she stayed cool, breathing in through her nose. Michele missed the next two as Lila ducked to the side then she landed another on Lila's arm again.

"Good job, Lila," Noah said, distracting her from her already altering irritation. "Way to block."

Michele hit her with a combination of jabs, and up until the last one that came up under her chin, Lila blocked them all, but it rattled her. She spit her mouthpiece out, walking away from Michele. "So, we *are* landing big ones?" she asked, trying to keep it together because she knew this was nothing yet then turned to Gio. "Because I can fucking land big ones too. We don't need to take it easy on my account."

Hector chuckled, but it was Michele's smirk that really pissed Lila off. "Alright, just go at it," Gio said, spraying her mouthpiece clean and jumping onto the side of the ring to put it back in her mouth. "No taking turns, but keep your cool, yeah? Getting hit is the nature of the sport. It's gonna happen. Make that anger work *for* you not against you."

Lila turned around and took a deep breath before getting in the center of the ring with Michele. Michele blocked the first few jabs Lila took at her then landed one on the side of Lila's head. Lila responded immediately with a big one that had Michele tumbling back.

Lila stopped and waited. "No, no, no," Noah said as Hector clapped. "That's when you go in for the kill." He turned to Michele. "I mean we'll stop it before she does, but I wanna see her skills. I wanna see if she knows how to finish."

Pissed at herself that she hadn't gone for it all the way because she just assumed she shouldn't, Lila got back in the middle of the ring with Michele, who'd now recovered. Michele came at her again with a combination that landed under her chin. Apparently, this was her move. As pissed as it made her, Lila did what Gio said, made her anger work for her. She landed a combination of her own, pretended to wind up for a left then swung at her with her right. Again, Michele stumbled back, and Lila didn't hold back this time. She went at her, landing hit after hit that had Michele against the ropes and Hector cheering and whistling. The adrenaline rush was awesome, but Gio was in there now and stopped her.

"Fuck yeah!" Hector said, jabbing a fist in the air. "That's what I'm talking about. *That's* what you use that anger for. Just like that, baby!"

"You okay, Michele?" Noah asked as Michele walked it off in the ring, and she nodded even though her nose was already bleeding. Noah handed Gio a wet towel, and Gio cleaned her up.

"And this is really her first time sparring?" Abel asked, staring at her in complete disbelief.

"I told you she's a natural," Gio said, turning to him after cleaning Michele off.

"She's a badass," Abel said, shaking his head. "You're a badass, sweetheart."

He turned to Noah as she smiled at the irony of hearing *Aweless* Ayala first call her a badass then a sweetheart all with that same look of complete awe in his eyes.

"Felix will be here in a couple of days," Abel said with a smile. "He should see this." He turned back to Lila. "You work Sunday?"

Lila shook her head as Gio took her mouthpiece. "No," she said, feeling slightly excited about this now, especially because, even though Sonny would be back in town, he had mentioned needing to be somewhere for a few hours on Sunday. "But I can come in if you want me to."

"What time is that meeting on Sunday?" Noah asked Gio.

"Noon," Gio said, smiling even bigger. "But it doesn't matter. He'll probably be here all day." He turned to Lila. "Can you come in about one? We should be done by then."

Lila nodded as the excitement about this sunk in even more. Maybe she could do this. Maybe she was born to be a *badass*. Maybe her mother passing so young wasn't all for nothing. She still wouldn't tell a soul, not yet anyway. But she was glad to know Noah had been right. Her biggest fear was getting hit too many times in the face. This was only her first time in the ring, and she'd nearly knocked Michele out.

With a little more practice, she could work on *never* getting hit in the head. It was how she'd explain it to Ali anyway. But she'd wait until she was much better at this before she'd let Ali witness her skills in the ring.

# 9

# Sonny

This was insane. Even with the few surprise stops to see Lila during his weeks on the road, and that incredible FaceTime sex they'd had, *Sonny* had cut his trip short to get home a day early because he couldn't stand it anymore. He *needed* to see Lila again. Now he was standing here outside her apartment building, waiting for her to get home from work. Just like the first few times he'd been in the area, he'd been getting strange looks from passersby and he knew why. His Maserati stuck out as Sonny would in this neighborhood if he got out of the car. It was why he wore a hoodie over his head and sunglasses. The good thing was it was getting dark. Only that made his dark glasses even more suspicious. In this neighborhood, anyone eyeing his car was probably doing it more out of fear than curiosity. They probably thought him the kingpin of all the drug dealers that lived around here or the main pimp of all the *pimps* of the area, here to collect his money or something.

That made him chuckle; though it was short-lived. He remembered now how Lila said she wished she could move to a better area. The thought of her and her sister having to live in this area was now one that would worry him. All he could hope was, if things went well and they moved things along fast enough, he could get her out of this building. Maybe not move her in with him just yet since, obviously, she'd made it a point to say she needed to take things slow, but at least get her into a safer area.

He peered at the girl walking up the street toward the apartment building he was parked in front of. The closer she got, the harder his heart thudded, not just because he'd been dying to see her all week, but when he realized it was Lila, his first thought was *She walks these streets?*

As soon as she was close enough, he got out of the car. "You walk to work?"

Startled, she turned to the sound of his voice then smiled big. "*Sonny?* I thought you said you wouldn't be back until tomorrow." She rushed to him.

Before he could ask her again, she was in his arms, and *damn,* it felt good. He hugged her hard, groaning into her neck. "I couldn't stand it anymore. I needed to get back to you already, and since tomorrow I have those commitments I need to attend to, I cut my trip short just to see you tonight."

He didn't let her respond to that because he needed to get his mouth on hers already. As always, she kissed him as hungrily as he kissed her. It wasn't until he pulled away and saw the thugs down the street he remembered. "I thought you said you have a car?"

"I do. But me and my sister share it. Her school is farther away than my job. I'm a short bus ride away, and it drops me off right at the corner."

Sonny tried not to frown at that, but he couldn't help feeling concerned. Maybe he wouldn't be able to move her out too soon. But he might be able to swing *lending* her a car first.

He leaned in and kissed her again, keeping his thoughts to himself. "You hungry?" She nodded with a smile. "What do you feel like having?" They started back to the passenger side of his car. She crinkled her nose as he opened the door for her and he *had* to kiss her again.

"Chinese? There's a good mom and pop one around the corner."

"Okay Chinese?"

"Yeah." She smiled even bigger than earlier. "How did you know?"

"I'm telling you I grew up in this area, and that place has been around forever. Okay Chinese it is."

Because it was one of the few that had a drive-thru, they could get their food and head back to Hollenbeck Park to eat it. By then, it'd be good and dark again, unless she wanted to come back and eat it at her place. While he'd made it clear he'd be making things official once he was home and she hadn't protested, he wanted to come clean first about what he'd been keeping from her. He planned on doing that tomorrow. He had it all set up.

They started off with him telling her why he'd gotten here a day early. "I would've been back even sooner, but my second Vegas trip plans had been made a while ago, and last night's fight was the main reason I was there in the first place. So, I figured I should at least stay for that."

"Fight?" she asked then glanced away. "What kind of fight?"

"A few up-and-coming boxers. I have a friend who follows boxing—"

His phone ringing over the speakers interrupted them. Sonny frowned when he saw the name on the dash screen: Tatiana. Using the controls on his steering wheel, he sent the call to voicemail. "Sorry about that." He turned onto the street where Okay Chinese was.

Seeing Tatiana's name threw him off his thoughts, and he couldn't even remember what he'd been saying. "Anything particular you like from this place?"

"The fried pepper chicken wings, hands down," she said without a flinch. "But I also like their tangerine chicken."

They discussed the other menu items as they sat in the drive-thru until his phone rang again and the same name popped onto the dash screen. Once again, Sonny sent it to voicemail, but seeing Lila's eyebrow arch forced him to give her at least a short version of who Tatiana was. "Business colleague," he said as indifferently as he could.

It *was* the truth, partially anyway. Like with many of his female business colleagues, though, Sonny did his best to keep things on a professional level. It always amazed him how easily even the most professional ones were willing to take things a little further. He always made it clear his career didn't allow for anything more serious. Again, most were all for it, despite the stipulation. Some, like Tatiana, however, were far more persistent than others.

"Maybe it's important." It was a statement that sounded more like an inquiry—in invitation to further explain what kind of business colleague.

"Nah, she's part of the team I'm meeting with tomorrow. Technically, everyone still thinks I'm out of town, and if it's for pleasure, they know I usually don't respond to business stuff. I'll see her soon enough."

That seemed to satisfy her, and she didn't ask for more, but turning his phone off might seem suspicious. So, when they reached the park after getting their food, he left his phone in the car, instead of bringing it with him to the picnic table where they sat and ate.

They didn't sit on opposite sides of the table either. The time since he'd last seen her in person had felt like an eternity. No way was Sonny wasting a minute of having his hands on her. Even as they ate, his hand caressed her back, and he kissed her nonstop between eating and drinking their sodas.

He felt like a hormonally-charged and lovesick teen, not an almost thirty-year-old grown-ass man, but he didn't even care. Something about Lila made him nervous. His lifestyle was so different from hers. Already he knew enough to be certain she wouldn't have the patience for some of the things in it, like all the *Tatianas* she'd have to hear about among other things. Regardless, nervous or not, he was doing this tomorrow, for sure.

But before that, he wanted her to know how genuine his feelings were. Albeit it was crazy that he'd feel *this* much so soon, he needed her to know that what he was feeling was absolutely true, not just how much his cock ached for her as she'd seen for herself. He needed her to know how much more she meant to him now. So, letting her see his lovesick-teen side might actually be a good thing.

"You work tomorrow?"

She shook her head. "No, but I do have to go in for one quick thing. I shouldn't be there for more than an hour."

"In the morning or afternoon?"

"Mid-day," she said as she lifted her finger to his forehead and fixed a strand of his hair with a smile.

Sonny took her hand and kissed it then kissed her. *Jesus, how could he have it this bad after just a little over a month? Okay, maybe showing his lovesick side might be a good idea for some reasons, but he had to tone it down a little, before he crept her out.*

Clearing his throat, he picked up a chicken wing, hoping it'd keep his hands and lips busy for at least a little bit. "That's perfect," he said, taking a bite then wiping his mouth after swallowing. "My meeting's around that time, so we should both be free around the same time. We can drive out to Los Feliz where I live, and I'll show you around, since you said you've never been."

She nodded, smiling brightly, and that relieved him. His plan was to talk her into going back to his place, not just so he could officially claim her, but because once there, she'd inevitably know the truth about his life—*see* who he was—and what that entailed. There was evidence of it all over his house. It was crazy that all these years he'd worried about women being into him solely based on what he did. He'd never know for sure if they were genuinely into him or if they just liked the *idea* of being with someone like him. Now, here he was worried about Lila being put off by it.

But it was exactly what had drawn him to her to begin with—the fact that she *didn't* seem the least bit interested in how he'd made so much money. She hadn't even asked much about his cars. This entire time he'd known her, she'd been more interested in much simpler things about him. But they were the kinds of things that ultimately had him falling for her. She asked about the things that count, such as his likes and dislikes and his relationship with his siblings. They discussed goals, aspirations, even silly dreams. To his surprise, she admitted to possibly being interested in fitness modeling, something Sonny thought would be perfect for her, given what he'd seen and felt of her body so far. It was obviously a subject she was still not completely comfortable discussing. And since Sonny himself was still holding back on some major things about his life, he didn't want to be a hypocrite and push for more.

Compared to all the high-profile and high-maintenance women he'd been dating for years, Lila was such an exhilarating breath of fresh air. And her not knowing about him made more sense now that he knew she wasn't much for social media. She said she only had a Facebook profile and even that she logged onto so infrequently she was always having to reset her password. Because of the low budget she and her sister and roommate were on, they didn't even have cable. As crazy as that sounded, she said she and her sister were fine watching stuff on Netflix and YouTube.

Sonny only hoped now that, after tomorrow, things wouldn't change. That she wouldn't see or think him any different from the lovesick guy who, after just a little over a month of knowing her, was already cutting his own trips short just to get back to her.

They ate, talked, giggled, and did a whole lot more kissing and cuddling until they headed back to the car because she said she was getting chilly. He was in no hurry to get home, and while Sonny wouldn't mind just hanging out with her, he was dying to do a lot more of what they'd done during his quick visits. He suggested they might head up to Griffith Park, a place he knew well and had plenty of beautiful scenic spots they could park and get cozy.

"Marcelo used to take me up there a lot," she said softly, gazing out the window.

That said, Sonny made a hasty right turn in the opposite direction of Griffith Park. "Mulholland Drive has even better views," he said simply as he got on the freeway.

Fuck that. He wouldn't be taking her somewhere where she'd be thinking of her ex while Sonny's tongue and lips made the most of his time with her. Halfway up their drive, as she cheerfully told him about her sister's journalist sleuthing and how close she was to uncovering who the on-campus drug dealer might be at her college, his phone rang again. It'd already rung once with a different girl's name popping up, which he hadn't explained and she hadn't asked about. Now it was Tatiana *again,* and Sonny felt like banging the damn steering wheel, but he refused to answer, not with the call coming through the speakers. Tatiana was an insatiable flirt, and there'd be no way Lila wouldn't pick up on it. The last thing he wanted when he was so close to coming clean was to piss off Lila.

"Are you sure she's just a business associate?" The sweet expression of Lila wore earlier was gone now. "Three times she's called on a Saturday night."

"We have this meeting tomorrow," Sonny explained, picking his phone up from the center console, *pissed* that he hadn't just turned the fucking thing off earlier. "She probably wants to compare notes, but I'm *not* interrupting my time with you for business."

That last part he'd nearly said through his teeth. He'd since heard the rest of the story behind her breakup with her ex. Not only had he enlisted in the Army without even telling her, just up and left, he'd cheated on her, and he'd knocked someone up after Lila had forgiven him for leaving. Apparently, Lila didn't approve of all the illegal shit he was doing, so before she could dump his ass, he'd left on a whim, to prove he was willing to go to such lengths to change for her. Then he went and fucking cheated on her.

Sonny and Lila may not have been an official couple yet, but he'd meant it when he claimed her as his, even if, at the time, he'd been sort of playful about it. He'd definitely consider it cheating if she saw anyone else, so he knew she had every right to be pissed about this.

Shutting his phone off, he put it down then reached for Lila's hand. Their eyes met for a moment as he came to a stop sign, but she didn't say anything, except she wasn't gazing at him in that whimsical way she'd done all night.

"I turned it off because I don't want to keep getting interrupted all night. I looked forward to tonight all week. I don't want anything spoiling this."

"Who's Frances?"

If their eyes weren't locked, he might've been able to squeeze them shut like he wished he could do. Frances was the other girl whose name had popped up on his screen earlier. "Frances *is* someone I went out with in the past." Lila started loosening her hand from his, but he held it firmly. "But I haven't seen her in months. Just kept in touch on the phone. Only I'll be letting her know even that's gonna stop now."

They drove silently the rest of the way to a spot that overlooked the Hollywood Bowl. The view was awesome. In Sonny's opinion, it was one of the best in the entire Los Angeles area, only now Sonny wasn't feeling it.

As soon as they parked and he killed the engine, he turned to Lila. "Look. Before I met you, I was a single guy, and while I didn't have time for any real relationships, I did date. There are girls who have my number, and I haven't even had a chance to let them know my situation has changed now." She started to say something, but he went on because he had a feeling what her response to this might be. "As fast as things have moved, I know you originally said you wanted to take this slow. Despite everything we've already done, I'm still more than willing to take this slowly. But based on how tense things got there for a moment, I'm assuming, regardless of how slow we're taking this, you feel the same way I do. Seeing anyone else while we're doing this, no matter how slow, isn't gonna fly, right?"

She stared at him, and now that hardened expression appeared a little vulnerable—nervous. "I hadn't really thought of it"—her expression hardened a little— "not until all the phone calls you sent to voicemail tonight, but no, it's not gonna fly."

Relieved, Sonny exhaled. "Good." He leaned in and kissed her. "Then agreed, we're both off the market, and anyone who thinks otherwise will be informed accordingly."

Finally, he got a smile out of her, and then he was kissing her again, long, deep, and devouring her mouth after waiting for what felt like an eternity to do again. After a few more marathon kisses, they got out of the car. He'd parked near a grassy knoll that overlooked the view. Sonny had come prepared with a blanket they could sit on and a small ice chest. He pulled them out of his trunk. Lila came around just before he could close the trunk. "A sweatshirt, perfect! It's even chillier up here."

Sonny's heart pounded a little because it was one of his new baseball sweatshirts, and it was personalized with his last name. He pulled it out and handed it to her. "One of my favorites actually. My mom had it personalized for me not too long ago."

She read the last name on the back—something he'd already been honest about, and she still hadn't had a clue—and smiled. "This is cool. So, I take it you're a big fan?"

"Yeah, I am." He smiled as she pulled it over her head.

It was huge on her, but she looked adorable in it. The thought of smelling her in it the next time he wore it was one that had him smiling like a crazy person again. He kissed her, throwing the blanket over his shoulder, as he closed the trunk. He took the cooler in one hand and her hand in the other. He set up the blanket, explaining he'd brought a bottle of wine but also brought some *Mocktails* he'd seen down at the store where he picked up the bottle of wine, since she didn't like drinking. He pulled one out of the cooler. "*Piña colada,* non-alcoholic."

"It's not that I don't like alcohol," she explained, glancing down at the bottle of wine. "I've been told a glass of red wine here and there is good for your heart. Drinking just makes me nervous because, as bad as I am controlling my emotions . . ." She frowned as if even talking about it made her uncomfortable. 'I'm afraid of what kind of reaction I might have. I already had a pretty bad one once when my ex convinced me to take some shots of Jack Daniels way back."

That irritated Sonny as much as it almost made him chuckle. "Yeah, wine and Jack are way different. I know people who are used to drinking who still stay the hell away from Jack because that shit can really light you up and not in a good way. Wine is more mellowing than anything. I mean I guess, if you drink a whole lot of it, you might get a little crazy, but a glass or two should be fine. If anything, it might put you to sleep. But unlike your ex, I'm in no way insisting you drink any. I just thought a glass of wine up here would be perfect. But I'll pour you your piña colada, and it'll be just as romantic."

She peered at him curiously. "Is it bitter?" she asked. "I heard the white ones are."

"They can be. Oddly enough, *White* Zinfandel," he said, pulling the bottle out, "is not white. It's pink and it's light and sweet, but not too sweet like pink moscato. Anything too sweet can give you a headache the next day. You can have a sip of mine if you wanna try it."

Lila nodded, smiling a bit nervously, so Sonny leaned over and kissed her, lifting her chin. "You'll be fine," he whispered, smiling when he got a sweet smile out of her.

He opened the bottle and poured himself a little in one of the plastic cups he brought then handed it to her. Lila took a sip, licking her lips, pondering for a moment, then tilted her head with a smirk. "Not bad."

"You can keep that cup for yourself if you want. I can pour me another."

She nodded, so he took the other cup out of the cooler and poured himself some wine. They sat looking out at the beautiful view and made small talk about the weather. He told her a little more about his trip, keeping what he was out there doing a little vague.

Once done with his glass of wine, he set it down in the cooler and kissed her a little deeper than he had most of the night. She set her cup down then lay back on the blanket, allowing Sonny to lie over her, and their kissing got even heavier. Sonny did the impossible again just as he had the times he'd stopped by and surprised her. He refrained from getting too carried away. Only he couldn't keep his hands off her entirely. He brought his hand over her belly. The undeniable six pack she had going on underneath her clothes that he'd seen several times now was a fucking turn on. He sucked her tongue until she moaned.

Lila caressed his arms and back as his hand went lower onto her legs. Despite their FaceTime sex, his heart nearly stopped when she let her leg fall open ever so slightly. He *did not* want to push, but it felt like an invitation, so he caressed her inner thigh over her spandex pants. His hand moved up a bit, feeling the heat that radiated from in between her legs, but he didn't go there. Then her hand was on his, and at first, he thought she was going to stop him, until she moved it between her legs, and this time *he* moaned.

Running his fingers down the middle, even over her spandex pants, he could feel how hot and likely wet she was. He touched the spot he knew would have her squirming, and she arched her back, kissing him harder. This was definitely an invitation for him to do more.

"Has it been over two years"—he kissed her lips then nipped them— "since you last had sex?"

"Since I've last had it in the flesh? Yes," she said breathlessly as he caressed her a little harder. Her response had him moaning again, and he felt her squeeze his shoulder. "I told you. You're the first person I allowed to even kiss me since then. And you're the only person ever who I've done what I did on FaceTime with. It's been hard for me to trust, so . . ."

Sonny stared at her, swallowing hard. "You can trust me. I promise." She nodded, staring in his eyes as his heart thudded in response to her go-ahead. "I've been dying to touch what's rightfully mine now," he said, bringing his hand up and under the waist of her pants.

While she tensed a bit, Lila wasn't stopping him. Sonny wasn't about to make love to her right there. He had a feeling she wouldn't want that anyway. But just like during his surprise visits, he got the distinct feeling of what she *did* want—what she might be *needing* for someone else to do to her—badly. So, he slipped his hand into her pants and under her panties, making his way down slowly as she spread for him a little.

"Jesus," he muttered, trying to keep it together before the touch of her burning wet flesh against his fingertips had him messing his pants.

Lila moaned, squirming as he slid his fingers down her hot slit and then slowly into her. She was tight, and ever since he'd seen it, Sonny's mind had been going wild imagining what she'd taste like when he finally got to go there. For now, he'd concentrate on making her feel good without having any accidents in the process, because even just doing this to her was *such* a fucking turn on.

Sonny kissed her, mimicking with his tongue what his fingers were doing to her pussy. He hoped he could soon be tasting her down there too. He worked her, sliding two fingers in and out as his thumb caressed her engorged clit. The visual of what she'd done for him had him moaning in her mouth as her body began to tremble.

With a whimper, Lila pulled her mouth away, needing to catch her breath as her body really began to tremble, and she moaned, arching her back. "That's it, baby," he said, stroking her a little gentler as he felt her begin to grip around his fingers. "Come, Lila," he whispered against her lips. "Come all over my fingers."

Sonny squeezed his own legs shut because the incredible feeling of her slick wet flesh pulsating around his fingers was too much. Feeling her entire body tremble against his and hearing her soft moans nearly had him coming too. "No more," she said, breathless, and he pulled his hand away to let her enjoy it.

He watched her beautiful face as she smiled in woozy satisfaction, then brought his hand out from her pants. Just when she gazed at him, he stuck his fingers in his mouth, sucking her juices off them, then groaned, squeezing his eyes shut. "Fucking delicious," he said as his aching cock throbbed just from the taste of her. "Next time I'll do that to you with my tongue." Her eyes widened and he smiled. "Yeah, that's definitely happening."

The meeting hadn't even started, and already, all Sonny could think of was getting the hell out of there. He could hardly wait to get Lila back to his place today. He only hoped after he came clean today she'd still trust him.

At least today's meeting didn't require him to wear a monkey suit, but given the number of other celebs in attendance, there were bound to be cameras, maybe even paparazzi, so he didn't dress completely down. He wore comfortable jeans and shoes, but still wore a sports coat and a button-down shirt.

Leroy Deck, the starting center for the LA Clippers, was the first one to greet him when he arrived. "Hey, man," Leroy said, holding out his hand to shake it then tapping his back with the other. "Feeling at home yet?"

"This has always been home to me," Sonny said with a smirk. "But, yeah, it feels great that I'm back for good."

Noah and Gio came out to greet him and Tatiana. Unlike everyone else who was dressed down a bit like Sonny, Tatiana was in her power skirt suit with the skirt a little shorter than the norm and big fuck-me shoes. She'd been wearing them when he met her months ago, the kind that *used* to have his cock awakening just from seeing her strut that nice little ass of hers after tapping it a few times. She knew it too, because he'd told her so. He was certain it was why she was wearing this today. Only now, none of it did anything for him. The moment she got the chance, she linked her arm into his and leaned into him. Her heels were so big, even as petite a woman as she was, she was tall enough to murmur into his ear, "I called you last night. I heard you'd ducked out of Vegas a day early. I was hoping we could get together. What are you doing after this?"

"Hey, if it isn't Mr. LA." Sonny and Tatiana both turned to see a smiling Felix walking toward them. Even then,

Tatiana made no effort to move away from Sonny. "Glad you made it. Everyone's excited about this season. What are you thinking? You getting us a championship title? We're due."

"I'll do my best. We got a good team this year."

"We sure do," Tatiana added, tightening her grip on his arm. "And with you in it now, we should at least make the play-offs."

"Play-offs my ass," Noah said, joining the conversation. "They paid a fortune to get this guy out here. He better make it happen."

A couple of the other guys from the team arrived and then more reporters. They were all here to discuss the next 5th Street charity event they'd all be part of. But Gio let them know they were also in for a surprise, something they all might be interested in being part of.

They were taken into one of the private training rooms where they'd set up tables and chairs. They went over some of the events scheduled for the coming months: the silent auction for the signed sports memorabilia they'd all donated, the signing they were having in a few weeks, and the celebrity 5k walk coming that summer. The whole time Tatiana sat next him, her legs were crossed so he had a nice view of her long bare thigh, since her skirt was so short. There was also no shortage of her hand on his thigh and her leaning in to whisper comments into his ear. He'd previously enjoyed Tatiana's forwardness. He appreciated a woman who wasn't afraid to go after what she wanted. But for the first time since he'd known her, he moved her hands away a few times. It just felt wrong now.

Then Gio clicked something on the Power Point he'd set up earlier. Everyone had busted his balls because he was being so formal about today's meeting, since normally they all just tossed ideas and opinions around, even just chatted and caught up with each other.

That was how the other two of these meetings Sonny had attended so far had been. He'd known the guys of 5th Street for years from other sporting events award shows and even TV spots on sports talk shows. But it wasn't until now that he'd be considered an Angelino again that they'd asked and he'd agreed to be part of this charity program for the gym.

"*Assholes*," Gio said, laughing as they started busting his balls again for the Power Point thing as he flicked and hit a few things on the laptop. "It's just one thing I want you to see before I show you the real thing since she's here now."

He hit something else on the laptop and then a photo appeared on the wall. Two female boxers were in the boxing ring, wearing headgear, both brunettes, both sporting cornrows, and both with impressively fit bodies. The photo was perfectly timed to where the one with her back slightly turned away from the photo just landed what looked like a killer knockout punch on the other. Gio pointed at the girl landing the punch.

"That," he said with a big smile, "is what women's boxing desperately needs. She's a powerhouse and a natural. This photo was taken yesterday, only the *third* time she's sparred against anyone in her *life*. We had her in there for the first time on Thursday. Even then, she almost knocked out a girl who's been training for years. She'll be the next badass in women's sports since Ronda Rousey. And you, Tatiana, get the exclusive of unveiling this beautiful thing to the world."

Tatiana leaned into Sonny. "Beautiful?" She scoffed under her breath. "Yeah, she seems lovely."

"We just need to get the buzz and excitement going for this program," Gio continued still looking very keyed up, "and with you guys endorsing and talking it up on your social media and such, that might just happen faster. But don't just take my word for it. We have her here today. Before I tell you any more about her, let me have you guys come see for yourself." He turned to one of the guys standing by a double door. "She ready?" The guy nodded. "And she knows there's more than just Felix coming in to watch?"

For whatever reason, that made the guy chuckle. "Yeah, she knows."

"And she's okay with it?"

He chuckled again. "Yeah, Noah just told me to tell you that he'll handle the introductions and you guys just go along with it all, until *after* the presentation."

"Got it." Gio turned to everyone sitting in the room. "Let's go check this out."

Again, Tatiana hooked her arm into Sonny's and leaned into him as they walked out, but his new teammate Toby Nixon walked alongside him. Then Felix was there on the other side of Tatiana. This made it impossible for him to tell Tatiana what he wanted to: to get the hell off him. But he knew it was his own fault. The last time he'd been here, she'd done the same thing, even playfully called him her boyfriend. Only he hadn't given a shit then, and since he'd been looking forward to nailing her after that meeting, he just went along with it. Unlike today, where he hadn't done a thing to encourage the behavior except not tell her to stop, the last time he'd gone along with all the discreet touching and even groping when no one was watching.

He was just glad he was coming clean with Lila today. There were too many cameras here today, and with this unveiling shit, he had a feeling there'd be more. The moment he was out of here today, he'd be calling her.

# Lila

Lila loosened up, hitting the speed bag, and shook her head from side to side. Gus, the meathead cocky guy Gio had sent in to help warm her up, advised her how to stretch her jaw too. He'd already cracked a few jokes about warming her up being his pleasure and other ways he could help her loosen her jaw. He was that close to her unleashing on him what Gio and Noah now called her lethal combination knockout jab. After a few glares, he'd gotten the hint and was being somewhat professional.

She still wasn't sure what to think. When she got here earlier, she'd seen the crowd of what appeared to be big wigs or maybe other famous boxers that often came in to 5th Street. That bitch-face reporter was there, so Lila could only assume something big was going on. Either that or that meeting the guys were having with Felix was a big thing. The reporter didn't look to be doing much reporting though.

She'd been too busy hanging off one of the guys in particular. Neither had been facing Lila when she walked in, but some of the other guys had been, and she didn't recognize any of them anyway. Although the two very tall black guys were likely basketball players. Some of the Lakers and Clippers players were known to come in here from time to time. Though, pathetically, Lila wouldn't recognize any of them either. She'd just never been a fan of basketball, or any sport for that matter except for boxing, and that only started recently when she seriously began giving boxing some consideration.

Since she'd run into Gio as she got here, he'd been happy about her being here early. He'd asked her to go into the training room, and he'd sent Gus to warm her up. But she got the feeling he wasn't telling her something. Just as Lila's eyes met Gus's, who annoyingly kept trying to prolong the eye contact, the door to the training room opened, and in walked Noah and Hector. "How we doing?" Hector asked.

"She's doing *beautifully*," Gus said, smiling at her from the other side of the speed bag.

Lila nearly rolled her eyes but managed not to. "Couple things," Hector said as Noah went and grabbed more tape to finish taping her hands. "We brought in Odessa Cantor, someone a little more experienced with a few knockouts under her belt, for this sparring. She weighs just a little more than you do. I still think she's got nothing on you, but we wanted someone who might hold out a little longer than the last two did for this presentation. Another thing, we'll have a few more people in here watching than just Felix."

"Like who?" she asked, feeling alarmed, not to mention a little pissed because she remembered all those people earlier. "Did you bring in reporters and cameras?"

"No, not for this," Noah said, rushing toward her. "They're here for that meeting we had. But we would like to show you off to some of the people *in* that meeting. Big names."

"Celebrity athletes?" she asked as more alarm and heat inundated her. "You never—"

"Relax. They're just people like you and—"

"*Bullshit!* You never mentioned—"

"Listen, listen, listen," he said, urgently holding up a hand. "Do you know Leroy Deck? Tony Nixon?"

He rattled off several other names, all of which *maybe* sounded familiar, but Lila had to admit she had no idea who they were. She shook her head, glancing at Hector and Gus. Both looked appalled that she didn't know any of them.

"Sylvester Sabian?" Hector asked as if she *should* know that. "Only the best shortstop in the big leagues, who *everyone* in Los Angeles has been talking about, even my *mom*, because he just signed with the Dodgers?"

"I think," she lied, feeling even more embarrassed about her lack of sports knowledge.

But hearing the last name of the shortstop did make her insides flutter because it made her think of Sonny. Up until him, it was the first time she'd even heard the last name.

"Well, there you go," Noah said, already wrapping one of her hands. "They may be well-known athletes to other people. But to you, they're nobody. You'll be sparring in a room with a few strangers watching. Just think of them as other trainers like Gus here watching you."

"Yeah, with cars that cost more than my parents' house," Gus said, shaking his head.

Noah glared at Gus then got back to wrapping Lila's hands. Once he'd managed to convince Lila to just get in her zone like Gio had been training her to do and drown out everything else in the room, he told her more about Odessa. He wasn't at all worried about Lila being able to handle her and gave Lila the go-ahead to give it her all.

"No holding back," he said, lifting a brow and looking her straight in the eyes. "Odessa's a big girl and is ready to take it. We want these guys to see your power and your strength."

Odessa walked in just a few minutes later. She was a tough-looking black girl wearing cornrows as Lila did, today. Odessa was bigger than the other two girls Lila had fought, but just like no one ever had, she didn't scare Lila. It was how she'd felt her whole life. Unless anyone Lila brawled with had a gun or another weapon that could take her down, the only way she'd go down was if she couldn't move or breathe anymore. As pumped and enraged as she could get, she'd fight to the death if she had to.

The only thing that scared her was that there'd be a room full of people watching. If this girl did get a good hit on Lila, they'd be witness to the ugliness it would spawn. She punched her gloves together, glancing at her reflection in the wall mirror. Ever since that first time in the ring when her hair had given her such issues, she'd since decided cornrows were the way to go. She'd been watching women's boxing matches on YouTube, and it was how most wore their hair in the ring. It made sense. In Lila's opinion, it wasn't the most attractive, but then she wasn't trying to impress anyone with her looks when she was in the ring. Just her skills. And just like with the first girl and now Odessa, it did make her look tougher—harder. Gio said getting in your opponent's head was another aspect of fighting.

Noah had told her they'd explained to this girl and her manager they needed to borrow her for a friendly spar so they could unveil what they thought might be the next big thing in women's boxing. They needed someone who could last a little longer against her than some of the girls she'd gone up against. If this girl was any better with sports knowledge than Lila was, then seeing the *big names* here today for Lila's unveiling would be enough to get in Odessa's head. Lila looking even tougher than normal was just another plus.

After several minutes of punching the pads with Gus for a little, with Hector coaching while Noah walked over and spoke with Odessa and her trainer, Noah turned back to Lila and asked if she was ready.

She was as ready as she'd ever be, if that meant anything. Noah told Gus to go tell Gio she was ready, and Lila's insides were instantly roiling. She had this. She knew she did, but it was still nerve-wracking. Gus came back in the room first. "They're on their way," he said, walking over to Lila, who was stretching her legs a bit and then jumping in place to loosen up some more. "So, what's your deal?" Gus asked, sizing her up as she continued to stretch from side to side. "You single or what?"

Lila didn't even look at him. That should be answer enough. Single or not, she wasn't interested. That was all he needed to know. Felix walked in first, holding the door open for the rest of the guys that filed in behind them. She glanced away, taking a deep breath when she noticed all eyes focused on her immediately. When she glanced up again, she made eye contact with Gio, who smiled and waved her over as more people continued to walk in. She'd nearly reached him when she saw him.

Sonny. With that bitch-face whore hanging on his arm.

He glanced at her, began to look away, then did a wide-eyed double take. The whore leaned into him and whispered something in his ear. Felix closed the door just as Gio placed his hand on Lila's shoulder. Her eyes were fixated on the slutty outfit bitch-face wore, but more infuriating was the way she continued to paw Sonny and giggle. Sonny appeared as stunned as she did, only her insides were already doing what they did best, turning the incredible hurt and utter jealousy she was feeling into seething *rage*.

"Gentlemen," Gio began. "I'd like you to meet Lila Rico, women's boxing's up-and-coming sensation."

Lila did her best to concentrate on what Gio was saying, but it felt *impossible,* with every hair on her body standing at attention. Was this the big-name athlete boyfriend that bitch had been talking about in the employee bathroom? Lila had felt many types of anger throughout her life. But this was different. She felt fucking *played*. He'd been so damn good at lying to her all this time, even last night and just this morning when he emailed her to tell her he'd thought of her all night and first thing when he woke. She didn't even want to look at Sonny and the bitch, but it couldn't be helped. Her eyes inevitably traveled down to their hands where the bitch nearly slipped hers into his until Sonny fisted his shut. *Really? You're going to try and save face now, you fucking bastard?*

Noah took over the talking. "We'll save the introductions until after we give you a little taste of what we're all in for when this badass makes her debut later this year." He turned and pointed in the direction of Sonny, but Lila refused to even look his way again. "Tatiana, no photos just yet, okay? You'll have the exclusive when we're ready to make an official public announcement, but for now . . ."

Whatever he said after that was drowned out by the shrilling sound of fury in Lila's ear. Lila had turned the moment she heard the name, only because she had to confirm who he was talking to, and of course, Tatiana was the bitch all over Sonny. The shrill got even louder. It was the one she only ever heard *after* she'd lost control, so this was new to her, and she managed to take in a deep breath and *not* lose it.

This was his *business associate* who he'd turned his phone off because of last night? From the looks of it, as cozied up and *not* upset about Sonny blowing her off last night as she was, maybe he'd made up for it. Maybe he'd gone and picked the whore up after he dropped Lila off last night. It'd make sense he might want to relieve the massive hard-on Lila knew he'd driven away with. Maybe he'd spent the night and been with this bitch all morning.

"You okay?" Noah asked Lila, snapping her out of the stupor she hadn't even realized she'd fallen into.

She nodded, unable to even speak, afraid she might snap, taking an even deeper breath because she felt like a complete idiot who'd been taken in by the smooth-talking *asshole* with his beautiful kisses and flowers. His twenty-nine-year-old ass had probably perfected the act over the years. He'd probably been using all his cunning to take advantage of *stupid* girls, other stupid girls who'd fallen for his bullshit "I have no game" act. If Tatiana wasn't his girlfriend and just another girl he was playing, infuriatingly now, Lila had something in common with the cunt.

Feeling like the girl in the movie *The Exorcist*, it took great effort not to spin her head around and spew every filthy word she had in her at him. But somehow, she managed to stay in control. She'd like to think the room full of *big names,* not to mention all her bosses being present, was her reason for not exploding. Only she knew there was an even bigger reason.

In all the years she'd completely lost her shit, it was nothing more than fury she'd felt. This time there was also pain and humiliation; although, the pain outweighed the humiliation by a ton. It was, however, neck and neck with the fury she was feeling. While she'd never felt so close to exploding, she'd also never felt so close to completely falling apart either.

Climbing into the ring, she cursed herself inwardly. *Why* hadn't she gone with her gut? This just proved her theory that all guys were horny *dicks* after just one thing. Sonny wasn't special as she'd begun to truly believe. Five weeks. *Five weeks* she'd known this asshole, and already she'd fallen so hard she couldn't even explode on his ass for fear of letting him see the tears. She doubted she'd be able to refrain from unleashing her wrath on him the moment she got the chance, but she fucking *refused* to let him see her cry for him.

"Remember to focus," Gio said as he placed her headgear on her. "Don't lose your cool. She lands anything that pisses you off, let the anger work for you, not against you. Then do your thing. You got this."

*Focus. Don't lose your cool.* What a joke. Lila was having a hard-enough time trying to steady her breathing, let alone focus. And not losing her cool would be harder than ever now. She was so close to it already.

The giggling made the hair on the back of her neck stand. Tatiana wasn't the only other female who'd walked in the room with the group of athletes, but Lila already knew that fucking giggle. Turning very slowly, she watched as Tatiana leaned into Sonny, still giggling, and whispered something in his ear, even as he attempted once again to save face and pull away. Then her eyes went from Tatiana to Sonny's as she stared him down.

The asshole actually looked unnerved—remorseful even. But Lila knew damn well that, just like Marcelo, he was only sorry he'd been caught. If she hadn't been wearing her mouthpiece, Lila would've mouthed the words she wanted to scream at him so bad. *Fuck you!* She already knew it was *exactly* what she'd be saying to him the moment he attempted to lie his way out of this. Fuck him *and* his little whore. Lila was only glad she'd found out about this now and not later, because after last night, she'd seriously considered moving the relationship along a lot faster than she'd first intended. It was the only thing keeping her from jumping out of the ring and telling him the hell off right there in front of everyone, because if he hadn't told her last night that he had a special day planned for them today, which she was certain included him officially *claiming* her, she might've encouraged him do it last night. There'd have been no way she would've kept her cool even this long.

## Sonny

Clearly, but understandably so, Lila was *livid*. Disgusted might be a better word to describe the way she'd stared Sonny down. He couldn't even blame her. What wasn't clear was if she knew who he was yet. Had she been told or was she mostly pissed about Tatiana and her utterly unprofessional behavior? Never in his life had Sonny been more annoyed with anyone as he was right then.

Gio introduced Lila's opponent, Odessa Cantor. Even though Sonny had been witness to the power behind Lila's lethal fists, it still made him nervous to hear Odessa's impressive record. Lila might be good at defending herself on the streets, but fighting in the ring against a trained fighter was different. And Gio said she'd only been in the ring for the first time *that* past week?

"I get that they wanna look tough in the ring," Tatiana whispered, not so quietly in his ear. "But do they have to be so butch?"

Just as he had from the moment he realized it was Lila they'd be watching fight today, he ignored Tatiana and stared straight ahead. Lila was at the corner of the ring while Gio and Noah gave her some last-minute tips.

For a moment, Sonny considered walking over and saying something to her, but he couldn't think of a single thing he could say without having to give her a full explanation. There was no time for that now. He watched as Gio jumped out of the ring and then rang a bell cueing the girls to start the sparring.

Sonny observed the girls jumping around the ring, not making any contact yet, with his insides still in knots. The more he thought of it, the more his stomach balled up because he could only imagine what she must be thinking. Just last night he'd promised her she could trust him. As aroused as Lila had been, her uncertainty about allowing things to move forward was just as palpable. This was *bad*. All he could hope for now was that she'd give him the opportunity to explain himself. He knew better than to try and throw in the argument that she also had kept a few things from him. Like the fact that she was an up-and-coming boxer.

No surprise Lila landed a few good left hooks; then her opponent landed one that seemed to rock Lila a little. The moment she recovered, she was all over Odessa. Sonny had to wonder how much of the sudden fury he saw in her expression had to do with Tatiana still hanging on him, despite his shoving her hands off him now, more rudely than earlier. If it weren't for how close others were standing to them, he might tell her to get the fuck off him, in those very words, too, because judging from what he knew about Lila, nothing short of his telling off any woman who came on as strong as Tatiana would be satisfying enough.

At this point he knew his not making it clear to Tatiana that he was in a relationship already and that her behavior was inappropriate, could be grounds for getting dumped. If Lila hadn't already mentally done so, which could very well be the case if he had to go by the deadly glare he'd been assaulted with.

He was distracted momentarily from his worrisome thoughts when Gio had to jump in the ring and pull a rabid Lila off Odessa. There were people whooping, hollering, and clapping their hands, as impressed by Lila's speed and power as Sonny had been that first night. He'd been excited for her. Without a doubt, she had more skills in the ring than he'd given her credit for, but this only made the knot in his stomach tighten further. She walked away from Odessa when Gio pulled her off, and the first thing she did was turn and glare at Sonny. She continued to stalk around the ring in what looked like a struggling attempt to calm herself. Yeah, she was furious with him, and he hadn't been off in his observation that she might be taking out on Odessa what she was feeling about seeing him with Tatiana—the girl who'd called so much on a Saturday night Lila had finally questioned it. And now she knew Sonny hadn't been entirely forthcoming about that either.

"She's an animal." Tatiana hissed outright since there was so much noise going on in the training room now there was no need to keep her voice down. "Figures. She has the manners of one too. No wonder I can't stand her."

Sonny's head jerked to look at Tatiana the second he heard that last part, and for the first time since he laid eyes on Lila today, he responded to one of her comments. "You know her?"

"We've run into each other a few times here at 5th Street, and each time she's been a total bitch to me."

Feeling his insides sink impossibly lower than they'd already had, Sonny nearly groaned. Lila *already* hated

Tatiana before today? He needed to get the hell away from Tatiana *now*.

"And there you have it folks," Gio said, lifting Lila's arm. "That's as much as we're gonna get today because we don't want anyone hurt. But all this power and skill come from someone who's only been in the ring a handful of times."

Noah hopped in the ring with them, smiling big as Gio pulled Lila's mouthpiece out. "And, Lila, just so you know who came here to see you today, we have Leroy Deck, the Clippers starting center, Tony Nixon, right wing for the LA Kings . . ." He named a few of the others and then he got to Sonny. ". . . the exciting and newest member of the LA Dodgers, shortstop and living legend, Sylvester 'Double S' Sabian."

An added dose of distaste or disgust filled Lila's expression when she turned to meet Sonny's eyes again. He shook his head discreetly, hoping to somehow convey that he hadn't completely lied. His middle name *was* Sonny. He'd had every intention of telling her everything today, damn it.

As Noah finished his little speech, he let everyone know Lila hadn't been prepared to take questions today and that technically it was her day off. "Both Lila and Odessa were gracious enough to come in on their days off. So, if we can just get a round of applause for them, we can let them go and I can do a quick Q & A."

The group clapped, and Sonny walked away from Tatiana before she could make any more comments. He was in no mood for her ass anymore. He worked himself closer to the area of the ring where Lila now stood as Gio helped get her gloves and headgear off. He waited until she was out of the ring and walking toward the door to the ladies' locker room.

"Lila," he called out softly to not interrupt the Q & A Noah was now doing about their newly discovered *badass*.

As expected, she ignored him and even started walking a little faster, so he sped up too. "Lila, please, I can explain."

He made the mistake of reaching out to touch her arm, and she immediately flinched, jerking her arm away just as she reached the door. "Don't you ever touch me or talk to me again," she said loudly but thankfully not loud enough to stop the Q & A.

"I was gonna tell you today," he said, holding up his hands.

"About what?" she shot back even louder, and this time Noah did pause.

Without looking around, because Sonny couldn't take his eyes off Lila, he knew everyone's eyes and ears were on them now.

"That you lied to me this whole time or about *Tatiana*? Is that why you've only taken me to parks at night and places no one can see us together because you don't wanna be seen with the *hood rat* you're trying to bag?"

"No!"

"Go fuck yourself, *Sylvester!* Or better yet, go fuck *Tatiana*. That nasty bitch certainly looks to be in heat. I don't give a fuck what you think of me, asshole! I *know* I deserve better, so just stay the hell away from me!"

With that, she stalked out of the room, slamming the door behind her and leaving Sonny there in a completely silenced room. Taking a deep breath, he turned to face the gawking crowd. Even Noah and Gio, who were still in the ring, seemed to be at a loss for words. "Just a little miscommunication," he said, trying to make light of what just happened with a shrug and a forced smile. "Carry on."

Noah cleared his throat and a took a few moments, but he finally went back to what he'd been saying before Lila's outburst. Felix and Hector were at his side almost immediately. "The fuck was that about?" Hector asked in a lowered voice.

Sonny shook his head, knowing he had no choice but to just tell them. "Long story short, I met her last month at a concert nearby here. She had no idea who I was, and I didn't tell her. I even introduced myself with my middle name, not my first. But we really hit it off. We've talked day and night ever since." He shrugged, feeling like the biggest idiot ever. "It was just nice having a chick interested in me for *me* and not for who I am, you know? For years, it's been impossible to find one who doesn't. But I wanted to make sure she wasn't just putting on an act. Anyway, let's just say, in the past few weeks, things started to get a little heavier and promises were made. Then I walked in here with Tatiana all over me." He shook his head then let it fall back. "*Fuck!* I had no idea she even worked here. She told me she does youth training."

"Yeah, here," Abel confirmed with a nod as he walked up and joined them. "She assists Gio's wife with the youth program we have here."

"So, what?" Hector asked with a slight glare. "Were you not planning on telling her about Tatiana?"

"Did I hear my name?" Tatiana moseyed on up to their group. "Wow, but that girl has a mouth on her. Please tell me you're not seriously—"

"Not now, Tatiana," Sonny said nearly through his teeth. "This doesn't concern you. Give us a minute, will you, please?"

"This doesn't concern me, yet my name—"

"I'll explain that later," Sonny said even more dismissively, trying not to snap.

She stared at him for a second before lifting her brow and thankfully walking away. Sonny turned to Hector, who was still eyeing him questionably. "This all happened so fast I hadn't even had a chance to let anyone in on it. I was gonna see Lila later today, take her down to my place."

He explained how there'd be no hiding who he was after that. Then he suddenly had a thought. "You guys know her well? Can you talk to her? Help me explain?"

Hector shook his head with a smirk. "Fuck that. I'm not getting *my* head bit off. That girl's a walking time bomb."

Gio suddenly joined them. "What the hell was that about, Sabian? You and Lila?" he asked, and Sonny turned to him now with the tiniest bit of hope.

"Your wife works with her?"

Gio nodded but still looked lost.

"It's a long story." Sonny explained quickly what he'd just told the guys then shook his head, completely exasperated. "You think Bianca could get her to just hear me out?"

Gio shook his head. "Lila's not working today. You heard Noah. It was her day off. She came in just for this. She's probably gone already."

*Fuck!* "I gotta go then. Fill me in on anything else I need to know about the charity stuff later. I need to go find Lila."

Before they could say anything more, he rushed out the same door Lila had stormed out of. Sonny pulled his phone out, immediately, wondering if maybe she hadn't already sent him any *colorful* messages. At this point, he'd take anything, even that, but there were no such messages. He hit speed dial, even though he knew how dismal the chances of her answering his call were. It rang once then went to voicemail, which meant one thing: she wouldn't be taking his calls. With no other choice, he tried to rush out but was stopped a few dozen times. One of those times was by Roni, Noah's wife, so he had no choice but to stop and chat with her about a surprise party she and Felix's wife were planning for Felix's birthday. Almost forty fucking minutes later, he was finally out of there.

He'd just begun to put an email together on his tablet when his phone rang with a call from Tony Banks, his publicist. Grudgingly, he answered it. "Hey, Banks. What's up?"

"A lot. I got you booked on *Ellen* tomorrow, *Live with Kelly* on Tuesday, and then *Conan* on Thursday, but keep Wednesday and Friday open because there are a few local radio shows I'm trying to get you in before spring training starts."

With a groan, he brought his hand to his forehead. Before today, he thought he'd have all week with Lila. Spring training was rolling around soon, and his time with her in the next few months anyway would've been limited as it was. Then today happened and now Banks was filling up this week fast. Part of the record-breaking contract he signed included his agreeing to doing a lot of promotion about his coming to Los Angeles. The city was hoping to stir up as much excitement about this and sell as many season tickets and home games as possible.

"Listen, Banks, this is a bad week for me. Any chance you can get some of this shit pushed back to next week?"

"Are you kidding me? You have any idea how long I've been trying and what I've gone through to get you on *Ellen*? I was this close to asking whose dick I had to suck and I'm not a gay man, Sabian. She's been booked solid for—"

"Alright, alright," Sonny said, frowning instead of laughing as he normally would at his publicist's exaggerated response. "Maybe not the *Ellen* show but at least one of the other ones and leave Wednesday and Friday as is. I need to take care of some shit this week."

"*Conan* and *Kimmel* are huge, Sabian," Banks said immediately. "They're only fifteen or twenty-minute spots. You'll be there an hour tops."

Banks promised to leave his Wednesday and Friday open, and Sabian agreed to do all three talk shows, mostly so he could get off the phone already and he could get his email to Lila written up. As soon as he was off the phone, he checked again for anything from Lila, and again there was nothing, so he clicked on his email and started his groveling email to her.

He went over it a few times before trying to decide if it was enough, too much, or if he should just send it already. So, he reread it out loud to hear what it sounded like.

"Lila, technically, I didn't actually lie about my name. I just gave you my middle name. You not knowing who I am is not completely unheard of, but lately, especially here in Los Angeles, there's been nonstop coverage about my signing with the Dodgers. I also do a lot of commercials and such. I've even done a few cameos on television shows. It's why, at first, I just wanted to make sure you were being honest about not knowing who I was. After that very first night we spent time together, I knew you were the real deal, but it's been SO long since I've met a girl who I could be certain was interested in me for me, not for my fame. It's why I kept on with the whole Sonny thing. I was afraid you might Google me and the jig would be up. Honest to God, I had every intention of telling you today. It's why I wanted to take you to Los Feliz. I was going to show you my home. There'd be no hiding who I am there, with all the stuff on my walls and what not.

"About Tatiana, I'd lie and say nothing's ever happened between her and me, only I want to be perfectly honest with you from here on. I do have a business relationship with her, but I've also been involved with her intimately."

He stopped to replace the word *intimately* with *on a more personal level*. If she ever asked for specifics, he'd give them to her, but for now, he'd leave it at that. Taking a deep breath, he continued reading out loud.

"But not anytime lately and certainly not since I've met and started talking to you." Sonny stopped to highlight and make that last sentence all caps then continued to read. "Yes, she was all over me today. She's always been like that. Today was the first time I'd seen her since I started seeing you, and I hadn't had the chance to let her know about you.

About us. We were in meetings and around others the whole time. But I swear to you I meant what I said last night. I will make it perfectly clear to her, and *any* other women I've been involved with in the past, that my status has changed. That I'm in an exclusive relationship now. I understand completely why you'd be so angry, and I can't apologize enough, but please, *please*"—he stopped again to make that last word all caps too then read on— "give me the chance to explain myself further to you in person or at the very least on the phone. Please, Lila, I'm begging here."

"Good enough," he said under his breath.

Sonny didn't see how he could possibly grovel any more than that. Lila might be a spitfire with an explosive temper, but Sonny had seen her sweet vulnerable side. He'd also felt what his kisses did to her—the same thing her kisses did to him. And all of what he'd just written was true. Every last word damn it. He'd like to think, despite knowing him for just a few weeks, it'd be harder for her to dismiss him so easily.

He sent it off then started toward her apartment building. It wasn't even until he got there that he realized that only two of the times he'd been here he'd gotten lucky and the security door had been left open. One of the times like now it was locked and he'd had to call Lila to come down and open it. There was no one around now. "Fucking hell," he muttered as he stood there looking up at the building with endless doors.

He walked around for a while with no luck in finding anyone who might let him in, getting more and more anxious by the minute. Just when he'd decided to give up for now, loud screams distracted him. He turned to see two terrified-looking young girls turning the corner and running for their lives in his direction. He watched curiously, glancing around to see what they might be running from, but saw nothing. They reached the same apartment building Lila lived in. One of them opened it with a key, and they ran through the gate.

Before Sonny had the presence of mind to try and run to the door, it slammed shut behind them. He was once again distracted when a car came screeching around the corner they'd just turned from.

The girls were out of sight now. The car slowed as it got closer. Sonny could see there was only one person in the car, a young guy who searched the area furiously. For a moment, Sonny wondered if maybe the girls hadn't stolen something from him and maybe he should let him know which direction they'd run. But his gut told him otherwise. If anyone was the guilty party here, it was the thug in the car.

Sonny peered at him until the thug's eyes met his. His stare was a hard one, but it was fleeting. It went soft the moment Sonny could tell he recognized him, but Sonny looked away. He wasn't about to indulge this guy, who'd clearly been terrorizing those girls, in any type of exchange.

Instead, he walked toward the gate again, hoping he might see the girls or anyone else somewhere. The car skidded away, and a few minutes later, the girls peeked their heads out from around the corner of one of the buildings inside.

"He's gone," Sonny informed them, glancing back to make sure he really was and not still lurking up the street.

"Where are you going?" one of them asked the other anxiously.

Sonny turned to see the taller of the two girls rushing toward him. "I have to get to work," she said, peering out into the street before opening the gate.

"You can't," the shorter girl with the thick glasses urged. "What if he drives by the bus stop again and sees you?"

"I can't be late to work again, Al." The first girl opened the gate, and Sonny took advantage of it, holding it open for her.

"Can I help you?" the shorter one with the glasses asked Sonny, blocking the entrance with her body. "Only tenants and their guests are allowed in here."

"But I am a guest—"

"Jen"—the girl questioning him turned back to the other girl, losing interest in Sonny's response when the other girl started out— "please wait. My sister should be home soon if she's not already. I'll give you a ride."

"I don't have time. I'll be late," Jen argued, despite the fear in her eyes.

Sonny glanced up at Lila's apartment then exhaled, knowing what he should do. "You need a ride?"

They turned to him, their expressions both surprised and a bit unsure. Then they exchanged glances. "It's better than you taking the chance of that guy coming back," the short one said with a shrug then she turned back to Sonny. "What's your name?"

"Are you . . .?" Jen started to ask; then her jaw dropped. "You're that baseball player, aren't you? The one everyone's been talking about lately."

The other girl peered at him through her thick glasses that made her eyes look huge as her brows pinched together. "Who?"

"Yeah, I am," Sonny confirmed then turned to the other girl, whose giant eyes indicated she evidently still had no clue who he was. "I'm Sly Sabian. I used to play for the Padres, but I'll be playing for the Dodgers this year."

"I'm Alison," the girl with the glasses said in response, looking more relieved than impressed or starry-eyed as most girls did when meeting him. "This is Jenny. Can you really give her a ride?"

"Sure." Sonny smiled even as the disappointment of knowing his talk with Lila would have to be put off grew heavier. "Where you going?"

"Not too far," Jenny said, smiling big now. "I work at the Payless on Soto and Cesar Chavez."

Sonny smiled. "The one with the mural."

It wasn't a question. It was a statement. He knew the area all too well. He'd been to the shoe store plenty of times with his mom and sisters growing up. The bus stop dropped them off right there at that corner.

"Yeah, that's the one," she said with a nod but was looking past him with the same look of awe as she'd been looking at Sonny just seconds ago. "Is that your car?"

Alison followed Jenny's amazed eyes. Sonny didn't think her eyes could get any bigger than they already looked under those thick glasses, but they did. Then her mouth fell open.

"Yeah, that's my car." Sonny smiled, glancing back at the sports car.

"Oh, wow," Alison said, walking toward it, then turned back to Sonny. "What in the world are *you* doing in this neighborhood anyway?"

The reminder of why he was here and what he still had to deal with later made his smile flatten. "My girlfriend lives here."

Normally, referring to any girl as his girlfriend would've nearly choked him, but he actually liked the way it felt saying it. Though it almost hurt to think that it may no longer be the case.

Both girls turned to him, a little incredulous; then Jenny smiled big. "So, you're coming back here after you drop me off?" Sonny nodded even though he wasn't sure it'd do him any good. "Can Alison come with us, then? You can bring her back since you're coming back anyway, and she's a car enthusiast. This is probably the only chance she'll ever get to ride in one of these."

He almost agreed immediately then thought better of it. Jenny looked like she might be eighteen, but Alison didn't look much older than fifteen, maybe sixteen. She was a short little thing still carrying some baby fat, and those glasses made her appear even younger and more innocent than Jenny. Not that there was anything *not* innocent about Jenny. Alison just looked a little more fragile—docile somehow. Most importantly, if she was underage, this could mean trouble for him. The media was just looking for anything to get the next big headline. They were notorious for sensationalizing everything just so they could make even the most innocent and otherwise boring headline that much juicier.

"How old are you?" he asked Alison before he'd agree then added just to be safe. "Both of you?"

"Eighteen," they said in unison and that surprised him.

Sonny peered at Alison suspiciously. "Are you really?"

The question appeared to annoy her. "I'm almost nineteen," she informed him; though the annoyance was short-lived because her eyes were back on his car again, taking every detail in.

"You don't look eighteen," he said even at the risk of pissing her off, but he needed to be sure.

"She's actually the older of the two of us," Jenny confirmed. "I just turned eighteen two months ago. She'll be nineteen next month."

"Hmm," Sonny said, pulling out his keys and clicking the doors unlocked. "I would've thought the opposite."

He kept the rest to himself—that petite little Alison might even pass for a high-school kid. "Hop in. You too, Alison. I'll bring you back."

Once in the car and after answering some of their more pressing questions, mostly about the car, what other cars he owned, and about some of the other players he knew, Sonny finally asked them what he was curious about. "So why was that guy chasing you two?"

The shoe store was just a few miles away from Lila's apartment building, so they were almost there. "Long story," Jenny chirped from the backseat. "Basically, I may've taken a photo of him doing something shady and he saw me."

"Did he see what building we ran into?" Alison asked, her eyes once again big and full of concern.

Sonny couldn't help but smile. The glasses gave her an almost comical look, a human version of the little bookworm with the oversized glasses. Only her glasses weren't oversized. Her eyes just appeared to be because her lenses were so damned thick. This close, Sonny could also see she wore no makeup.

Normally, he'd attribute *that* to why he'd assumed she was so young, but Lila was proof that wasn't necessarily always the case. Aside from the night he first met her where she'd worn *some* makeup but not nearly as much as most girls wore to clubs, the other times he'd seen her, she wore little if any at all. She didn't need makeup to not look like a kid. She just carried herself with such self-confidence it exuded a maturity far beyond her twenty-one years. But then she'd probably lived through and seen far more than most twenty-one-year-olds.

"I don't think he did," he finally said, trying to shake off the thoughts of Lila. Alison exhaled, visibly relieved. "He slowed, but he was looking in every direction like he had no idea where you two had gone."

"Oh, thank God," Jenny said as he pulled up to the shoe store.

"But we'll likely still see him at school," Alison said, turning back to face Jenny.

"School?" Sonny raised a brow. "I thought you two said you're eighteen?"

"College," Alison said without a flinch.

Jenny opened the back door and thanked Sonny. She got out then came up to the front window on Alison's side and raised her phone up to her face. Before Sonny knew what happened, she'd snapped several pictures. Then she turned around and hunched down so she could take a selfie with Alison and Sonny in the background. Sonny at least had a chance to smile and give a thumbs-up this time. "It's the only way my brother will ever believe this." She smiled big when she was done. "Thanks again," she said to Sonny then pointed at Alison. "I'll talk to you as soon as I get off tonight."

We can't stop now, Ali. No matter what. *Real* investigative journalists stop at nothing to get their story."

With that, she winked and rushed away. "You're a journalist too?" Sonny asked as he pulled away from the curb.

"Studying to be one," she explained.

It wasn't until the words sunk in that a few things registered, making him feel like an idiot for not making the connection sooner. He didn't even really listen to the rest of what she said about her major and college classes. All Sonny could think of was *Ali* lived in Lila's building. She was eighteen, a journalist student, and she mentioned a sister earlier.

"Are you Lila's sister?" he asked, unable to believe his luck.

Her eyes widened again in that way that made Sonny smile every time now. "How do you know my sister?"

## 12

As meek and docile as Sonny had pegged Ali to be, she turned out to be anything but. She was also far more mature than the middle-school kid he first thought her. Apparently, the fierce need to protect your sister ran both ways and just as strongly. First, Ali listened quietly as he explained about him and Lila. How they met, why he'd kept who he really was from her, and that despite their time apart, they'd since established exclusivity. Then he briefly told her what happened that morning at 5th Street. That was when the protective sister claws came out slowly but boldly.

"So, you mean to tell me that my sister is probably somewhere very upset right now?"

"Well, hopefully not anymore," Sonny said as they parked in front of Lila's apartment building. "Not if she read the email where I explained it all."

Then the rest of the inquisition followed. "Why was this reporter all over you? Why did you let her? What exactly are your intentions with my sister? If it's not baseball season, then where have you been all these weeks? Who've you been with?"

Sonny answered every one of her questions as quickly as she threw them at him. Tatiana is . . . well . . . Tatiana and he'd be cutting all ties with her the moment he got the chance.

He's already crazy about Lila, so his intentions are to hopefully keep moving forward with the relationship.

He'd been in meetings, shooting commercials, and, as part of his contract, making guest appearances on countless shows to promote his move here for the upcoming baseball season. And part of his trip had been scheduled long ago, personal stuff with friends and family, so he couldn't cancel.

Mostly he travels alone, but sometimes, he meets up with friends, other teammates, or his publicist and agent.

At first, he'd thought Ali and Lila were completely different. Now he could see they were definitely cut from the same cloth. Lila had told him some of the stories of her defending her sister while growing up in foster care and about some of the bullies in school. The only difference was he'd yet to hear Ali cuss. But he didn't doubt for a moment now that she wouldn't roar just as loudly as Lila if she ever had to come to her defense. At one point, she started tapping at the screen on her phone.

"What are you doing?" Sonny asked, hopeful that she might be texting Lila.

"Give me a sec," she said without looking up.

She tapped away and sat silently reading for a few moments as Sonny sat there staring at her impatiently. Then she tapped again, glanced up at him, peered without saying a word, and then went back to reading whatever it was she was reading on her screen.

"Who's Mona Fellini?" she asked without looking up.

This surprised and unnerved him. "Why? Who's asking?"

"I am." She glanced up from her screen finally and pushed up on her glasses. "You were spotted with her in New York couple weeks ago. You said you started seeing Lila over a month ago."

She lifted her phone screen so he could see the photo of him and Mona strolling down the Manhattan street together. Ali slid her finger across the screen to scroll the photos then stopped on one that had Sonny gulping, one of them holding hands. *Fuck.*

"She's an old friend."

"You hold hands with all your *friends,* Mr. Sabian?" She brought the phone back down in front of her as she tapped away again.

"Call me Sylvester. Sly." He shook his head as the exasperation began to build. "Better yet, call me Sonny. It's what your sister calls me, and no, I don't hold hands with *all* my friends." Damn Mona and her constantly slipping her hand in his. "It was cold and she slipped her hand in mine, but she really is just a friend."

"You went out with Frankie Nunez?"

*Now* she seemed starry-eyed, but it was fleeting. In the next moment, she was lifting her brow in disapproval. Sonny was pretty sure what photos she was looking at now. "I was her date for the Grammy's. We had brunch a few times and attended a few charity events, but we were never really a thing."

"Did you sleep with her?"

Sonny laughed, nervously glancing away. "That was . . . I mean those were the Grammy's. Last year. Not this year. Way back. Like ancient history," he said, pissed about his bumbling answer.

"That's not what I asked."

"That's irrelevant, don't you think?" Sonny asked as the exasperation grew with every one of her inquiries. "I hadn't even met your sister then."

"Leslie McHugh, Ivette Adams, Shannon Solis, Michelina?" She glanced up at him. "What's she like? Is she a true vegetarian? I know a lot of celebrities claim to be, but they're really not."

"I have no idea." He huffed.

"You've had *a lot* of girlfriends, Sonny." She slid her finger over the screen. "I hope you get checked often."

"I'm a well-known athlete, Ali. Just because my picture's been taken a lot doesn't mean I've slept with every girl I've posed with."

*Almost* true. He hadn't slept with *every* one of them. But he did make sure to use protection with all the ones he had. And being a professional baseball player, he was required to have regular physicals, so he knew he was clean.

"Are you gonna help me out here or not? Will you talk to your sister for me?"

"Look." She finally put her phone down. "I won't sugarcoat this for you. If Lila hasn't already kicked you to the curb because of your slutty reporter friend or because you lied to her all this time, she will once she sees what a— And I apologize if this offends you." She lifted her brow; though she hardly looked sorry. "What a man whore you are."

"I'm not a man whore," he insisted, even if some might argue with that. "The stories about my personal life, most of them, are exaggerated. And the photos with me and all those women just come with the territory—"

"If you expect Lila to just accept that—"

"No!" He shook his head. "I don't. I just mean constantly being photographed and even followed by the paparazzi is just a part of my life, but I have every intention of keeping my promise to her that I'd never hurt her or do anything that might *accidently* hurt her."

"Like today?" She regarded him, completely unimpressed.

"Exactly," Sonny said with conviction. "Like today. That'll *never* happen again because, from here on, everyone will know I'm not a single guy anymore. So, any behavior like Tatiana's today won't be tolerated. In fact . . ."

Sonny pulled out his phone in desperation because it didn't appear he was making any progress in convincing Ali of his loyalty to Lila. If she wasn't buying this, he was sure as shit Lila wouldn't either. This was a risk but one he was willing to take. He hit the call button after locating the last call he'd had from Tatiana. It rang over the speakers in his car so Ali would hear this for herself.

"Hello, Sly," she murmured the moment she answered. "If you're calling to apologize, don't. I'd prefer you drop by and *show* me how sorry you are."

"Nope, not calling to apologize." He raised his brows and nodded at Ali, who was leaning against the door, looking almost bored. "I'm just calling to get something clear with you. I'm seeing Lila now, and after this morning, I need to cut all ties with you, even business ones. It's just not gonna work anymore."

"You can't be serious—"

"I am," he said before she said anything insulting about Lila. "I can't risk you being so fucking unprofessional the way you were this morning and causing any problems between Lila and me. It's just not worth it."

"Does this mean—?"

"It means what I just said it means, Tatiana," he said, feeling a little more heated the more he thought about what Tatiana *pretending* to not get this, might cost him. What it could've cost him already. "I don't think I could've made this any clearer. Next time I see you, I don't know you, and you don't know me. The moment I get the chance, I'll be blocking all your shit. Got it?"

The phone clicked, and Sonny looked down at his screen. Yep, she'd hung up on him, but he was glad that hadn't been as ugly as he'd been dreading.

"How many more of those calls are you gonna have to make?"

"None." He put his phone down. "Believe it or not, women are not what takes up most of my time. My work does. But I already told Lila that I'm done letting my career get in the way of my personal life. I'm making her my first priority from here on. If she lets me, that is."

His phone rang and the screen on the dash lit up with the name Olivia. Ali's brow went up again and she shook her head.

"That's my friend's sister."

Ali shrugged as if that didn't make it any less of a girl calling him. "My friend's *married* sister," he clarified, hitting the answer button. "Liv, what's up?"

"Hey, Sly." Her cheerful voice came through the speakers again. "Sorry to bother you. I'm just trying to get a final headcount for this Friday. Will you be there?"

"I will, actually, and unless she's working, I'll be bringing my *girlfriend*." He turned to Ali, who again didn't look the least bit impressed.

"You have a girlfriend?" Of course, Olivia would sound *way* too surprised. "Like a *real* girlfriend? One you're actually taking serious? Why didn't you bring her to the Baptism?"

He frowned, glancing at a smirking Ali, who, if he wasn't mistaken, was beginning to enjoy his unease. "Things were just starting off for us back then, and I didn't want to push anything as big as an overnight trip on her yet. But I'll definitely be bringing her around from here on."

"Well, congrats." She still sounded way too giddy about the news. "I'm so excited for you. Does AJ know? Because you know he's always said you'd *never* settle down."

Sonny pinched the rim of his nose, closing his eyes, and didn't bother looking at Ali this time. "No, he doesn't, actually. I haven't really told anyone yet, but if she's off Friday, I'll bring her for sure."

"Yes! For sure bring her. It's the only way AJ and the guys will ever believe it."

"I gotta go, Liv," he said, pissed at himself now for answering the call.

He'd had enough of her overly surprised reaction to his *finally* getting a girlfriend. It was horse shit. He had a good reason for not having settled down yet or not having a serious girlfriend in so long.

The moment he was off the phone with Olivia, he turned to Ali, whom he was sure had gotten a big kick out of that. "The only reason why she's so surprised is exactly what I explained to you earlier. It's been *years* since I've met anyone who I could be sure was into me because of *me,* not just for my fame. I honestly was beginning to think I never would, and obviously so did AJ and a few of my other friends." He took a deep breath. "But you see why this is so important to me, right? I finally met someone who's genuinely into me and who I've fallen for *big time.* Will you please help me out here?"

"If I do this," she began, her big eyes peering at him guardedly. "You have to promise me two things. First, that you *will not* toy with her or do anything to hurt her *ever.*"

"Done," he said immediately and without the slightest hesitation. "I abso-fucking-lutely promise."

"I may look small, Sonny, but I swear to you, if you ever hurt her, I will hunt you down and make you pay dearly."

Sonny chuckled, despite the exasperation he was still feeling. "I believe you."

She peered at him a bit more and then finally spoke again. "Second, you can't mention to her about the guy chasing me and Jenny today."

This time he wasn't so quick to agree. He was certain Lila wouldn't be happy about him keeping something like that from her, especially if this guy chasing them could potentially be dangerous. "Ali, I can't—"

"Ah-ah." She shook her head. "You want me to do this for you, then you have to promise. This isn't a big deal anyway. He was just being a jerk trying to scare us."

"And he did," Sonny shot back. "I heard your screams and saw the looks on your faces. You really should let her in on this. She could—"

"She worries enough about me. That's the deal. Take it or leave it. You never saw what you saw today. We both got here at the same time today, and you asked me if I knew Lila then you explained everything to me. Going once." She reached for the door handle. "Going twice." She turned the handle. "Going—"

"Fine," Sonny agreed but didn't promise.

"You promise?"

He nearly groaned, letting his head fall back against his seat. "I promise." *Damn it.*

"This is good." Ali smiled, straightening out, and started tapping her phone screen again. "If you keep this promise, then I'll know you should be good for the one you made about never hurting Lila. As long as I know your word is good, if you ever need any more favors, I'd be happy to oblige."

*Great.*

"Let me check if she's home and get a feel for how angry she might still be." Her words were foreboding. "I don't know how well you know my sister yet. But you don't wanna get on her bad side. You might not wanna see her just yet if she's still pissed."

In Sonny's effort to get through his story as quickly as possible earlier, he'd kept it vague. He'd been at 5th Street for some business when he ran into Lila, and the reporter had been all over him the whole time. So, Ali didn't know he'd not only been witness to Lila's temper before but that he'd watched her pummel an established boxer today as well. Only he didn't get a chance to tell her because she started speaking into her phone. Just knowing Lila was on the other end made him strangely nervous. He'd gotten so used to being in constant contact with her; not hearing from her in almost two hours now made him anxious.

"What are you up to?" Ali asked.

Sonny watched her anxiously as Ali listened to whatever Lila was saying.

"Are you in the mood for company or no?" Ali bit the corner of her lip. "A friend of mine. We can all hang out."

Ali frowned but then nodded at Sonny. He had no idea what that meant. He just hoped he'd at least get a chance to explain himself. Maybe drop to his knees if need be.

She hung up and smiled. "Let's go. She sounded alright, and I can usually tell just by her tone if she's in a foul mood. Maybe your email did calm her some."

"So, what's the plan," he asked nervously as he came around the car and met her in on the sidewalk.

"Plan?" She turned to him, wide-eyed. "That's it. I'm getting you in to see her. You're on your own after that."

Sonny wasn't sure why that surprised him. What did he expect her to do? Vouch for what a good guy she thought he was after having just met him? They got through the security door then walked up the stairs. Every step he took he was more anxious than the last.

Ali put the key in the door lock, and Sonny held his breath as she turned and pushed the door open. Lila had her back turned as she walked out of the front room with her phone at her ear and waved a hand back at Ali.

"She's on the phone," Ali stated the obvious, and suddenly, she looked as nervous as he felt.

They exchanged tense glances as they stood there in the middle of the front room. "Have a seat," she finally said, fidgeting with her blouse and biting her thumb nail.

"Maybe I should go warn her that you're here." Ali started toward the door Lila had just walked out of.

"Wait." Sonny stood up from the sofa he'd just sat down on. "What if she refuses to see me? I need to talk to her, explain it all in person. This could be my only chance."

Ali looked as unsure about this as he did, but it was true this could be his only chance. Lila had been *beyond* angry today. She might still be. Now he was glad Ali would be in the room when he did see her again. It might help keep her calm. Keep things from getting out of control if she happened to lose it again.

Even Sonny would've been pissed had the tables been turned and another guy's hands had been all over her. His temper had never been what some of his teammates' tempers were—what Lila's was—but just the thought pissed him off. He was actually impressed now that Lila had kept her cool as long as she had because he sure as hell wouldn't have.

Ali started to protest, saying something about not being so sure anymore if it was a good idea to just spring this on Lila, when the door to the room Lila had walked into opened. The smile on her face when she saw Ali flattened the moment her eyes met Sonny's, and the room was suddenly filled with a suffocating silence.

# Lila

"Lila, I heard him out," Ali said, sounding almost panicked. "For what it's worth, I believe him."

"So did I," Lila said before Ali could feel even the slightest bit of guilt. "He's that *good.*"

"It's the truth," Sonny said, holding a hand up and taking a step toward her.

As if dreading this man wasn't already *way* out of her league, seeing him here standing in her tiny front room again with such a huge presence might just confirm it. He stood next to her sister, who he towered over, and it made him appear larger than life. Now she knew he was a major sports celebrity to boot. She'd Googled all the photos, articles, videos, and countless YouTube videos made by his adoring female fans. They were endless, videos put together of him and one of the many celebrities he'd been linked to. Like their fantasy couple. It made Lila sick. Not just sick, but it made her realize how unbelievably impossible it'd be for her to deal with this.

"I heard the call he made to that reporter you saw him with." Ali took a step forward toward Lila. "He cut her off for real, business relationship and all. It was no act, Lila. She was pissed and hung up on him."

Ali knew Lila too well. If he'd really explained it all to her, then she'd know *that* part of today was what Lila had been most pissed about, especially once she'd read his email explaining about why he'd kept his true identity from her.

Lila nodded, still staring into Sonny's eyes; his intense gaze bore into her now. She was still unsure what she wanted to do with this information. On the one hand, her heart and soul yearned for his feelings for her to be true—as genuine as hers were for him. But on the other hand, she couldn't for the life of her even begin to believe she'd be able to deal with this without fucking it all up. She was nowhere near grasping any kind of control over her unpredictable outbursts. Or rather *very* predictable very explosive reactions. She already knew how she'd react *when* not *if* she was in the inevitable position of having to see him around other women again. Women who'd be all too ready to offer themselves up to him. Women like the ones she'd already seen countless photos of him with. Glamorous, sophisticated women who were the epitome of class and poise.

Everything Lila was not.

"I'll leave you two to talk," Ali said, stepping out of the room and closing the bedroom door behind her.

"I'm so sor—"

"What do you want with me?" Lila asked before Sonny could begin his apologies.

"What do you mean?"

"Why me? Of all the girls in the world you can obviously have, why should I believe you want me and *only* me?"

The tension in his rigid expression softened a bit, and he smiled, taking a few steps closer to her. Lila swallowed hard, willing herself to stand strong and not give into him just because he was such an insanely perfect specimen of a man. Infuriatingly, he was just as beautiful on the inside. At least it was what her first impression of him had been so far. But after the bombshell she got this morning, she wasn't sure how much of that was true too. Could he really be this perfect?

Now she knew all too well he could have any girl he wanted. She'd spent more than an hour, confirming that fact while she dug online obsessively about everything and *anything* she could find on the guy. The whole time she'd thought the same thing. The same question begged to be answered, and now he was gazing at her like the answer to that should be obvious.

"Because ever since the day I first laid eyes on you"—he took a few more steps closer to her— "and then got to kiss those sweet lips, you've been the first thing on my mind when I wake and the last thing I wanna think about when I go to bed at night. That's *never* happened to me before."

Lila gulped, feeling her heart swell and her entire body warm as he neared her, bringing his hand to her face.

"But why me?" she whispered. "All those girls. All those glamorous celebrities . . ."

She paused when he shook his head and caressed her cheek gently with his fingers. "You're nothing like any of those girls, Lila. And that's exactly *why* you. I don't want any of that phony Hollywood bullshit. I didn't even know *what* I wanted until I met you. What I want is a *real* girl. And you're as real as it gets. You're everything I've missed about my life since I became famous. You're everything I've been searching for, for years, and it hit me like a freight train the night I met you. *Everything* about you. Your distaste for me when you thought I was just some guy trying to get lucky that night. The burger joint you preferred over my offer to take you to a steak house. You being so familiar with Hollenbeck Park and not being the least bit afraid of being there at night. Even that damn temper and mouth on you. I grew up here in Boyle Heights just like you. On the streets. Playing ball in empty parking lots, breaking windows, and running amuck. Don't you see? You're not the first girl I've seen beat someone's ass." He brought his hand around her waist roughly and pulled her to him. "Just the first one I've seen look hot as hell doing it. And for what it's worth, only in my professional world am I known as Sylvester or Sly. It's my grandfather's name, but my mom has always called me Santino, and my sisters call me Sonny. So, I'm pretty used to going by it."

His eyes suddenly went a little dark as he stared into hers, and he pressed his hard body against hers, lighting every inch of Lila's body on fire.

"You're not the first girl who's cussed me out either."

"I'm sorry," Lila said, chiding herself when she remembered the ugly words she'd spat at Sonny today. "I just—"

"Don't apologize," he said before she could finish. "Don't ever apologize for not holding your feelings back. I'm not mad about that. I understand why you'd react the way you did." He smirked, gazing into her eyes with that same heat she'd only seen when she knew he was aroused. "And you're hot as hell even when you're pissed and telling me to go fuck myself."

Lila winced at that, but he hugged her even tighter—rougher. "What does piss me off is that, even for a second, you'd believe I think you're a hood rat or that I'm just trying to bag you."

She stared into his now menacing eyes, breathing deeply and remembering how hurt she'd been when she really did believe that.

Sonny shook his head, pressing his lips as his expression morphed from disgust to frustration, then took his own deep breath before going on. "Understand this. I *love* that you're different. I love your passion, and I've already accepted that my spunky-ass girlfriend has a wicked temper that's gonna keep me on my toes. But I *will not* tolerate anyone putting you down, including yourself. So, unless you want me spanking that sweet ass of yours, I don't ever wanna hear you do that again. The only reason I kept our outings to parks and places people wouldn't see us was to avoid being mobbed and you finding out who I was before I'd planned on telling you. But I guarantee you, *when* you agree to take me back, not *if* because I won't give up until you do, the whole world will know who my girl is. And just like you with your sister, I won't be letting anyone fuck with you in *any* way—physically or verbally. So, don't ever think for a second that I'd be ashamed of you." He leaned in and licked her bottom lip before nipping at it until she gasped in both pain and arousal. "How could I ever be ashamed of my beautiful badass?"

Normally, Lila's cynical ass would be wracking her brain to come up with reasons not to believe him, for excuses to continue to push him away. It'd be for her own good because, despite all his mesmerizing words, she was still skeptical. Only it wasn't him that she didn't trust. She still didn't trust that *she* wouldn't fuck this up royally.

"I don't think I'm ready for all this, S—" She caught herself before calling him Sonny then thought better of it because she'd never call him anything but "*Sonny.*"

"What's there to be ready for?" he asked, searching her eyes, as panic filled his eyes.

Lila thought of how tempted she'd been today to jump out of the ring and claw Tatiana's eyes out. Each time she'd seen the whore paw at Sonny, it'd been a struggle not to stop, spit her mouthpiece out, and scream, "Get your fucking hands off him!"

If her feelings of entitlement had been off the charts then, *before* she'd ever heard him call her his girlfriend, his beautiful badass, *his*, which only meant one thing—he was saying he was *hers*—how in the world could she trust herself not to explode if she ever saw something like that again?

"I don't trust myself," she whispered, glancing away from his eyes.

"So, trust *me*." He lifted her chin, forcing eye contact. His eyes were warm but at the same time full of determination. "I promise never to put you in a situation like today again, Lila." He leaned in and kissed her softly then spoke again, staring seriously into her eyes. "It's not just you. Feeling anger over something like that is normal. Trust me. If the tables had been turned, things would've gotten a lot uglier than me just telling *you* off."

Lila found that hard to believe, but she was glad she hadn't had to explain what she meant by saying she didn't trust herself. He'd known exactly what she meant. In spite of the unease she was still feeling about this whole thing, the enormous relief outweighed it. There wasn't even a full smile on her face, and Sonny was already wrapping his arms around her and burying his face in her neck with a groan.

He kissed then sucked her neck, igniting the now familiar ache between her legs instantly; then he pulled away. "So, now that I'm forgiven and all is well, how 'bout that trip to Los Feliz we were supposed to take today?"

"But—" She began to protest when his lips crashed onto hers again.

His amazing tongue did things to her she was afraid might have her moaning soon. The moment she could pull away take a breath—she licked her lips, breathlessly staring into his beautifully intense eyes. "I still have a million questions, Sonny."

"You can ask me anything you want on the way to my house. I had everything planned until . . ." He shook his head with a frown as he tugged her along toward the door.

"Wait. I need my purse and to tell Ali where I'm going."

Sonny let her hand loose, and she rushed to the bedroom, her heart beating erratically. Her mind was all over the place. Was this a mistake? Had she forgiven him too easily? Were they moving too fast? Should she be feeling *everything* she was feeling for him so soon? Yet, at the same time, in the middle of terrifying uncertainty, a part of her wanted to screech like a school girl full of excitement, just another thing she'd never done nor had even the slightest inclination of doing before she met him. Even Ali said she believed his sincerity.

Ali sat up on her bed where she'd been lying studying, the moment Lila walked in the room. "So?"

Lila couldn't even begin to try and hide the giddy smile already plastered on her face. This day had gone from one of the worst in her life to one of the most nerve-wracking. Wishing she could just enjoy this more as she should be, she placed her hand on her belly to try and placate the enormous knot in there. She was only glad now she'd taken such a long shower when she got home today to try and calm herself.

"I think everything is okay now, but I still have so many questions."

"Well, ask them," Ali said with an excited smile. "I did."

"You did?" Lila asked, grabbing her purse on the dresser.

Once again, it was a reminder of just how unglamorous she was compared to all those women she'd seen photographed with Sonny. Her purse was more of a backpack than a purse. Although the lady at the second-hand store where she'd purchased it called it a backpack satchel, so technically it *was* a purse. All Lila cared about at the time was that it was something she wouldn't accidently forget on the bus.

Swinging the *satchel* over her shoulder, she turned to face Ali, who was already telling her about some of the questions she'd asked Sonny. Of course, her sister had covered one of the burning questions Lila had for Sonny, about that Mona girl he was holding hands with in New York just a few weeks ago.

Though his answer to the question had been anything but satisfactory, even to Ali. *It was cold?* Really? That was his excuse? It was the kind of bullshit Lila would have no patience for and even less intention of dealing with. These were the things they'd be discussing today before she made the final decision on whether she was moving forward with this insane situation.

Ali let her in on a few of the other things she'd quizzed Sonny about before Lila finally started toward the bedroom door, until she remembered something and turned back. "You're not going anywhere today, right?"

"No, I have to cram for a test this week."

"Good. Check with me if by chance you leave for *any* reason. I'll be home early. I have work early in the morning, and I need to talk to you."

Ali stared at her curiously then glanced at the door and smiled. "Right. I have lots of questions too. So, I'll be waiting."

There was more than just Sonny she needed to talk to Ali about, but she wouldn't get into it now. Finally, she got out of there and met Sonny in the front room. A couple of the kids downstairs recognized him and stopped them so they could take a photo. Sonny obliged while Lila stood and watched, trying to make sense of how surreal her life suddenly felt.

Watching him kneel and take a few photos with some of his much younger and clearly awestruck fans only made this more real. It'd be a while before it fully registered that Sonny was a celebrity. After seeing all the recent and ongoing headlines about his signing with the Dodgers, she felt so completely ignorant. How could she not have heard about it? Her head was obviously buried when it came to sports stuff, which was so stupid, considering she might soon be a sports figure herself. Not that she thought for a moment she'd be anywhere as big as Sonny was.

Once done with the photos and because they were beginning to draw a crowd, Sonny and Lila made a quick exit. "That's probably the biggest thing you'll have to get used to," Sonny said as he waved at the small crowd standing on the sidewalk, watching and still taking photos of his car as they drove away. "And I don't mean just because of me." He turned to her. "Something tells me you, too, will be making headlines soon. So why didn't *you* tell *me* about your boxing? You're being such a badass makes total sense now. Of course you'd be."

Lila shook her head, glancing out the window even as he laced his fingers into hers. "You heard Noah," she reminded him. "I've only been in the ring a few times. I've never fought professionally. For the longest time, I refused to even consider it."

"Why? You're so good."

Lila shrugged, not sure if she was ready to share this with him yet. "Personal reasons."

"Lila." He squeezed her hand. "You don't have to tell me now, but I'd eventually like to know *everything* about you and for you to know everything about me. I don't like the thought of keeping even our most intimate secrets from one another."

There was no way Lila could refrain from scoffing at that. Sonny turned to her and gave her a remorseful look. "Alright, I deserved that, but I mean from here on. So, when you're ready, I'd love it if you shared."

Lila glanced at him, her insides fluttering as they'd only ever done for him. His eyes were on the road again but then glanced in her direction. The intense expression softened immediately when their eyes met.

She squeezed his hand, and despite her reservations about all this still, she took a deep breath, ready to share. "My mom was an amateur boxer who, like me, was told she had great potential. My grandpa was a boxer back in his heyday. Even boxed professionally for a while there, and it's probably where my mom and I got our natural talent. But my grandpa ended up with all these medical issues that I'm certain had to do with his days of constantly getting punched in the head. No one ever said it, but I'm positive the stroke he had that left his face partially paralyzed had to do with all the beatings he'd taken over the years."

Sonny turned to her when she paused. "Did your mom have any medical issues because of it?"

Lila laughed humorlessly. "Yeah, boxing took her life."

She stared out the window, remembering and then contemplating on the ironic fact that Sonny had brought out yet another first for her. She'd never once discussed her feelings about this with anyone, not even any of her therapists and many counselors who tried in vain to get her to open up about it.

"She'd been warned it was dangerous to get back in the ring after the second concussion. But she did anyway. After her third one, the doctor refused to sign off on allowing her back in the ring. Only the guys at the gym she fought at didn't give a fuck."

Lila stopped to take a deep breath, angry that she couldn't clean up her filthy mouth for more than a few minutes. It'd be a constant reminder of the lower class she'd always be a part of. How different she and her perfect boyfriend were.

"It's okay to be mad," Sonny said, kissing her hand. "I'd be pissed too."

"Yeah, well, she didn't have to get in the ring again, but I guess it was her dream, and she refused to give it up, even if it meant she was risking leaving us orphaned, which was exactly what happened. Because of my grandpa's age and medical issues, he was considered unfit to become our legal guardian. With no other family, we were carted off to foster care."

Lila paused, glancing up when Sonny kissed her hand again. "I'm sorry."

She shrugged. "Even if he'd been able to fight to get custody of us, we would've been right back in foster care that next year when he passed from another massive stroke."

"And your father?" he asked, sounding cautious.

"The prick left us before Ali was even born. I don't even remember him, and my mom didn't tell us too much about him, but I remember overhearing her once on the phone, years after Ali was born. I was still very young." Lila chuckled and again felt zero humor in it. "I remember it clearly because it totally confused me. She told whoever she was talking to that when my dad found out she was pregnant again he told her not to have the baby and she refused. So, he left. I kept thinking how could she *not* have it? Could you just choose to never let it out of your belly?"

Sonny turned to her with a sympathetic smile. Lila tried smiling, but it was weak at best.

They came to a stop, and Sonny leaned over and kissed her softly. "You're beautiful," he whispered before pulling away. "I just had to say that. Carry on."

Lila smiled again despite the mood her story had put her in, but she was ready to move on to the subject of him and all his female friends. Only she'd do her best to stay cool—remain civil in spite of herself. This was her chance to prove to her doubtful heart that she could handle a relationship of this magnitude without blowing it.

## Sonny

There was no way she could know this, but with every new thing Sonny learned about Lila, he fell even harder for her. Even her outburst today at the gym had garnered her more respect. She had a roomful of superstar athletes, some of which were her bosses, and she didn't hold back for the sake of appearances. Most women would've sucked it up—refused to make a scene—and worried about looking bad.

Not Lila.

She wasn't holding in shit for anyone or anything, and he'd meant every word of it when he said he fucking loved that about her. He loved that she was so different. It was exactly why he was so curious about something now and he had to ask.

"So, what made you change your mind about fighting?"

"A few things," she said with a frown. "Gio pointed out that if I was good enough, which he's confident I am, that I'll likely almost never get hit in the head, at least not hard or often enough to cause any serious damage. But also, I need the extra money. My other roommate is moving out, and that means I'll have to come up with the extra third of the rent she was paying. Unless I can find another roommate I can trust to live with me and Ali, I need more money coming in. And you know me. I trust *no one*."

Sonny chuckled, even if hearing her say she needed more cash had him tempted to offer to move her into a safer neighborhood where he'd pay all her expenses. Already he felt completely compelled to take her and Ali in under his wing, tell her she didn't need to fight another day in her life if she didn't want to and he'd take care of their every need. Only one thing kept him from putting it out there. He'd already known she would adamantly refuse the offer. This soon anyway. But he'd definitely be working on it later. For now, he'd just put it out there so she'd know it was eventually coming.

"You do realize that, when things move forward with us and this relationship gets even more serious, you won't need to fight or even work for that matter. I'd love nothing more than to take care of you, and I, of course, understand you and Ali are a package deal. She'd be more than welcome."

Not surprising, Lila had already started shaking her head even before he finished. "I fought tooth and nail to be able to take Ali with me when I was eighteen and out of the system. My goal the moment I got her was to get a job and move us out of the assisted-living facility they put me up in until I could get on my feet. When I was finally able to, I vowed never to get myself in a position where I'd have to count on *anyone* for anything. As generous and amazing as it is for you to even be thinking this way so soon . . ." This time she squeezed his hand back and smiled sweetly. "And it is very generous and *beyond* sweet of you. I just can't do that, Sonny. I refuse to count on anyone *ever* again."

Although this didn't sit well with Sonny because he had every intention of taking her and Ali out of those projects and getting them settled in somewhere safer, he couldn't help but smile. Sonny brought her hand to his mouth again. He kissed it several times before turning to her.

"Don't ever ask me *why you* again, because this is just one of the many reasons."

Instead of smiling as he expected her to, the sweet smile she'd already worn slowly went flat. "Okay, but I do have other questions."

"Ask away." He tried not to sound as nervous as this made him.

"My sister said she already asked you some of what I was wondering myself."

He nodded, staring straight ahead. Figures she'd be wondering about that too.

"The girl you were with in New York—"

"I wasn't *with* her," he said immediately.

"Okay, the girl you were photographed with strolling through Manhattan and then holding hands."

Sonny let out a breath. "It was cold—"

Lila pulled her hand out of his. "That's a bullshit excuse, Sonny, and you know it."

"You didn't let me finish," he said before she could get too heated.

"So, what? This exclusivity thing is only weather permitting? What else did you do to keep her warm?"

Sonny pulled off to a smaller street then stopped altogether and parked because he could already hear it in her lethal tone. This would escalate fast if he didn't address it head on.

"Okay." He turned to her, bringing a hand up in front of him. "I'll admit she is someone I've gone out with in the past. She was there at the same studio where I was filming a commercial. She's a sports agent—*not* mine. But we're often in the same circles, charity events, parties, etc. I hadn't seen her in months, so we walked out and grabbed some coffee, and yes, at one point, she slipped her hand in mine and alright . . ." He conceded with a reluctant nod. "I went along with it. But that's all that happened. When she found out I'd be there for another night, she suggested we get together for dinner or drinks that night, and I swear to you on my mother this is exactly what I told her. 'I can't. I just started seeing someone, and I don't wanna do *anything* that might screw this up.'"

Somehow, he thought she'd be more impressed with his whole swearing on his mother thing and after telling her verbatim what he'd really told Mona. Lila looked anything but impressed. Just as her sister had earlier, she lifted an annoyed brow. "How often do you just *go along* with allowing women to slip their hands into yours or all out paw you like today?"

"Honestly?" He did his best to tread lightly, but he was determined to be *completely* honest. "When I was single, always." He shrugged, lifting a hand up again before she could retort. "I'm a man, Lila. It's different for us. We don't mind and it didn't matter then. But it does now and things *will* change. I promise you."

She stared at him for a few moments without saying anything then frowned, shaking her head, and glanced out the window. "This is what scares me, Sonny. I don't wanna be in a relationship where we'll be arguing over petty shit like this"—she turned to face him again, her expression more worried now than mad like she was earlier— "arguing over some girl slipping her hand in yours. I wish I could say it won't bother me—that I'll be able to shake it off without getting pissed. But I know I won't. I *will* be pissed and even worse, hurt, *every* fucking time." She pressed her lips as if admitting that last part really irritated her.

"I don't understand why you think that's such a bad thing, babe." He reached out for her hand because he needed to get something straight with her right now. "Having a bad temper is one thing. Getting pissed over someone else's hands on what belongs to *you* is perfectly understandable. I hope you don't think that kind of reaction to something like that is exclusive only to you because of your short fuse. Like I warned you earlier, Lila, expect things to get ugly if I ever have to deal with what you did today. It's why I'm so sorry you had to and why I'll make sure it never happens again."

"But you can't control all of them, and you already know what'll happen if any idiot even *thinks* of pawing *me*."

Sonny laughed. "Yeah, I know. It's why I was so careful that first night when I took the risk and asked if I could kiss you." The very thought had him leaning into her and kissing her softly; then he stopped and gazed into her eyes. "I promise you I may not be pummeling any girl that tries to put her hands on me. Hitting women just isn't for me, but I'll put a stop to it. Besides . . ." He kissed her again, sucking her bottom lip and smiling when he felt her body's trembling reaction to that. "I'm pretty sure once the word gets out about who my girl is, especially because I'm certain your name and what you're so good at doing will be out for the world to know real soon, any girl who might've *pawed* me in the past will definitely think twice about doing so now. And when it comes to the fans, just like all the 5th Street wives, I promise you in time, you'll be just as unfazed."

"I doubt it." She smirked. "But for now, I guess I'll have to take your word for it."

"Yeah, you will," Sonny said, leaning in and taking her mouth again.

Sonny kissed her again even as she smiled against his lips. He hoped they were done with this, at least for now. He preferred to occupy his mouth in a better way. The hypocrisy could only be muted so much and for so long. He'd seen the way some of those guys eyed Lila's finely toned body today in that sparring room. She'd soon be dealing with overzealous fans or admirers herself. Or rather Sonny knew all too well he'd have to be dealing with watching them ogle her and take *too*-close-for-comfort selfies. Her comfort *and* his.

After another deep exchange of frantic tongue wrestling and feeling her body's usual reaction, which had already tightened his crotch, he pulled away and stared into her eyes. "You'll just have to take my word for it because I ain't going anywhere. I know where to find you now, and I have no qualms about stalking you until you hear me out anytime you send me packing."

Unable to keep his mouth off her, he was at it again. Jesus, what tasting her mouth and then feeling her hard body under his did to him. When he was finally able to tear himself away, he glanced out the window, still licking his lips. "We're not far from my house now. Are you hungry? We can pick something up and take it back to my place."

Lila nodded eagerly. "I didn't have much breakfast. I was so nervous and then after . . ." She pouted and even that had Sonny gazing at her, feeling completely lovesick. "I sort of lost my appetite."

Well, that wiped the damn smile off his face. He leaned in and kissed her nose. "But we're all good now, right?" he asked, feeling like scum all over again.

Lila nodded, surprising him when she reached over and ran her fingers through his hair. With her seemingly nowhere near as disgusted and pissed at him as she was earlier, Sonny had to wonder. Maybe even after the debacle at the gym he might still have a chance of possibly feeling those fingers dig into his shoulders and back later today.

"So, you must be starving." He pushed any thought of having her under him away before she'd notice his aching cock pushing against his pants already.

"I am." She continued to run her fingers gently through his hair with a smile.

Before he'd even asked, he'd already had an idea of the best place to pick something up from. But then he thought better of it. "Are you on any kind of special diet?"

Lila laughed. "I should be, and I imagine once I confirm I'm all in for this, they'll get me on one, but I work out so much right now, I've actually been afraid of losing weight."

Sonny turned to eye her. "Could you be any more different from *any* girl I've ever met. What girl is ever afraid of losing weight?"

She smiled big. "One who'll be counting on her power and muscle to make sure she doesn't get pounded in the head."

"Then I know just the place." Sonny pulled out onto the street. "Something tells me you probably work out enough that you can eat pretty much anything you want."

"I've been blessed with an excellent metabolism." She confirmed with a smile.

"Good. Because after the day we've had, I'd say we could both go for some good comfort food."

He told her about the greasy spoon they'd be picking up food from and named all the comfort dishes they served, and she groaned after each one. The place had an odd drive-thru, so they didn't have to get out, but they did have to park to wait since it wasn't burgers they'd be waiting on.

Unfortunately, Lila's excitement about the food and lighthearted mood was short-lived—for both of them. As soon as they turned the corner onto the street with the downtown shopping and trendy restaurants, Lila was distracted not by what she saw but *who*. Sonny saw her do the double take. "Is that . . .?"

She craned her neck back as they came to a red light to get a better look then turned to Sonny with that same starry-eyed look so often directed at him. "Zac Efron?"

The twinkle in her eyes was cute. It was innocent, so unlike Lila, whimsical even. It *pissed* the shit out of him.

"Could be." Sonny stared straight ahead but refused to look back then stepped on the gas the moment the light turned green. "I heard he lives in the area."

"You live in the same neighborhood as *Zac Efron?*" she asked, her words again way too dreamy like.

Sonny clutched the steering wheel tightly, trying not to get worked up over this because he'd be ridiculous to. "Yep" was his only response as he continued to stare ahead.

The whole world had been talking about Sonny's signing with the Dodgers, and Lila had never heard of him, but Zac fucking Efron had her craning her neck?

She glanced around now, taking everything in. "I don't know why I just assumed all celebrities lived in Beverly Hills, high rises in New York, or the Hamptons. Los Feliz." She turned to face Sonny. "Who knew?"

"We're not too far from Hollywood or Beverly Hills, and it's a pretty exclusive neighborhood, so there's a lot of celebrities in this area," Sonny informed her, feeling a little stupid now for his inane jealousy. Still, he reached over and slipped his hand in hers, squeezing slightly. "Abel and Felix live in the area too."

As they drove up the long driveway to Sonny's estate, she was visibly stunned. All the lighthearted chatter came to a sudden halt as her wide eyes took in what now felt like a never-ending stone driveway and a professionally kept landscape on either side.

Finally, they reached the gate at the top that opened to his circular driveway. He'd never thought it before, but suddenly the huge fountain that adorned the middle of the driveway just in front of the home's entrance suddenly felt like overkill.

"That was there when I bought the place," he explained as if that made the extravagance any less his.

He'd known from the moment he dropped off Lila that first night that his lifestyle would be a bit of a shock to her— that it'd take some getting used to. But he hadn't anticipated this. He couldn't make out if she was just staggered or maybe disgusted. She hadn't uttered a word since they'd started up his driveway.

"You're probably wondering if I really need all this, and the answer to that is a resounding no." He let go of her hand to turn off the car once he'd rolled around to the very front of his estate's entrance. "When you're fortunate to make the kind of money I do, Lila, you have to have tax write-offs. Lots of them. Because even—"

"You don't have to apologize for your lifestyle, Sonny." She reached out to touch his hand. "If you earned it, then enjoy it."

"Yeah, but a single guy like me doesn't need all this. I'm just trying to explain—"

"You don't need to explain anything about that to me." This time *she* kissed his hand. "One of the things that popped up a lot today about you is all the charity work you do. The youth baseball camp you run during the off-season. My head was spinning, and now I understand why you're gone so much. I'm not disgusted if that's what you're thinking. I've just never seen anything like this, not in person anyway. But since we spoke of not keeping anything from each other, if you want to tell me all about your *real* life now, I'm all ears. You can do so while you give me the grand tour."

Relieved, he leaned in and kissed her. "Yes." He pulled back to look at her in the eyes. "I wanna tell you all about it."

⭐

# Lila

The mansion, or rather estate as Sonny referred to it, was beyond anything Lila had ever seen. From the *long* lavish entrance with the extraordinary waterfall in front of the sprawling Spanish Colonial home, every room in the house was bigger than Lila's entire apartment. And every room was professionally decorated wall to wall, so it looked like something out of a magazine. Lila had been speechless throughout the tour Sonny gave her.

Her bookworm sister would appreciate the lobby/library, but the enormous ballroom was something else. The full bar in the ginormous ballroom was bigger than the one at the club where she'd met him. And then there was the maid's quarters. That alone was more than Lila would ever dare hope to live in one day. It was a full home attached to the side of the house with a full bathroom, living room, and its own private luxurious kitchen, two-car garage and even its own entrance.

They'd taken the grand tour after they'd eaten their dinner. Lila had teased that the walk around the enormous property would be enough to work off the large portions of comfort food they'd eaten. It'd taken long enough because they'd gone through all his trophies, awards, and posters for the many products he'd endorsed over the years. Now she knew why he had so many Rolexes. It was just one of the countless products he endorsed.

At one point, Lila shook her head, exasperated that he was this famous and she'd never heard of him. "What?" Sonny asked when he noticed.

"I still can't believe I had no clue who you were. In my defense," she said before further confirming how clueless she'd been, "remember I don't have cable and for the most part stay off social media. I'm not much for pop culture."

Sonny muttered something as he turned away.

"What was that?"

He shook his head. "Never mind."

"No," she asked curiously now, especially because strangely he sounded irritated. "What did you say? Honest to God, I really don't watch much television at all."

Startling her, he spun around suddenly then pinned her against the wall. "I said but you knew that fruity bastard when you saw him."

"*What*? Who?"

"Zack fucking Efron." He kissed her then nipped her bottom lip. "Today when we picked up lunch."

Lila laughed because it felt *ridiculous* that Sonny might be jealous of her affection for *Zack Efron*. "It's not funny," he said. "You've never struck me as someone who'd get all dreamy-eyed and shit, but I saw you today. It's exactly what you did."

Laughing even more, Lila caressed the side of his face and kissed him, even though he tried to pull away. "First, I seriously doubt he's fruity. Seems more of a lady killer to me." That only made Sonny's expression harden. "But *Charlie St. Cloud* is one of me and Ali's favorite movies. We cried like babies because of the whole brother bond and his losing his brother in the movie the way he did. It's one of the few movies I've watched many times. So, obviously, I'd recognize him."

"Well, don't expect me to ever watch it with you."

Lila shook her head. "My God, you're adorable when you're jealous, but really? Of a movie star?"

Sonny kissed her again—hard. "Don't forget I'm around a lot of celebrities of all kinds. The fact that he's a movie star doesn't mean shit to me."

With that, he pulled her along and the tour was officially over. Lila hadn't realized how long the tour had gone on, but by the time they sat comfortably on Sonny's oversized sofa in his family room, watching TV, the competitive cooking show they watched actually made her hungry again.

One comment about how good the food they were working on looked and another bragging one about her very discriminating palate and Sonny had jumped all over it. He bet her she couldn't win the challenge he had for her. Within minutes, he'd gone into the kitchen and come back with a box full of things. She'd now been trying to guess what they were while blindfolded as he fed them to her. He'd given her the opportunity to choose the stakes for their bet. Pathetically, she couldn't think of anything, so he'd taken it upon himself to name the stakes. For every one she got wrong, he got to take a piece of her clothing off. For every one she got right, she got to choose something he'd take off. Though it didn't seem fair because she'd been blindfolded the whole time and would be until they were done. So, it's not like she got to enjoy his bare chest.

Lila sat there in her bra and jeans, while Sonny had lost his shirt and both shoes.

"Open wide," he said as she braced herself for her next taste.

He slipped her a small spoonful of something soft, slightly pasty, and a bit sour. "Sour cream?"

"Close, but nope. I want your pants."

Feeling her face warm, she flinched when she felt his hand at her waist. "Wait," she said, giggling nervously. "How do I know you're not lying? That tasted just like sour cream."

"It was cream cheese," he said, spreading something on her lips with his finger.

The moment she tasted it she knew it was the cream cheese again. Sonny licked it off her lips, even as his hands continued to work the top button of her jeans.

Remembering what he'd said last night, Lila wasn't sure if this was leading to that or more. Her body trembled at the thought, and already she knew if things went further today, she'd be helpless to resist. She was so ready to be with him already.

She moved her hips, helping him slip her pants down, then shivered when she felt his lips on her thigh as he sprinkled kisses down her legs. Now she sat there in just her bra, panties, and socks, and her heart beat wildly as she heard his overly playful comment. *"Next up."*

Lila gulped, knowing she needed to get this one right. "This isn't liquid or soft. It's solid. You'll have to bite into it. Open up."

She opened her mouth as she felt a small pea-like object on her tongue. It was a little bigger than a pea but not smooth enough, and it made her nervous about biting into it. "This better not be a garlic clove."

Sonny laughed. "I wouldn't do that, especially because that'd be too easy. She bit into it, scrunching her nose in reaction, even though it didn't taste too bad. Just unfamiliar. The taste as well as the consistency. "I have no idea," she said, continuing to chew.

"Yes!" he said, and already his finger caressed the bottom of her bra.

"Wait," she said again with the nervous laugh. "I still get to guess. You have more?"

Sonny huffed but complied, pulling away. He put another in her mouth. This time she made note of the oddly shaped food and thought maybe he cut something bigger small to trick her. "Is it a potato?"

"Nope," he said, leaning her back onto the sofa and pulling the strap of her bra down her shoulder.

He quickly made himself comfortable over her body, and that was when she noticed. "Hey," she said, pulling on his shirt. "You didn't take your shirt off, cheater."

Sonny laughed, pulling away as she removed the blindfold and watched him pull his shirt off, exposing his gloriously muscled upper body. She'd seen the tattoo on his upper arm in some of the posters of him shirtless and asked him about it then. But now she touched it for herself. It was a tree in US flag colors. Underneath, the roots spread out just as wide as the tree above. Only they were red, white, and green. In between the two words, it read, *American grown with Mexican Italian roots*. He'd explained how perfect he thought it was when the tattoo artist pitched the idea since he was looking for something that would express that sort of thing. And since Italy's and Mexico's flags bear the same colors, it worked out beautifully.

"You haven't won," she whispered as his kisses moved down her chin to her neck, making her entire body tremble in reaction.

"I won the moment I laid eyes on you." He nipped her neck then moved farther down.

His words made her heart swell. "What was it," she asked, breathing deeper.

"Hmm?" He pulled her bra down, exposing her breasts, and began to suck her nipple, her toes curling in reaction.

"The food I couldn't guess."

He stopped for a moment. "Garbanzo bean," he said then went right back to sucking.

It felt so damn good she squirmed and arched her back. It went on for a while. The longer he sucked her nipples, the more comfortable he made himself—like he could be there forever—but she could hardly stand it anymore.

Running her hands over his big hard shoulders, she shuddered every time he'd suck a little harder.

"Sonny," she whispered, in aching need now, but he didn't respond. Instead, he sucked harder then slipped his hand down into her panties. "Sonny," she said again as she felt his finger caress her slick folds.

"Yeah," he said, sounding just as breathless as she now felt.

"Make love to me," she heard herself practically beg.

It'd been way too long, and the thought of waiting even another minute was just too much. Without doubt, she knew she'd regret *not* following her heart and just giving into her feelings for him. Besides, he'd been right when he said technically they'd already made love. She just could hardly wait to feel him inside her.

"Make love to me, *please*."

Sonny looked up at her, his eyes a bit uncertain. "You sure about this? Just because I said I'd make it official the next time we were together doesn't mean I'm not still willing to wait for as long as I need to, Lila. I still have every intention of going along with your request of taking things slow."

The sincerity in his words only made Lila more sure about this. She sat up, taking his face in her hands. "Fuck me, Sonny or so help me God—"

Before she could finish, his lips were on hers. She gasped in nerve-wracking delight when he easily ripped her panties off her with one pull. "As you can see, I did plan on taking my time, but since you're threatening me . . ." He smirked as he pulled off her and flung off his jeans in two seconds.

"Yeah, don't take threats from me lightly," Lila said, watching his near naked gorgeously massive body move swiftly as he reached for his wallet on the coffee table.

Pulling out the condom from it, he ripped it open, and Lila refrained from gasping when he lowered his boxer briefs and out he popped, fully erect and ready to go. Even though she'd seen it already, seeing it in person was even more breathtaking. Wasting no time, he stared at her as he slipped the condom on. Her eyes went from his back down to what he was doing. Words couldn't describe the mixture of excitement and panic she was feeling now. She was really going through with this.

Once done, he pulled his boxer briefs completely off, and her panic was quickly replaced with anxious anticipation as he lay back down over her and she was buried under the gloriousness of hot naked muscle. Running her hands over his hard back, Lila kissed his shoulders and upper arms until their lips met again.

He kissed her hard and deep as he spread her legs under him, then sucked her bottom lip and began to enter her. It felt almost like a soothing technique, to help with the raw stretch he had to know she was feeling. "You're so tight," he grunted as he slipped in deeper, stretching her as she'd never been stretched before.

She and Marcelo had been kids when they'd been together. Sonny wasn't just a full-grown man; he was a beast compared to Marcelo. The delicious burn had her spreading wider to help accommodate him as he pushed impossibly deeper. Lila could feel him to her very core, and that sensation had her moaning with pleasure.

'You okay?"

She moaned again then smiled against his lips. "Do I sound like I'm not?"

Sonny finished slamming into her all the way and stayed there for a few moments not moving. He swayed his hips a little as if making enough room in there before pulling back and sliding in and out. Lila spread wider, as Sonny moved onto his knees. He lifted one of her legs, adjusting her so he could fuck her even deeper.

With one hand, he held her leg up and the other played with her clit. "Oh!" she cried out as he slammed into her harder with each thrust.

Again and again, he thrust in and out of her, his own moans beginning to get louder. The buildup was fast, and just like when she'd played with herself for him, she could already tell this would be explosive.

Panting and moaning louder and unabashedly as she felt it building, building, until she reached that heavenly place, she cried out in ecstasy. With her entire body trembling now, Sonny slowed just as an explosion of pleasure seared through her body and she continued to moan. He buried himself deep inside her with a groan, and they came together breathlessly as tears escaped the corner of her eyes. Lila knew all about angry and sad tears. But she didn't know there was such a thing as tears of pleasure.

He brought his body down onto her and lay there, for a few long moments as they both struggled to catch their breaths. "Oh . . ." Lila said, sucking in a chunk of breath. "My God, that was brilliant."

Sonny chuckled. "Brilliant, huh? That's a first."

Lila nudged him playfully. The last thing she wanted to discuss right now was how many other things his lovemaking had been called. Finally, he pulled away from her, offering his hand and helping her up. "Let's go to my bedroom. That was just an appetizer, sweetheart. I have a lot of other *brilliant* things I wanna do to you."

Her heart rate had just begun to normalize, and just like that, it spiked again.

# 15

"So how'd it go?" Ali asked as soon as Lila walked in the kitchen

Lila eyed Ali's plate: a cheeseburger patty—ground turkey no doubt—on lettuce and tomato, minus the bun. Ali had spread a little mayo, ketchup, and a sprinkle of cheese on them. She had what looked like a spinach salad on the side.

"It went well." Lila said, trying to hold in her excitement about just how good it'd gone.

She was still trying to wrap her head around it. Today had been far more than good. It'd been *too* good, so amazing it still made her nervous that she might wake up and it'd all be a dream.

Ali wiped her mouth after chewing her food. "He's officially your boyfriend, then?"

"Yes," Lila said, walking over to the fridge. "I guess he was before today, actually. I just hadn't said it out loud. I was afraid to jinx it. Still am."

She grabbed a water bottle out of the fridge and walked over to the table to take a seat across from Ali. "Is that what you wanted to talk to me about?" Ali asked, cutting into her patty with her fork. "You're nervous about this? Because let me tell you. He seemed pretty desperate to explain himself today, Li. I don't think anyone is *that* good about pretending to genuinely be into someone."

"Yeah, I know, but even before I found out who he really was, I felt like he was too good to be true. Too good for me." That last part she added cautiously because she knew that'd likely piss her sister off.

As expected, her sister's brows were already pinched together even as she continued to chew. She covered her hand with her mouth as if she wasn't willing to wait until she was done chewing. "*Why?*"

Lila laughed, opening her bottle of water. "Why? God, where do I start?"

"First of all, let me ask you something." Ali let her fork down on her plate with a loud clink. "You said you're officially a couple, right?"

"Yes." Lila nodded.

"So, do you still feel that way? That he's too good for you?"

Lila lifted a shoulder. "I don't want to, but, Jesus—"

"Jesus nothing," Ali said with a scowl. "He seems like a smart and nice enough guy. If he's gotten to know you, then he knows better than to just be blowing air up your ass to get you in bed. And you're not stupid either. You're an official oouple now—two equals in a relationship, no matter how famous he is. If we're going on just looks alone, he may be a hot celebrity athlete"—she shrugged— "with a body to die for. I've seen some of his underwear ads. But look at you. You're fitness model material for crying out loud, and you're beautiful both inside and out. I bet you anything that's what he loves most about you. Unlike those celebs and models with the fake boobs and lips he's dated, you're *real*, Li."

"That's exactly what he said." Lila smiled, feeling all warm and fuzzy again like when Sonny had first said it. "Didn't mention the celebs boobs and lips, but he pretty much said what you're saying."

"You see. Don't sell yourself short, sissy. You have so much to offer, and he knows this. If he didn't genuinely care about you, there's no way he'd be staking out the building the way he was when I got here today. Then he practically begged me to help him out because he was so worried that you might not give him a chance to explain."

Lila sighed. "I know. I get it now, and after today, I do believe that he really cares about me. But it's hard not to be nervous about this. I mean I was even before I found out about him being famous. Now this just ups my anxiousness about this a million times."

"What are you worried about?" Lila stared at her sister, surprised that she wouldn't know. "*What?*" Ali asked, clearly still not understanding Lila's unease about all this.

"What do you think, Ali? Did you not see all those glamorous women he's dated? All the places he's been? How in the world will I fit into all that?"

Lila wasn't even sure why she was still asking. After today, there'd be no turning back. Even if she tried to back out now, her heart would protest so adamantly she'd be putty in his hands the moment he tried to talk her out of it. Today was proof of that. She'd been so ready to spit in his face one minute, and then one reluctant read of his email—a few more explanations from him, sprinkled with more promises—and she'd been sold. Just like that.

"If that's what you're worried about, then that's an easy fix. I guarantee you most of those *glamorous* broads weren't born glamorous. Like with everything, it'll take some practice and getting used to. Think of all the audition tapes for some of the now famous American Idol alumni. *None* of them were the least bit glamorous back then. Some are unrecognizable now. Oh, and that chick"—Ali pointed at Lila with her fork, trying to remember— "that MMA fighter girl we watched on YouTube the other day. As hard as nails as she looks, have you seen how good she cleans up?" Ali picked up her phone, which was sitting right next to her plate. "What was her name again?"

"Ronda Rousey." Lila frowned as Ali started tapping on her phone screen because this was a reminder of that other thing she needed to talk to Ali about.

"Look," Ali said, handing Lila her phone. "Now you know that girl wasn't born into the lap of luxury and then just decided she wanted to get into the ring and kick some ass just for giggles. Yet, you wouldn't know she wasn't born with the essence of glamour by looking at her all done up like the girls in the photos with Sonny."

Lila scrolled through a couple of the photos of the fighter girl, nodding in agreement. Her mind however was now on something else. Only there was something even more important she needed to ask about first. "I talked to Marcelo today." She handed Ali her phone. "He called to ask if I'd talked to you today because he couldn't get a hold of Jenny since she turns off her phone at work, but he was worried."

Ali's eyes widened, but it was clear she knew about what. "Hmm."

"His friend works at the corner market up the street. He saw you two running and screaming then a car screeching around the corner. He thought maybe the guy in the car was chasing you two, so he called him to tell him about it."

Ali let her head fall back. "Jen mentioned him asking her about it when she got home from work, but he didn't mention having called you."

Instantly, Lila's entire body went taut. She knew her sister was fine, and when Marcelo let her in on what he'd heard, Lila knew for a fact Ali had just walked into the front room, safe. Seeing how unaffected Ali appeared, Lila even thought maybe Marcelo's friend had confused her and Jen with two other girls. So, she'd postponed asking about it. But now Ali had that look on her face, the same one she always wore when she was trying to keep Lila from losing her shit over something going on with her. Like the bullies back in high school.

"What's going on? Who was chasing you?"

"God, this world is too small." Ali huffed.

Lila peered at her, not sure what she meant by that, but feeling her patience thin. "Allison—"

"First, this guy happens to drive by the bus stop where I'd walked Jenny to and sees us. Then Marcelo's stupid friend sees us too."

"Who is this guy, Al?"

"We're still investigating the allegations that there may be drug trafficking going on in the school. We're getting close to blowing the thing wide open, but we need more." Ali shook her head, and taking a drink of her milk, she went on, milk mustache and all.

She explained about Jen taking a photo of what she thought might be a drug exchange on campus and how she'd been seen. She'd been chased through the campus but got away. Then the same guy saw them at the bus stop and did a U-turn, so they ran. "He didn't see what building we went into."

"Okay, that's it," Lila said, tapping the table with her water bottle because halfway through Ali's explanation she'd gone cold. "No more investigating this case."

"We can't just drop it—"

"Leave it to the authorities, Ali. I mean it. This is starting to sound dangerous."

"But we're so close."

"*Allison,* what if that guy had caught you? What if he decides to do random drive-bys until he runs into you guys again?" Lila shook her head adamantly. "It's bad enough I'll have to worry that he might now, but I don't want to worry that the daring duo will keep looking for trouble and find more. Promise me this ends now, or, so help me, I'll attach myself to your hip, even if it means having to sit with you in class."

Ali exhaled loudly, letting her shoulders drop as she wiped her milk mustache away. "Alright, alright, we'll keep any investigating we do strictly online."

Lila was going to add a few more things for Ali to promise she wouldn't do, but she stopped when she had another worrisome thought. Ali was brilliant and beyond goal-oriented. Lila hadn't even given much thought to the real dangers of investigative journalism. This was community college and very likely a local small-potatoes dope dealer. What kind of danger was Ali in for when she started snooping around the bigger stuff? Corrupt politicians and corporate wrong doings of big wigs who'd be willing to stop at nothing to keep from being outed by a relentless investigative journalist like Ali.

"Maybe you should stick to just regular journalism, Al. You just started and already you're being chased by the bad guys."

Ali grinned, her big eyes nearly sparkling. "Isn't it exciting?"

"No," Lila said, feeling exasperated. "No, it's not exciting to realize my sister's career choice is *this* dangerous."

"Oh stop," Ali said, eating the last of her cheeseburger patty then wiping her mouth. "It's edgy not dangerous. Most of my work will consist of me sitting in front of a computer, researching. So, how was it talking to Marcelo after all this time?"

The sudden random change in subject caught Lila by surprise. She tried to shrug it off as if hearing from him after all this time hadn't rattled her. But the truth was she'd hated the weirdness she'd felt during the entire short conversation she'd had with him—couldn't get off the phone with him fast enough. She'd always thought, if she ever spoke to him again, she'd be mean. Rude. She'd wanted to hate him, wanted to be cold and indifferent, but the damn subject matter had thrown her, and she'd sounded more grateful for his heads-up than anything. Worst yet, she'd even promised to get back to him as soon as she knew more. Only the distraction of walking out into the front room and seeing Sonny then Ali's seemingly unfazed demeanor had derailed that promise.

Now that Ali had mentioned talking to Jenny and that she'd apparently spoken to her brother already, Lila didn't see any reason for having to get back to him anymore. This relationship with Sonny was just getting started, and even though his jealousy over her interest in Zac Efron was cute, if not all out hilarious, she could already tell he wouldn't take too kindly to her allowing her jerk of an ex back in her life. Not that she planned to, but even her calling him back when it wasn't necessary might piss Sonny off. She'd already decided she wouldn't be doing anything she knew would piss her off *if*, as he put it earlier today, the tables were turned. And Lila knew just how *little* it'd take to piss her off, especially when it came to this stuff.

"I think I was too concerned with what he told me about you two being chased to even think much about anything else. He called just before you walked in, so the call was real short."

Ali stared at her for a moment, somewhat lost in thought. "Did Sonny mention something about Friday?"

Lila lay back on her bed with a groan, bringing her hands over her face. "He told you about that?"

"I was in his car when he took the call from his friend's sister asking if he'd be there. He told her he was bringing his *girlfriend*." Lila peeked out at her sister through her open fingers and saw Ali tilt her head. "What's the matter? It's just a party or gathering, right?"

"Not just *any* party," Lila said, sitting up and leaning against her headboard. "Not like the only ones I've ever attended or any I'm used to attending. It's his best friend's thirtieth birthday party, but his wife and sisters are making him think it's a wine-tasting charity event to get him there. And this isn't just any guy either; apparently, he's another superstar baseball player from his previous team, so there will be other celebrity athletes in attendance, which I don't even care about," she added with a frown because she really didn't. "Just like this morning, I doubt I'll recognize any of them."

"So, what's the problem, then?"

"Sonny said it really is a charity event. The guests are being asked to donate to their charity in lieu of gifts. But because of this and because he says most are very generous when donating, they've made it a *black-tie* affair."

Ali was still looking at her, as unmoved as previously. "So?"

"*What* the hell do I own that I can wear to a black-tie affair, Ali? I can't afford to buy anything fancy right now."

"You didn't tell him you couldn't go, did you?" Ali asked, tapping away at her phone.

"No, but I didn't give him a definite answer either. I said I had to work, which I really do."

"In the day," Ali said, lifting her brow at Lila before going back to tapping her phone screen. "I'm assuming this thing is in the evening, right?"

"Yeah, but he doesn't know what my regular hours are. I told him my shifts always vary."

"And you need this dress by Friday, right?"

"Yes," Lila said, frustrated now that her sister obviously didn't share the same anxiety about this as she did.

"Done!" Ali said, glancing up from her phone screen with a big smile.

"What do you mean done? I told you I can't afford anything."

"You don't have to pay. Jen's mom is a seamstress, remember? She'll do it for free."

Lila stared at her, remembering now the many times in the past when Marcelo's mom had hemmed up and even made her and Ali outfits as gifts. She'd forgotten all about that since she barely ever saw the woman anymore. "She's gonna be able to make me an evening gown by this Friday?"

"It's already made." Ali smiled smugly. "Don't you remember she always has dresses and stuff around the house that's she's working on for one reason or another? Jen says her mom has several gowns available for you to borrow. All she needs is for you to stop by at least a couple days prior and choose the one you like so she can get it specially fitted for you."

Admittedly, it was a relief. She wouldn't have to admit to Sonny this soon that fitting into his lifestyle was already going to be an issue. Although Ali's simple fix wasn't so simple. Going to get fitted for this damn dress would mean she'd very likely have to see Marcelo, something she had no desire to ever do again. But this might be the only answer. She needed to save her pennies now that Stacia had confirmed this was her last month living with them. Paying this last month's rent was clearly just a courtesy for her since she pretty much said she'd only be coming by to pick up her things little by little.

Which brought Lila to the next big thing she needed to discuss with her sister. "I guess I can do that. But can you discreetly ask Jen when would be the best time that I'd least likely run into Marcelo?"

Ali told her he's never there in the evenings, which worked for Lila, so they set it up for the following evening and she got right to it. "Only reason I don't just break down and go get a dress at the indoor swap meet or garment district downtown where I know I could get one for a lot cheaper than at the mall is because I have to watch every penny I spend this month."

As expected, she had her sister's interest. "Stacia's moving up north with Derek. His dad decided to retire early after that massive heart attack, and Derek put in for a transfer ASAP. Stacia didn't think he'd get the transfer so soon, but he did. This is her last month here." That had Ali's eyes widening, and Lila saw the moment the concern hit. "But don't worry. That promotion I mentioned? I got it."

Lila smiled, even though she was nervous as hell about admitting what exactly that promotion entailed.

Ali smiled too, her expression swelling with pride. "Really? What are you gonna be doing now?"

"Boxing," Lila blurted out before she could change her mind.

Instantly, Ali's smile flattened but not in an angry way. Lila saw more disbelief and confusion in her eyes than anything else. "Boxing? Like in the ring against other girls?"

With a nod and a wince, Lila confirmed. "It seems I have this natural talent for it. The trainers down there saw it in me, asked me to try it a few weeks ago, and they were right."

She explained in depth about Gio saying she'd be able to snag more fitness modeling jobs and endorsements if she had a title or two; how impressed he and all the owners of 5th Street had been with her natural skills, power, and ambidexterity; then about that morning's presentation and how seeing Sonny with that reporter had nearly ruined it.

To her surprise, Ali smiled big. "So, that bitch knows what she's up against now? She saw you in action then heard you tell him off. I love it."

Shaking her head, Lila laughed then asked the burning question. "You're not upset?"

"About what?" Ali asked as her smiling expression morphed into confusion.

"That I'll be boxing?"

Ali reached out for Lila's hand and laced their fingers together. "I know you were angry about mom and grandpa for a long time. Maybe still are. But I never have been." She shrugged. "I think I was too young at the time to understand what it was you were so mad about. But even as I got older and I overheard adults say you were still so angry with mom for risking her life fighting and stuff, I wasn't. I've always been of the belief that when it's your time it's your time. Mom could've been a librarian working in the safe confinement of a library, surrounded by books, but if her time to go was at the age she went, then she would've, no matter what. Maybe in a freak accident at the library." She smiled sweetly. "She might've plummeted to her death off one of those giant bookshelf ladders."

Of course, telling her Alikins about this turned out not nearly as painful as Lila had worried it would be. They talked about Lila's new career, new relationship, and this crazy day's happening until they were both too exhausted to talk anymore and called it a night. Lila lay there for a while, still unable to believe what a massive change her life was about to take. Thanks to Ali, however, she was more excited about it all now than scared. Though a tiny part of her, deep inside, was still absolutely *terrified* something was going to go very wrong.

# 16

It was Tuesday, and the week was moving along with Lila having gotten a few awkward but inevitable to-dos out of the way. She'd been fitted for the dress without incident because, as promised, Marcelo wasn't anywhere around. And she'd faced her bosses at the gym after Sunday's fiasco. They were now all aware that she and Sonny were in a relationship. Hector thought it was hilarious that she'd been dating *Sly* Sabian all this time and didn't know who he was.

Lila was just glad she was past all the inquiries. Though she didn't think Sonny would ever live it down. The cracks about him having a girl who'd whoop his ass if he ever messed up were still ongoing. While some were funny enough to have Lila smirking, she couldn't help being slightly bothered by it. She didn't want to be known as the girl who had her man by the balls out of fear. She hated to admit to finally feeling a little envious of the girlie girls.

Women like Nellie, Bianca, Ella, and Roni, all her bosses' wives, seemed to have their men in check out of mutual love and respect, not fear of having their nut sack ripped off. Even smartass Hector turned into a pussycat whenever his wife Charlee happened to come into the gym.

But then they all also had another thing in common that Lila had never felt. They were all so dainty and feminine. Not that being in Sonny's arms didn't make her feel daintier and girlier than Lila ever had. And she knew there was more to his attraction and respect for her than just fear of losing a limb. She just wished she could feel more like a lady now, especially since she'd be doing things like this Friday a lot more now that she was in a relationship with Sonny. She was even more grateful for Marcelo's mom now. She was certain this wasn't the last time she'd be needing her services.

"So, is it really true?"

Lila and Bianca had been busy cleaning up the youth gym so they could wrap it up for the day. They turned to see Ella and Nellie walking in.

Nellie smiled big. "I didn't know what to think when Abel told me about what happened Sunday. I kept meaning to get in here and ask you about it." Her expression went a little more sympathetic. "Mostly to see if you were okay because he said you'd been pretty upset. But I kept thinking he'd gotten something wrong. You really didn't know who Sly was?"

Lila shook her head, feeling her face flush. "Aside from boxing and that's only now, I've never really followed sports," she explained. "He introduced himself to me as Sonny, his middle name, and then kept to himself about being famous when he realized I didn't know who he was."

She went on and explained briefly about *why* Sonny had kept his identity to himself then about them not being around each other too often because of his traveling so much several of those first weeks. She'd already explained some of it to Bianca, who'd asked her about it first thing when Lila got back that week.

"But everything is okay now, right?" Nellie asked, looking genuinely concerned. "Between you and Sly, that is."

"Yes." Lila nodded, feeling a little weird about the girl talk. "He explained it all and we're good now."

"Well, it was a smart move, even if it did blow up in his face the way it did," Ella said with a smile. "When I first met Felix, I balked at getting involved with him *because* of who he was. Sabian may've have had a backward reasoning for not being forthcoming from the beginning, but you don't strike me as the type of girl who'd be falling all over herself for a guy just for his fame. Might've even been a turnoff for you if you'd known up front. Am I right?"

Despite her smiling with a confirming nod, Lila inwardly frowned. She was certain Ella meant she didn't strike her as the prissy fangirl type, more like the uptight aloof tomboy who'd never bend over backwards for a guy just because he's good-looking. Something she'd always been and still was proud of. She had no desire to be one of those kinds of girls, but a part of her wouldn't mind giving a more ladylike impression.

"You sure everything is okay?" Ella asked, staring at her, a bit unsure.

Apparently, Lila's inward frown hadn't been so subtle. She nodded again, trying to play it off, but Bianca, who she worked more closely with, cocked a brow. "I know you're a very private person, Lila, but sometimes talking about what's bothering you helps. I think maybe that's why you're wound so tight. Something tells me you hold a lot in. Not good for you, girl."

"No, not at all," Ella quickly agreed.

"I've told you from day one," Nellie said with a cautious smile. "You can come to any of us at any time, and we're here for you."

It was a foreign feeling to be surrounded by women—well-meaning mature women who Lila knew were sincere in their offers to lend an ear—not catty nosy women just trying to get the gossip. Strangely, Lila actually felt compelled to take them up on the offer. She was just so damn nervous about Friday; maybe talking about it *would* help.

"I just," she said, biting her lower lip. "I'm not like any of the girls I've seen him with on all those photos online."

"That's a good thing," Nellie said with a scoff.

Lila smiled, nodding in agreement. "I know, but I'm so unsophisticated it just makes me nervous. Like we're too different."

Ella put her arm around Lila's shoulder. "Oh, honey, you're preaching to the choir. When I first met Felix, I was told our worlds were so different they weren't even in the same galaxy."

"Yeah, but by who?" Nellie asked with a roll of her eye. "Your jerk ex who was so jealous of Felix he couldn't even see straight." Nellie turned to Lila, shaking her head but smiled. "Babe, not only were my life and Abel's different in the sense that he was a rising superstar and I was just a regular gal, I was also a divorcee eight years his senior."

Lila felt her eyes widen. "Sonny's eight years older than me."

Nellie laughed. "Take it from me: age makes as much difference in love as distance, time, color, and weight. None whatsoever."

"And like me," Ella added, "you'll soon see that your socioeconomic status will have just as much weight on your feelings for one another."

"We've all had to adjust in one way or another." Bianca laughed. "Even poor Charlee, who was once painfully shy, had no choice but to adjust to being married to someone so loud and outgoing as Hector."

"Don't let her fool you." Nellie smirked. "That girl was never that shy when it came to *some* things."

Ella and Bianca laughed, and Lila smiled, taking in a frustrated breath because she wasn't making herself clear. "I

know you guys were in similar situations as I am, but it was different for you." 
They all peered at her, but Ella spoke first. "How so? Because I grew up just a few blocks away from here." She stopped to giggle, bringing her hand to her mouth. "When I first met Felix, I was driving a car I had to warm up good and long before hitting the gas. Otherwise, it would backfire so loud I was afraid everyone around would dive for cover. Meanwhile, Felix drove a different luxury car every day."

As nervous as Lila was, the girls were all so down-to-earth that she laughed because she was beginning to feel a little comfortable talking to them. "I saw his home this weekend." Lila shook her head, wide-eyed. "I live in the projects, so yeah, huge difference, but that's not even what I'm most worried about."

"Then what is it?" Bianca asked, confused.

Lila glanced down at herself and then up at the mirrored wall. She was still wearing her hair in cornrows from her training with Gio and Hector earlier. "He's taking me to some black-tie affair thing this Friday, and I have *no* idea how I'm gonna fit in. I heard his friends are anxious about meeting me, and I just know I'm gonna blow it. I have a dress and all, but I'm seriously considering cancelling on him. Telling him—"

"No, no." Nellie shook her head adamantly. "Those things aren't as bad as you're thinking."

"Not at all," Ella agreed immediately. "And trust me. I'd never been to one either until Felix. I was nervous too, but I was fine."

"Yes, but you all are so"—she paused, trying to find the right word— "ladylike. And I'm so . . ."

"Look," Bianca said, chiming in. "The fact that he's taking you to meet his friends, who are anxious about meeting you, speaks volumes. Sabian's been one of sports' most eligible bachelors for years, and *he* chose you for a reason. Girl, look at you." She waved her hand up and down in front of Lila. "The guy's not blind. You got it going on. And obviously, *he's* not worried about you *blowing* it with his friends. But if *you're* worried about first impressions and being more ladylike, which we can be sometimes"—she laughed, pointing at herself and the other girls— "we can give you a few tips."

"Yes!" Ella said, smiling big. "Tonight's perfect, too, because we were just coming in to ask if Bianca was ready. Tonight, the dads are on kid duty and we're doing girls' margarita night over at Roni's. You're more than welcome to join us."

"Oh, this'll be so much fun," Nellie said, already tapping something onto her phone screen. "Roni will be so excited. She loves the idea of you and Sabian. She knows him better than any of us and says he's perfect for you. And Charlee and Drew will be there too. Drew's the resident single lady of our group, so she can set us straight in case our married asses are out of the loop when it comes to any of our tips."

Of course, Lila's first instincts were to object. She started to, but all her excuses were swiftly shot down. She didn't have to drink alcohol; they'd have plenty of other stuff including lots of desserts. Her sister was an adult and not disabled in any way, so she didn't *have* to get home to her just yet. And they had a driver picking them up and taking them all home. She couldn't even use having to see Sonny as an excuse since she'd already mentioned he was in New York until tomorrow.

Before she knew it, she was out of excuses, in a car similar to the one she'd driven around with Sonny that first night they met, and headed to Roni's place.

Somehow, Lila had been talked into having a margarita. They sat in Roni and Noah's outdoor sitting area that overlooked the lavish backyard. Roni lowered the music as she took a seat across from Lila. "So, first of all, I want details," she said with a wicked smile. "Have you slept with him?"

Lila's eyes widened and she felt her face heat. The girls all giggled, but all eyes were on her. She took a very slow sip of her drink before nodding. She was so not used to sharing such personal details with anyone. Ali was who she'd always been closest to, but when she'd been with Marcelo, she'd thought Ali too young to be sharing with her about her trysts with him. And last night the conversation hadn't even gone there. By the time she'd known Stacia well enough to share anything personal, the only thing she'd told her about her first and only boyfriend was what an asshole he turned out to be. The girl had been so busy lately, getting ready for her big move; she and Lila had barely exchanged a few texts in the past couple of weeks.

"Was it everything you imagined it'd be?" Charlee asked, wide-eyed. Her friend Drew sat next to her, nodding, equally excited.

"Um . . ." Lila licked her lips because she was *not* expecting to be having this conversation. What happened to the tips they were supposed to be giving her? "It was nice," she finally offered, knowing *that* was an understatement of epic proportions.

"You know," Nellie said, sitting up straighter and dusting off her crossed legs a little too properly. "This is normally where I'd chime in and scold the girls for making you uncomfortable with such a personal question."

*Thank you.*

"But I can't this time." She leaned over her legs and stared Lila down with a big grin. "Because I'm dying to know too."

The girls burst into laughter. "Seriously, he's just been so talked about lately," Bianca said, bringing her hand to her chest. "And now here we have his first serious girlfriend in years if *ever*. Which you gotta know will make headlines all over southern California if not the whole country for that reason alone, but then Gio assures me you're the next big thing in women's sports. You two will be sports lovers' royal couple. So, of course, we'd want the exclusive."

Lila brought her glass to her mouth, taking an even bigger swig of the sweet drink she was holding. Roni assured her she'd gone easy on the tequila. Now Lila wished she'd added an extra shot because this terrified her. Lila hadn't even thought of it in terms of being the tabloids' *it* couple.

"Oh, my God, B, you're scaring her now," Ella said, turning to Lila, then reached over and squeezed her knee. "You'll get used to the media faster than any of us did because you'll likely be in the spotlight just as much on your own merit. Not *just* because you're dating someone famous."

"But *do not* read the tabloid crap," Nellie warned firmly. "It's all a bunch of bullshit. What they do is they grab a tiny bit of the truth and sensationalize it by adding a whole bunch of lies for the sake of ratings and post hits. Only it'll drive you nuts because you'll always be wondering how much of it *is* true."

"Nothing will kill the mood and make you argue senselessly more than the stupid gossip shows and articles," Bianca added. "It's relationship *poison* if you let it be. Just do yourself a favor and stay away from them altogether."

"Okay, I think we've covered this enough," Drew said, holding her hand up. "You're forbidden to read the tabloids or ever argue with your boyfriend over them. Mmmkay? Now, let's get back to the important stuff. As fine as that man is, please tell me he delivers in bed."

Lila had known all these women for years now. She liked and respected every single one of them. But she'd never gotten personal with them about anything, especially about this kind of stuff.

"He does." She felt her cheeks flush then laughed nervously when they all sat up a bit, and Drew even moved to the edge of her seat.

Without giving away too much detail about her *fine man's* private parts, because that was all for her own visuals, she did assure them of one thing. "What you see in those photos he's modeled for is exactly what you get."

She indulged them a bit more by giving vague details. As much as Drew hoped he was a beast in bed, Lila only told them about how incredibly sweet and gentle he'd been. Finally, after a while of her very vague answers to their probing and sometimes silly questions, they got to what she'd thought she'd come here for.

"So, Lila here"—Nellie turned to Roni and then in Charlee and Drew's direction— "feels like maybe she's not ladylike enough for Sabian's world."

She explained about the black-tie affair and Lila's worries. Roni immediately turned to Lila. "What do you mean not ladylike enough? You're sexy as hell."

"I got this," Drew said, holding up her hand again. "Once upon a time my best friend here had to be convinced that she already had the attention of a certain boxing stud in her chess club. You, my friend, have *already* landed your stud. You just told us about how sweet and gentle he was with you. A guy like him knows full well most girls would bend over literally in either direction and let him have his way then thank *him* when it's over."

The girls all laughed as Roni stood and filled their margarita glasses all around. Lila gulped anxiously, not just about Drew stating what she thought were just her own insecurities as the obvious, but about Roni refilling her glass again. She made a mental note to sip her drink slowly and waited for Drew to continue.

"Yet, he was sweet and gentle, and you said it was the first time since you met him over a month ago? That's unheard of in his world!" All the girls nodded in unison, adding to Lila's already tightening stomach muscles. "Clearly, you've made a different impression on him than most of the easy lays he's so used to. You're already up, Lila. So, you'd like to be more ladylike to prove that, on top of being a badass athlete, you can purr like a kitten."

"I already have," Lila finally said, not sure if it was the tequila talking, but she giggled along with the girls. "I'd just like to not come across so *hard*. I realize it's probably good for my image as a boxer, since my career will be going in that direction, but I'd like to come across a little more . . ." She shook her head. "I don't know, approachable? Softer maybe?" Her mouth kept going, and she knew now the tequila was kicking in. "It's like I already know if I get any endorsement deals they'll all be for sports drinks, shoes, anything to do with being fast, athletic, tough. For the sake of him knowing his girl isn't *just* a badass, it'd be nice if I got approached to endorse something soft, ladylike. Some kind of cosmetic product or girlie shit."

Lila brought her hand to her mouth and frowned. "That's another thing. I don't want my first impression on his friends and family to be that of the foul-mouthed fighter girl from the projects."

"You're so much more than that," Ella said, smiling genuinely. "Don't sell yourself short, sweetie."

"And as hard as you think you come across to everyone," Bianca added, "I've seen you firsthand with those kids down at the youth center, Lila. There's no hiding what a softy you really are."

With that said, the rest of them stepped up with their similar opinions and the tips rang in left and right. They all agreed she had nothing to work on, on the sensual side. They said she oozed natural sensuality, and surprisingly, every one of them had a story to tell about when they'd seen one of the meatheads at the gym, sizing Lila up or literally eating her up with their eyes.

An hour later, she was practicing walking in Roni's super high heels. "I haven't worn those in a while," Roni said, sipping her margarita, then giggled. "Well, publicly that is."

The girls all giggled. "Yeah, I have my private stash too," Ella said, "for Felix's eyes only."

"Who in the world would wear anything this high in public unless they have a death wish?" Lila asked, struggling to look graceful in the dangerously high heels.

"I almost never stand in mine," Charlee said, bringing her hand to her mouth with an evil grin. "They're usually up in the air."

The girls all shrieked in laughter. Even Lila smirked, remembering a pair of shoes she'd bought a while back similar to the ones she wore now and wondering when she'd be wearing them for Sonny.

"We all have our private stash," Bianca admitted with a coy smile. "They may be for our personal fun only, but they're good to practice in. If you can perfect or come close to walking in these, then you'll have walking in the less lethal, but equally sexy, heels you'll wear in public down to an art."

Because Marcelo liked seeing Lila in big heels, she had walking in heels down. But these were ridiculous. Still, Bianca was right. She'd gotten kind of rusty since she hadn't worn any big heels in a while. If she could perfect these, then anything less would be a cinch.

"Now," Nellie said, reaching over for one of the puff pastry appetizers Roni had put out. "Personally, I think a foul mouth on a woman who's not afraid to say it as she sees it is perfectly fine. And most men love girls who talk dirty in bed. But maybe it is a good idea to start working on cleaning up the language, and not just for the sake of making a better impression on Sly's friends and family members." She waved her hand in front of her with a roll of her eyes. "We've all heard the song. 'When a man loves a woman, she can do no wrong. He'll turn his back on his best friend if he puts her down.'"

"Ain't that the truth?" Roni said, raising her glass.

The other girls lifted theirs, nodding in agreement. "Don't get me started on the bitches that take advantage of that," Nellie said with a huff. "We'll save that conversation for another day. My point is I seriously doubt you have anything to worry about when it comes to the impression you make on his friends and family. Only impression you need to worry about is the one you make on *him,* and it seems he's already smitten. But working on making a good impression on his friends makes for good practice. Abel mentioned they were going to talk to you about getting you signed with an agent and a publicist. First thing they'll discuss with you, aside from their fees, is your public image. You'll be interviewed a lot. With the Internet and YouTube nowadays, all these interviews are forever. So, cutting back on the F-bombs might be a good idea."

"It's just so automatic most of the time," Lila said, chewing the corner of her lip. "I don't even realize until it's already out there."

She hadn't even thought about all the interviews she'd be expected to make.

"Hector can be really bad," Charlee said with a wince, "especially when he's fired up. Most of the time you won't know what you'll be asked in advance, but you'll have an idea of the kinds of questions that might come up. So, if you prepare a few answers in advance, minus the F-bombs and other colorful language, you can just go with that."

They all offered more advice as Lila continued to practice walking around in the heels. She'd long ago switched to drinking water because she knew walking in those shoes and drinking alcohol wouldn't end well.

# LILA

As much fun as she'd surprisingly had, Lila cut her evening with the girls short because she was anxious to get home in time for Sonny's call. She'd since texted him to let him know she was having a girls' night with the 5th Street wives but would try and get home early so they could FaceTime. As usual, he said he'd wait up for it and for her to call no matter how late she got home.

Fortunately, most of them were antsy about getting home to their kids and babies too, so Lila didn't have to feel like the lone party poop. By the time she got home, Ali was asleep behind the closed door of what was now her own private bedroom—Stacia's former bedroom.

Sunday night they'd talked about Ali taking Stacia's room now that Stacia wouldn't be staying there anymore. Yesterday, when Lila had gotten home, it'd been bittersweet to see Ali happily moving things around in her first ever own bedroom. Now Lila was grateful for her privacy because she felt beyond anxious to see and hear from Sonny.

The moment she saw Sonny's gorgeous smile on her laptop screen, her insides went wild as was the norm now. "Hey, beautiful," he said with that twinkle in his eyes that made her breathe in deeply.

"Hey, Sonny. It's not too late for you?"

"Nope. I'm wide awake and wanna hear all about my baby's margarita night with the girls." His lips curved into a playful yet delicious grin. "Did you talk about your *boyfriend*?"

Lila laughed nervously as her insides fluttered wildly just from hearing that last word. No way was she telling him he was pretty much the focus of the *entire* night's conversation.

"Maybe a little," she admitted, chewing her lower lip and making herself comfortable against her headboard.

"Well, my flight isn't 'til noon tomorrow, so I have all night. Let's have it."

Lila could hardly believe this was what her life would be like from here on: thinking of her amazing boyfriend every moment she wasn't around him then ending the day staring at that breathtaking smile and him being the last person she spoke to *every* night. Best thing about it was that, after tonight, she was finally feeling a little more confident that she just might have a shot at not blowing this.

"Let's see. Where to start?"

## 17

## Sonny

Turned out the idea to unveil Lila to all the athletes attending the charity briefing had been genius. Some of those athletes had been so eager to share what they'd seen to everyone who'd listen, including some of the sponsors they had endorsement deals with. It was rumored that several had shown some interest. One had already contacted her. The guys down at the gym had scrambled to get Lila an emergency meeting with a publicist/manager that could represent her in such deals.

It hadn't even dawned on Sonny at first who she might be meeting with when she'd texted him to tell him about it and said she'd call him after. But he should've known. Since all the owners from 5th Street were represented by the same guy and this was so last minute, understandably they'd recommend the same guy they'd been working with for years.

Preston Styles was a powerhouse in the industry. He managed some of the biggest names in sports, but boxing was his MO. Sonny had met him a few times, and he wouldn't rain on Lila's parade because her text came across as excited, but his impression of the guy each time he'd met him was an arrogant prick. Even the guys admitted he could be, but said he was *that* good and had every right to be arrogant.

Sonny would give them that the arrogance came with the territory. Maybe the guy did have the right to brag. But this guy pushed the envelope. His own agent had gotten Sonny an unprecedented record-breaking deal with the Dodgers, and the guy was as down-to-earth and likeable as they came. Just because you were good in your field, didn't mean you had to be a prick. Abel, Felix, and so many of the guys Sonny had worked with for years were prime examples.

Still, he'd already decided he'd hold his tongue and not mention that because, for someone so new in the biz to be signing with such a powerhouse, this was awesome for Lila.

"He came in and watched for a little while I trained," Lila said, and her excitement about this was undeniable. "They showed him some footage of my sparring, including the one you saw in person, and he signed me on the spot."

"Of course he did." Sonny smiled big, genuinely happy for her. "He'd be an idiot not to, and the guy knows his stuff. If he saw the same sparring session I did and they told him it was only your third time in the ring, he'd know if he doesn't nab you someone else will."

"I'm his first female client ever too."

That surprised Sonny. "Are you?"

"Yeah," she said with a huff, and if he wasn't mistaken, her excitement was mixed with a little annoyance. "He actually said he'd never signed a woman as a client because 'he didn't mix business with pleasure.'"

Stopping in his tracks, Sonny squeezed the phone. "What the fuck does that mean?"

"Exactly." She sounded annoyed now too. "I guess he was trying to be funny, but you know me. When I didn't so much as crack a smile, because I sure as shit ain't encouraging that kind of talk or behavior, he apologized and assured me he was a professional. Though the sort of creepy way he eyed me the whole time wasn't missed."

This was *not* what Sonny had wanted to hear about the guy she'd just sign to work so closely with. Though the good thing about Lila was that he absolutely trusted she wouldn't be putting up with this guy's bullshit. But if the guy was already on Sonny's prick list, he'd just jumped to the very top.

Getting past that part of the meeting, she explained how he was in no way a fan of friendly fights as Gio had previously suggested. "Preston Styles doesn't do friendlies," she said in a lowered voice mimicking the guy. "He said, newbie or not, I was better than any female fighter he'd *ever* watched and why he'd never felt inclined to sign one on. He let a few comments slip about how he'd honestly thought he'd never be impressed by a woman in this sport. He didn't say it, but clearly, he thinks women have no place in boxing. But he did admit to having his doubts about me, even after everything the guys had told him. Then he adds . . ." she said, pausing, and it sounded like she was drinking something.

*As if Sonny wasn't already beyond annoyed with this guy, there was more?*

"Then he adds," she went on, "that I impressed him in more than one way, whatever that means. Sonny, I don't know the first thing about finding a manager. If it weren't for the guys assuring me he was eccentric and a little full of himself but otherwise one of the most sought-after managers in the industry, I might've passed on signing with him. But also, I have these Under Armour people very interested, offering what Noah called a lucrative deal. Twenty *thousand*," she said as if that were the biggest number in the world. "I don't think I've ever had even a thousand all at once sitting in my bank account for long, and Preston assured me he can get me fifty. Can you imagine?"

Sonny was about to offer her a million if she *didn't* sign with this asshole, when she chuckled. "I know for you that's chump change, but for me, Sonny, it's more than I ever dreamed of making in an entire year!"

"You'll be making a lot more than that soon. I promise. I'm so proud and happy for you, baby. Congrats."

"As far as my public image, he brought you up."

"Did he?" Sonny asked as his interest and annoyance took another spike.

"He likes that it'll be good publicity-wise, but he suggested I not be overly affectionate with you in public." This had her chuckling while it had Sonny gnashing his teeth. "He says my public image should be a hard badass."

That did it. Not once had Sonny's manager ever had a say in his intimate affairs. This fucker was already telling Lila how affectionate she should get with him in public? The guy had just moved up to the very top of Sonny's shit list.

This was definitely going to have to change. Sonny was pissed that he hadn't thought to call when he'd gotten nearer to 5th Street. Lila was so damn adamant that she'd be fine taking the bus home today, and with him coming all the way from Burbank, he didn't want her waiting on him to pick her up in case he got stuck in traffic. Which was *exactly* what had happened.

Per the guys at the gym, he'd missed her by about twenty minutes. She'd said she had errands to run after work as well, so he'd called her immediately to see where she was. He could pick her up where she was and drive her around. But she hadn't answered, and it took her a while to respond to his text. Even then her response to his offer to come get her wherever she was, was a vague one. All she'd said was she was on her way home.

He'd been sitting at the corner of her block so she'd at least not have to walk the rest of the way from the bus stop to her apartment in the dark. But still nothing. He texted her again to ask if maybe she'd gotten home. For all he knew, she may've gotten off the bus at another stop if wherever her errands had taken her were on a different bus route home. Just as he set his phone down, he did a double take when he saw the pickup truck turn onto her street. Lila was in the passenger seat and a guy was driving.

Instantly, his curiosity was piqued—among another emotion—as he turned on his ignition. He drove up her block and watched as the truck made a U-turn in the middle of the street then didn't just slow to drop her off. The driver parked and even turned the lights off.

Sonny pulled over before getting too close and waited. Maybe he'd been mistaken. Maybe that hadn't been her. He glanced down at his phone to see if she'd responded to his last text, but she hadn't. The longer they remained in the parked truck, the more he didn't know what to think. Lila had never mentioned any guy friends. But it made sense she'd have some working at a gym and all. Finally, the passenger door opened. Sonny was as relieved as he was annoyed to see it was really her, especially given that she normally responded quickly to his texts—usually immediately—unless she was at work. And this time she'd only responded the one short time and still hadn't bothered responding to the last one.

He watched as she walked toward her apartment building, carrying what looked like a dress or something in a plastic bag. Maybe she'd stopped at the cleaners. Turning his headlights and engine on, Sonny watched as the guy in the truck did the same. The guy drove away, and Sonny drove to the end of the block, made a U-turn, and parked in the same spot the truck had pulled out of. Just as he turned off the car he got the text.

> I'm home now.

Sonny stared at it for a moment. He never would've imagined being suspicious of a girl who'd yet to give him a *single* reason to be suspicious about. Still he reasoned, so far, their relationship had been mostly a long-distance one. He'd only known her less than two months. That and his being this crazy about her so soon was likely a bad combo. This was just another confirmation of how different he felt about Lila than he had about any other girl—ever.

"Don't blow it, ass," he muttered under his breath. Then went against his own advice and put the text together, sending it before he could talk himself out of it.

> Good. Can I come get you? I'm in LA now.

She responded that she was getting ready to jump in the shower but he was welcome to stop by. She said Ali wouldn't be home until later and they had the place to themselves. Then she added a smiley face.

Groaning, Sonny debated if he should ruin the night with his unfounded suspicions or enjoy what he might be in for. He decided to give it a few minutes, let her shower, and then wait and see if she mentioned her ride home. For all he knew, it could've been an Uber driver. Though as far as he knew, they were supposed to be four-door cars. Pickup trucks wouldn't qualify. And them sitting there talking for a few minutes afterward didn't seem right. But he'd give her the benefit of the doubt and texted her he'd be there in fifteen.

*Exactly* fifteen agonizing minutes later, he texted her to say he was outside. She texted back to say she'd buzz him in. As soon as he dialed her apartment, he was in and he headed up the stairs. She opened the door, wearing a bathrobe and

heels so high his crotch instantly tightened. He wrapped his arms around her and devoured her mouth.
*Be cool. Don't fuck this up.*
"How was your day?" he asked in between sucking her tongue.
"Good." She purred then sucked his tongue back.
Breathing in sharply, he kissed her deep then pulled away. "So, you had errands to run after work. I was hoping I could catch you and get you home."
"No need." She smiled, gazing into his eyes. "I finished and made it home okay."
With a fully erect cock, he pressed it against her, pulling on the string of her bathrobe. "I hate you taking the bus, especially when it's dark."
"The walk from the bus stop is a short one, Sonny," she said against his lips then licked his bottom lip. "I promise. It's no big deal."
Sonny stared at her. She rolled her shoulders so her robe fell off. In nothing but the high heels she'd walked out wearing, she looked utterly amazing.
*Do not fuck this up!*
Even his throbbing cock was begging him not to, but his possessive heart was already protesting. "So, you took the bus home, babe?"
"I told you I've been doing it forever." She pulled his shirt up and over his head, so he was now standing there shirtless in only his jeans. Then she kissed his pecks one by one. "It's no big deal."
He stared at her, breathing in deep. If she'd just said she got a ride home from a friend, he could've let it go, but he still didn't want to be accusatory. It was probably nothing, and he refused to ruin this night. So, instead of asking why she was lying, he took another route.
"Ever get a ride home from friends?"
His body was pressed against her so firmly he felt it the moment she stiffened. He never took his eyes off her, so he

also saw the obvious alarm even as she tried to hide it. Swallowing hard, he did his best to keep his cool. This meant nothing. This was Lila. *His* Lila. She wouldn't have slept with him just this past weekend or be standing here naked for him if she were doing something with someone else.

"Sometimes," she said in a near whisper.

"Tonight?" She nodded but didn't say more. "Who?" he asked, remaining calm.

"Marcelo."

*Now* he might lose it.

"So, why'd you lie?"

Lila shrugged as Sonny pulled away, lifting her chin when she tried to break the eye contact. She looked right into his eyes now. "Technically, I didn't actually say I took the bus *tonight*. Just said I've been doing it forever."

Trying not to sound annoyed by her response, he worded his carefully. He didn't want to sound like he was calling her on what *technically* was beginning to sound like *bullshit*. "But you didn't mention getting a ride from Marcelo—your ex-boyfriend."

"I just didn't see the point in mentioning it. It was a quick five-minute ride if that."

"From where?" Sonny was doing his best to try and keep his cool, but his calm was beginning to wear thin.

"His house," she whispered again then went on when she obviously saw the spark in his eyes. "Only reason I didn't want you to know about it is I didn't want to have to tell you why I had to be there this week."

"You've been there more than once this week?" She nodded again and again went on quickly because clearly Sonny's attempts to keep his cool were a joke. "I didn't want you to know I'm borrowing a dress for tomorrow. His mom's a seamstress. She always has extra dresses around that she's working on. It was Ali's idea, and I made sure to go in the evening when he works so I wouldn't see him. I didn't the first night when I went there to get fitted, but today was his night off. I had every intention of taking the bus home, like I had to get there. But his mom *insisted* he give me a ride home since it was dark."

She ran her fingers through his hair, and her other hand caressed his rigid chest. "For what it's worth, it was awkward as shit. I couldn't get it over with fast enough."

"But you sat in the truck with him for a while even once you got here."

Her eyes narrowed. "You saw?"

Sonny pressed his body against hers in case she thought to push him away and nodded, staring at her. "I was hoping to catch you when you got off the bus so you wouldn't have to walk the rest of the way in the dark, when I saw his truck pass with you in it."

She lifted a brow but didn't appear pissed. "He's a talker, Sonny. And I hadn't spoken to him in years." She lifted and dropped her shoulder. "I guess he felt like he needed to explain himself since I admitted to not having read any of his letters."

"What did he explain?"

"A bunch of bullshit. I didn't even wanna hear it, but only because he gave me a ride and his mom did me this favor with the dress, I let him finish when he dropped me off."

Sonny brought his hand around her and squeezed her firm ass. "You should've told me you didn't have a dress, and I'm getting you a car."

Her eyes widened. "No, you're not," she said immediately. "A nice car in this area wouldn't last long anyway."

"Doesn't have to be fancy, just reliable."

"You can't just—"

"Either that or I'll set up an Uber account for you. I hate you taking the bus. You said it yourself. This area isn't the best, and I hate knowing you ever have to walk the neighborhood at night."

She placed her hand against Sonny's chest, but he'd be damned if he'd let her push him away. So, he stood his ground firmly. "Sonny, you can't just—"

"I can and I will. I know this is just the start for us. I haven't known you long, but I know one thing for sure. I want you to be safe, and getting you a car or out of this building, into a better area, ain't shit for me. It'd be an enormous relief to know you're safe, so I'd be doing it as much for you as I am for my own peace of mind."

She shook her head but with less conviction, and Sonny was done talking. He put his hand on her other ass cheek and squeezed her ass with both hands then dove into her neck.

"Don't ever keep something like that from me again," he said, kissing her neck then sucking a little harder, "especially when it comes to him." He pulled away to look her in the eyes. "You might think you have a temper, sweetheart, but I can already tell things will get ugly *fast* when it comes to this kind of shit."

"I'm sorry," she whispered. "It's just that—"

Sonny stopped her from saying more by kissing her then nipping her bottom lip. "Don't tell me how sorry you are. Show me." He brought his hand around in between her legs and slid his fingers over her hot wet slit. "And then promise you'll never lie to me again."

Lila eyed him with a smirk as she undid the button on his jeans then pulled his zipper down. Sonny had every intention of taking her right there against the wall until she pulled his ready-to-go throbbing cock out of his pants and slid down until she was on her knees in front of him. She licked the pre-cum off the tip then took him in her mouth—deep.

Sonny's legs nearly gave as he let his head fall back with a groan. "I'm sorry," she said, licking the rim of his cock slowly, "that I lied."

Lila took him in again so deep he could feel the back of her throat, and he nearly lost it right then. "Oh, baby," he said with a grunt.

"It'll never," she said as she kissed the tip of his cock then licked, "happen again."

She took him in her mouth nice and deep again as she stroked him with her hand. Her tongue was fucking magic. It felt so damn good he almost felt like telling her to feel free to lie if this was how she'd make up for it every time.

Of course, the words *feel free to lie* were never coming out of his mouth. Not now that he knew just how easily he could lose his shit if she ever did. Especially about her asshole ex.

Lila sucked his dick so good for what began to feel like too long. Like maybe he should offer to finish by taking her against the wall as he'd first thought might happen. But amazingly, she seemed to be enjoying it as much as he was. Feeling just how deep she'd take him, had him ready to blow.

"I'm gonna come, babe," he said, desperately trying to keep from blowing in her mouth, but she nodded, giving him the go-ahead and took him even deeper.

It was all he could do to stop the inevitable. He came hard down her throat, and she moaned, swallowing every bit of it. It only made him continue to shoot more. Still grunting in pleasure, he leaned his hand against the wall because his legs felt like noodles now. Sonny watched as his beautiful Lila licked him clean and even sucked the tip of his cock for any lingering juices.

She glanced up at him after kissing the tip one last time then smiled, licking her lips slowly as she stood up. "Delicious."

He groaned again, leaning into her, already knowing he could easily be hard again very soon. He pressed his body over hers against the wall and leaned his forehead against hers. No way could he still be mad at her after *that* apology, but he did want to make one thing clear.

"Seriously, babe," he said, kissing her lips softly. "I'll be holding you to the promise about not keeping anything from me that might piss me off. And just to be clear, *anything* you keep from me about this guy *will* piss me off."

She nodded. "Like you said the other day, I won't be doing or keeping anything from you that I know would piss me off if the tables were turned." She smirked, soothing the brow he didn't even realize was still sharply arched. "And you know that covers a *whole* lot of ground."

Good," he said, kissing her longer and harder, then stopped to pull up his pants. "'Cause I was this close to spanking this fucking ass." He squeezed her ass again with one hand then nipped her bottom lip.

"I might've liked that," she said with a wicked grin.

That had him groaning again and tugging her towards her bedroom. "Let's go to your room in case your sister gets here. This might get loud."

# Lila

Just as Gio obliged with Lila's adamant refusal to be interviewed by Tatiana, Gio had also agreed to give Ali that interview she'd asked for. She'd done so yesterday and was way too excited about the possibility of interviewing some of the men on the work-release program. Lila wasn't thrilled about that. From the looks of some of the ones she'd seen around the gym already, she didn't care what anyone said. They looked dangerous.

"It's not like I'll be interviewing them out in their gritty turfs or anything," Ali had argued when Lila had expressed her unease about Ali interviewing them. "If I do interview them, I'd be doing it right there in the gym with Gio or one of the owners even. It's perfectly safe, and I told you Gio said they have to qualify to be in the program, and that means they must have had a good standing record when they did their time of being well-behaved. The smallest of infractions will get them kicked out of the program, as in *any* type of violation of their probation, including simply being late to check in with their probation officers. And the rumors about any of them being murderers is only half true. Gio said outright murder-one ex-cons don't qualify for the program, but manslaughter or second-degree murder ex-felons, who maybe killed someone in self-defense, do. There are also guys with manslaughter convictions from having killed someone by accident."

"How do you kill someone by accident and still go to jail?" Lila asked skeptically.

"DUI's."

"That's no accident. People who drive drunk do so knowing the risks."

Lila shuddered at just the thought. If anyone ever killed Ali by *accident* because they were driving under the influence, she'd make it her mission to make sure they never saw the light of day again.

"There's one guy in there who fired shots in the air for New Year's, and somehow the bullet hit someone, killing him," Ali had countered. "So, *it is* possible to kill someone by accident and still have to do time. He wasn't licensed to be carrying a gun and had priors, so he was sentenced to a few years."

"I've seen some of the guys, Ali. They've got bad news written all over them."

"I saw some yesterday too," Ali said. "But Gio even said, as hard as they look, they're actually pretty good guys."

Lila scoffed. "I'll try to swallow the whole 'they're trying to rehabilitate themselves crap. But good guys my ass. They did time for good reason and they look shady as shit."

"I don't know," Ali said with a sly little smile. "I think tattoos are kind of sexy."

Lila had peered at her, knowing her smartass little sister was just trying to rile her. "Don't you even think about it, Allison."

"What?" Ali had laughed, glancing up from her phone. "Am I not allowed to drool a little over some of them bad boys? It's not like any of them are going to be into this mess." With a huff, she'd added, "You should've seen the way one of them looked at me today when I gave into stupid temptation and walked out of the employee break room where I'd been interviewing Gio, devouring one of the donuts they had in there."

That alone pissed Lila off. "*How* did he look at you?"

"Like I should be in there working off this fat, not adding more to it."

Instantly, Lila got at her for continually being so self-deprecating. But Ali cut her off, saying she knew she wasn't fat. Her point had been that Lila had nothing to worry about. The good thing was that Ali said she'd likely not have time to come in and interview any of those *bad boys* for a few weeks. She had finals still and a couple of papers to write.

Another thing happened yesterday before Lila had to "run her errands" and be forced to see Marcelo. Bianca had cornered Lila to tell her that her friend Toni would be in town today. She was a cosmetologist who owned her own salon up in Big Bear. According to Bianca, Toni was highly skilled and willing to give Lila a makeover for her big night out. So, she'd be getting her hair, nails, and makeup done now.

Ali was excited for Lila. While Lila tried to get on board, it was nerve-wracking. She had to work and thankfully so or she would've worried about this all day if she'd had the day off like Bianca tried to give her. But Lila did agree to leave early with Bianca to her home where Lila showered and Toni was set up to work her magic.

To Lila's surprise, the other girls showed up bearing gifts such as different shoes, jewelry, and perfume she might want to borrow. They broke out the margaritas again; though Lila was so nervous she didn't have any.

The dress she'd borrowed from Marcelo's mom, while not a designer dress by any means, was quite glamorous. It was a long black lacy long-sleeved gown. Marcelo's mom had fixed it so it hugged her body perfectly. The flesh-colored slip underneath covered all the pertinent parts just so but was short enough you could see enough of her long legs underneath. The slit on the front left-hand side also went all the way up to her thigh where the slip underneath ended. The plunging neckline wasn't too low, but like her sister, being top heavy made the cleavage show that much more dramatically.

"Oh, my God, I love it." Roni said as the other girls' jaws dropped, and Drew whistled when Lila walked out of Bianca's master bathroom in the dress.

"Hot mama!" Drew said, taking her in.

"Oh, that Sly's gonna be drooling," Nellie added.

Lila laughed nervously, stepping in front of Bianca's closet mirrored doors. It *was* stunning, and Toni had done an amazing job not just styling her hair but doing her glamorous makeup. Lila couldn't get over how shiny and sleek her long dark tresses looked. It was amazing how far some expensive hair product and styling could go, which reminded her of something.

"My sister's birthday is just around the corner," she said, turning to Toni. "I'm getting her contacts finally, and now I'm thinking maybe it'd be nice if I can get her a makeover. She gets down about her looks a lot. If you can do something different to her hair then maybe give her some tips on how to do her hair and makeup on her own, it might give her a little more confidence. I could pay you."

Toni waved her hand in front of her as she sipped her margarita. "No need. I love doing makeovers. Just let me know when so I can plan a trip down."

Lila insisted she'd at least pay her for her gas. Though they quickly got back to the subject of her and Sonny. "Now comes the tricky part," Lila said, pulling the strappy high heel shoes she'd be wearing out of the box. "I've only worn these a handful of times but haven't in a while."

"Well, it's a good thing you practiced with those street walker shoes of mine." Roni laughed. "These don't look too bad."

She put them on and practiced walking around in them in Bianca's big bedroom. "Work it girl," Toni said, laughing.

They all agreed it'd be better if she'd forgo the necklace, leaving her cleavage to be the center of attention in that area, but she did go with the diamond-studded silver hoop earrings Nellie brought. She also wore the matching diamond-studded silver bangle bracelet.

By the time Sonny arrived to pick her up, she felt ironically like what he'd first called her the night they met at the concert—Cinderella, all done up and ready for the ball.

"Jesus, as if I didn't think you stunning already. You look amazing," he said, pulling her to him the moment he was close enough.

He looked beyond amazing himself in his black tux. She'd seen photos of him in tuxedos online, but seeing him in person was beyond breathtaking. Lila didn't think she'd ever get used to the fact that this was *her* man. It still felt so surreal.

The girls took a few photos before Lila and Sonny made their exit. Still nervous about tonight, Lila took deep breaths as she sat in the back seat of the town car driving them to the wine-tasting party. "What's wrong?" Sonny asked, running his hand up and down her thigh.

Lila shrugged. "I've never been to anything like this."

"Just relax." He lifted her hand to his mouth and kissed it. "You're gonna be fine."

When they arrived, she was glad Ali thought to ask Marcelo's mom about the dress. Everyone was dressed so glamorously. While she felt completely out of her element, at least she didn't feel underdressed. Lila glanced around as they walked into the posh restaurant bar. Was this the lifestyle she'd really have to get used to?

As if reading her mind, Sonny leaned into her. "I only ever do anything this fancy a handful of times a year," he whispered in her ear. Lila turned to look at him and he smiled. "Most of the fundraising stuff I do is sports-related: the baseball camp or visiting kids in hospitals and such. I promise you this isn't the norm or anything you'll need to prepare to be doing often."

They walked over to a group of people sitting at a long table. Fortunately, Lila had done her homework and looked up AJ "Rage" Romero, Sonny's friend whose birthday they were celebrating tonight. She also looked up more of his former teammates and some of his new ones. While his friend from his Padres days lived in the San Diego area, this event was taking place in Hollywood. So, there'd be teammates from both the Padres and the Dodgers in attendance.

Lila could at least say she'd heard of them now. The group greeted them as they arrived at the table. The guys stood up to shake Lila's hand as Sonny introduced her to AJ's family, his siblings, and their spouses. AJ had yet to arrive, but she knew who his brothers Nathan and Isaiah were before they were even introduced. The resemblance was uncanny.

Something about Sonny having such a close friend whose short fuse had earned him the nickname *Rage* gave Lila a tiny bit of solace. She'd seen some of the footage of him losing it on the field. It meant all these good friends of his were used to dealing with someone who had little control of his temper.

God forbid she'd ever lose it like she had in front of all those other athletes, but they might not be so quick to judge. "So, you *are* for real?" Olivia, AJ's sister, said with a big smile as she shook Lila's hand then winked. "Not that Sonny is that big of a ladies' man or anything of the sort. He's just been so picky all these years."

"Not picky," Sonny interjected, squeezing Lila's hand. "*Careful*. And my being so damn careful almost blew up in my face."

"It did," Lila reminded him with a smirk.

"That's right it did." He winced. "But I fixed it, and now I'm certain she's exactly what I'd been holding out for."

Lila's heart thudded as he continued to walk around the table and introduced her to everyone else. They took a seat and ordered drinks. Sonny assured Lila she'd be fine if she had a glass of wine or two. She agreed to have one but sipped it very slowly.

When AJ arrived, they did the big surprise thing as he entered. Then dinner was served, which Lila wasn't even aware they'd be having. She thought it was specifically a wine tasting. So, it was a relief since she hadn't had anything to eat since breakfast. She'd just been too nervous about tonight.

Sonny was asked to pose with a few of his old teammates and then some of his new ones, and Lila was left at the table with AJ's family. "Why do you call him Sonny?" Emi, AJ's younger sister, asked.

Lila smiled, wiping her mouth with her napkin. "That thing he said about him being careful blowing up in his face? I didn't know who he was when I met him. I've never followed sports."

She went on to explain about him giving her his middle name and her being so clueless. How because of his promotional tour, their relationship until last week consisted of mostly emails, FaceTime, and phone calls, with a few short visits in between. So, they hadn't even gone out in public where he'd be recognized and she'd know he was famous. She left out the real reason why she *refused* to call him Sly or Sylvester even. Ali had since mentioned that

Tatiana even *sounded* like a horny slut. Her sister had mimicked the way Tatiana purred his name when he'd answered the call she'd gotten to hear: *Sly* Just hearing someone call him that made her think of the bitch. So, she was glad most referred to him as Sabian.

"Oh, wow," Emi said with a laugh then turned to her brother Nathan. "You see. You said he was dreaming when he'd talked about holding out for someone who didn't know who he was."

"I always thought it was possible," Isaiah, AJ's other brother, said. "Just because *we* follow baseball so closely, it seemed like such a long shot that he ever would. But think about it. I bet we could run into an LA Kings player for example and not have a clue who he is since we don't follow hockey. At least I wouldn't be able to name a single player on the team."

"This is true," Emi agreed, and that made Lila feel less lame about not knowing who Sonny was before last week.

It also made her feel better to hear he really hadn't lied about why he'd kept the truth from her. Even his friends were aware of his desire to meet someone who didn't know who he was. It made him all the more attractive to her. Most guys in his position would use their status as a heartthrob superstar athlete to get as many women as they could. Sonny had done just the opposite, played his status down in exchange for a deeper connection with someone ordinary like Lila rather than a superficial one with one of the many supermodels and other celebrities so easily accessible to him.

Everything had been going smoothly. There hadn't been any uncomfortable situations, and Lila hadn't let any F-bombs slip. If it hadn't been for a couple things that happened toward the end of the evening, Lila might've called it a solid success.

First, they'd done enough moving about the restaurant, mingling and Sonny impressing Lila to no end with his charm and wit. But she'd spent most of her time talking with

AJ's sisters and sisters-in-law. They were all so sweet and welcoming, and Lila had no doubt that, like the ladies from 5th Street, she'd fit in with these women just fine, despite their different lifestyles.

Then it happened. Sonny had moved away to talk with AJ, his brothers, his cousin, and a couple of older guys he said were AJ's uncles. He'd warned Lila they could be loud and a little obnoxious, something they'd immediately confirmed when she met them. They could also give Lila a run for her money with the amount of F-bombs they dropped even with their nephews telling them to bring it down a notch—more than once.

They spoke so loud Lila could pretty much follow their conversation along with the one she was having with AJ's sisters. Someone in the crowd of loudmouths ribbed Sonny about finally getting serious with a girl. Then one of his uncles was quick to point out that Sonny had been *pretty fucking serious* about Emi once upon a time there.

Lila hadn't missed the way someone hissed at him to "shut the fuck up," and their voices were hushed, but instantly she was annoyed. If they were speaking of Emi, AJ's sister who'd she'd spent so much time pleasantly chatting with tonight, the least Sonny could've done was give Lila a heads-up. It was awkward as shit because just as Lila had heard the comment loud and clear, she was sure Emi had too.

Olivia continued what she'd been talking about, her expanding dog-grooming business. But the words were out there now, lingering in the air like the elephant in the room no one addressed. Just making eye contact with Emi felt uncomfortable after the fact.

By the time the evening was over, Lila was more than relieved. Despite the uncomfortable turn the evening had taken, she'd had a nice enough time. But aside from the surprise about Emi, her head had begun to spin a little with all the different athletes and even a few celebrities she did recognize. It felt like she had to be "on" the whole time, and she was ready to be off already. For as glamorous as she knew she looked, she still didn't feel as sophisticated as some of the other women there, who clearly did this often.

The moment they were in the privacy of the back of the town car, Sonny addressed what was obviously on Lila's mind. "In case you're wondering, yes, it is Emi, AJ's sister, who his uncle was talking about. And, yes, she is probably one of the few women I dated who I ever began to feel serious about."

Feeling a flash of jealousy and even more annoyed that he hadn't told her before tonight, she turned to him, lifting a brow, but before she could say anything he went on. "I would've mentioned it, but I knew you were already nervous about tonight. I didn't want you preoccupied with that. I figured, since the Romeros are a family I plan on staying close to, I did plan on telling you after tonight in case it ever came up later." He shrugged, kissing her hand. "I should've figured, with his loud-ass uncles there, it'd come up sooner than I anticipated. It's no big deal. We didn't date long, and as you can see, she's happily married now. In fact," he added with a chuckle. "She dumped my ass for her husband."

That floored Lila, not that Emi wasn't attractive. Despite the extra curves, she had a cute shape, something Lila kept trying to convince her sister of—that guys *liked* curves. Both Emi and her sister Olivia had some major hourglass figures, and both their husbands were damn hot; though Lila wouldn't be admitting that to Sonny. Except now Sonny was telling her even he'd had a serious thing for Emi and *she* dumped *him*?

"You might've shared that with me when I told you about Marcelo cheating on me."

"She didn't cheat on me," he clarified. "I guess she and Syd had been good friends for a long time, and she didn't realize her feelings for him until she and I started dating. She didn't start seeing him until after she broke things off with me, but she admitted he was the reason why she did."

Lila refrained from asking if he'd slept with her. Since he said she was one of the only girls he'd ever taken seriously, the answer to that was likely yes. Lila didn't need the visuals anytime she was around the girl again. Besides, obviously, Emi hadn't felt enough for Sonny. She was married now and had been more than gracious tonight. Lila didn't want to hate her, but she *was* curious.

"How long ago?"

"Years," he said. "She's since gotten married and even had a couple of kids. What happened between us is ancient history and never even brought up now for obvious reasons. Why make her husband or anyone I'm with uncomfortable, right? But Manny and Max are a different story. They don't do subtle or tact for that matter."

As if that little revelation hadn't been enough to nearly sour the otherwise pleasant evening, Sonny's phone lit up in the center console, distracting them both momentarily. It wasn't lit long because he sent it to voicemail. But it was long enough for Lila to see the name on the screen: *Tatiana*. Sonny set the phone back down after sending it to voicemail, and Lila glanced out the window, determined not to let the bitch ruin her evening. But she *had* to ask, so she turned back to him. "I thought you said you blocked her."

"I meant to." He reached for his phone again with a frown. "But I forgot to. I hadn't heard from her since the day I cut all ties with her. Not until tonight that is. It's the second time she's called."

The screen lit up again, this time with what looked like a text. "That from her?"

"Yeah." He nodded, unlocking his screen, then chuckled under his breath and tapped his screen. "She must be drunk."

He turned to Lila, leaning in to kiss her, but she pulled back, eyeing him curiously. "What did she say?"

Pressing his lips together, he seemed to think about it for a moment. "She's inviting me to stop by her place."

Lila's brow arched immediately. "Even after you dismissed her? What did you say?"

"I didn't. I'm not encouraging that shit with any kind of response. I just added her to my auto-reject list. I won't even see when or if she ever calls or texts me again."

He leaned in once again to kiss her. Lila let him this time as what he'd just told her sunk in. This bitch knew he and Lila were a couple now, and she was still inviting him to come down to her place? Taking a deep breath even as Sonny reiterated that Tatiana was officially blocked, Lila reminded herself of two things. She had to because he couldn't physically block her if he ever saw her again and he was bound to.

One: she'd never fight over a man. And two: a disrespectful whore throwing herself at a taken man—even if it was Lila's man—was *not* worth going to jail for.

## Sonny

In the following weeks after Sonny successfully blocked Tatiana from all his social media, phone, and email, she *seemed* to have taken the hint. It also seemed Gio and Noah were using her less and less for any press-related stuff around 5th Street, especially given that their latest up-and-coming prize fighter refused to work with Tatiana. But she'd still be an ever-present face at the press conferences that had anything to do with the Dodgers.

Sonny made sure to be completely honest with Lila about this. While it didn't sit well with her to know Tatiana would still have limited access to him, she understood that was out of his hands. All Sonny could do was promise her she had nothing to worry about. He wouldn't be allowing Tatiana's nonsense to come between him and Lila.

Lila now had other things to keep her preoccupied when he wasn't around. Her career as a professional boxer was moving fast. She'd had several official fights now under her belt, all won by TKO but not against anyone that mattered. Styles had just said she needed to start setting a record, even if it was against unknown fighters like herself. Getting a fight lined up against someone that really mattered would take having an impressive record. So far, Lila was undefeated and starting to make a buzz.

 Then Styles did it. He set up a match impressive even for him. It'd be her first *real* fight as he put it and just a month away now. She'd be fighting for the title. Lila would be boxing the former Gold medalist from the UK, and now welterweight world champ, Sadie Mannering. Sonny was certain Mannering's camp was likely thinking they were playing it safe and why Lila was given a shot at the title. Lila was still unknown for the most part. Champs did that when they wanted to hold onto their titles a little longer—fight "bums"—and in the world of boxing, despite Lila's talent, she was considered worse than a bum. This was her first fight *ever* against any real contender. Of course, they could mask the fact that they'd agreed to have Mannering fight Lila for that reason by pointing to her undefeated record.

 She'd signed her first endorsement with Under Armour, and as promised, Styles got her that fifty grand he'd said he would. She also filmed her first commercial, and much to her relief, she had one simple line. It was basically one of those slow-motion commercials of Lila working out and then running and looking like a hot badass wearing their product. All she had to do was read their slogan at the very end. She had a photo shoot later that week for the posters they'd be using to publicize her much-anticipated debut fight.

 Sonny walked into the gym to pick Lila up after her shift there. She'd since bought another car with her endorsement deal money. The car wasn't brand new and far from fancy, but it was more reliable than the one they had, which they were keeping. Since Sonny was certain he'd be able to pick her up on time, Ali had dropped her off today.

He did a double take when he saw Ali there, not just because she was there when she didn't need to pick up Lila, but because of how different she looked. Lila had mentioned more than once about Ali's preoccupation with her weight and the low self-esteem it created. He'd almost forgotten about Lila mentioning that she was getting Ali a makeover. She'd told him about it a few days prior, but he hadn't seen Ali in the last couple of days. Lila had been pleased with the outcome and now he could see why.

He'd thought Ali adorable from the moment he'd first met her. Not just because of those giant eyes behind the thick lenses, but she was a younger, slightly fuller version of Lila. Despite how much more womanly Lila appeared to be than her younger seemingly docile little sister, Sonny knew better. He'd been privy to her little sister's spunk from day one.

Though he wasn't stupid enough to say it out loud, Ali had the kind of curves guys would appreciate, even if they weren't as rock hard as Lila's. With her contact lenses now, a new sexier hairdo, and a little more makeup than she'd worn before, Ali might give Lila more to worry about than her sister's self-image. Already he could see the subtle turning of heads as she waited outside one of the training rooms with a notebook in her hand.

That reminded him of why she was there. Lila had also mentioned her unease about her sister coming down to 5th Street today to interview a few of the *thugs* from the work-release program. He'd just walked up to Ali when Lila walked up to them as well. "Hey." He pecked Lila hello then turned to Ali with a smile. "You look different."

Ali smiled sheepishly. "I'm still getting used to it, but I like it."

"Your friend did this?" Sonny asked as he slipped his hand into Lila's.

"Bianca's friend," she clarified. "I think she did an excellent job."

"She did," Sonny agreed, turning back to Ali. "You look"—he shook his head, trying to find the appropriate words— "very grown up now, womanly?"

He winced, turning back to Lila, hoping he hadn't chosen the wrong word. She smirked, peering at him. "Not too grown up though. She's still my baby sister." Ali rolled her eyes with a smile. "And even though I didn't think there was anything wrong with the way she looked before"—Lila turned to Ali with a stern look at first then smiled— "I do love the new look and the little pep in your step it seems to have given you. I've already seen the way some of these meatheads eyed her as she walked in here today."

Ali laughed. "You're too much, Lila. *No one* is looking at me. But I am grateful to be rid of those glasses. That alone would've been enough to have me walking a little happier. So, the rest is just icing." She smiled big, making Sonny smile with her, because she looked so happy. "Best damn birthday gift ever, but"—the big smile quickly waned as she eyed Lila suspiciously– "I know why you're here. And you need to be gone. I don't want you anywhere around threatening these guys I'm interviewing with your evil eye. I'm already nervous enough as it is. Not scared," she clarified quickly. "Just nervous about not botching this interview. I need to get this right."

"You'll do fine," Lila assured her. "And that would be the old Lila, thank you very much. The new Lila has since turned over a new leaf. My days of snapping without thinking are long behind me."

Ali scoffed and even Sonny couldn't keep a straight face when he heard that. Gio walked up to them, mirroring the same double take Sonny had done when he saw Ali. "Wow, you look different." Ali giggled while Lila smiled proudly. "Bianca said the makeover had made a big difference, but I didn't think she meant this much."

# LILA

"It's the bottle-cap lenses being gone that make the biggest difference," Ali said. "It's what feels most different to me anyway. My head feels lighter."

She laughed while Lila frowned. "They weren't that bad. I think you looked cute in them."

"Yeah, if you're into nerdy little bookworms with glasses so thick they could see into the future."

Sonny was distracted by the two guys a few yards behind Gio, walking toward them. One of them fit the description of what Lila had described to him just a few days prior: bald, built like a truck "like he had nothing better to do in jail but work out," and full of tats. He couldn't blame her for being uneasy about these guys being free to roam the gym. The guy with him wasn't nearly as big, but he looked just as thuggish and was equally inked up.

Gio was in the middle of explaining about the guys Ali would be interviewing when the two guys walked up and stopped just behind Gio. "Ready when you are, chief."

It was the other guy that asked, not the bald one. That idiot was too busy eyeing Lila curiously instead. Lila was facing them as Sonny was, but Gio and Ali had to turn to the guys behind them. "Hey," Gio, said smiling. "Right on time. Here she is."

Noah walked by on his phone, distracting Gio. Gio called out to him then turned back to Ali and the guys. "Give me a sec, guys. I gotta tell him something before he leaves."

He rushed away, leaving the two guys staring blankly at Ali. The bald one sized her up, his brows pinching as the corners of his lips began to curve up. "*Jelly.*"

The word silenced them all for a moment. Sonny wasn't sure what the guy meant, but it was clear what Ali and Lila were thinking by their scandalized expressions.

Lila was the first to snap everyone out of their stunned silence, and she did it like only Lila would. "*Excuse* me?"

"Yeah, it is *Jelly.*" The guy ignored Lila altogether yet continued to peer at Ali with a bemused expression.

"She has a name and it's not Jelly, asshole."

"Whoa!" the guy with him, who'd been just as stunned as the rest of them, finally spoke up then laughed nervously, turning to the *asshole*. "Dude, what are you doing?"

Ali, who didn't appear as stunned as she'd first been, reached out and touched Lila's arm. "Lila, no—"

"No, bullshit!" Lila said, taking a step forward, but Sonny held her back. "That is fucking rude. Who are you to—?"

"Lila, I don't think he means what you're thinking," Ali said, shaking her head adamantly.

"What *are* you thinking?" the guy asked with an attitude, so Sonny took a step in front of her.

"That Jelly's an offensive way to refer to someone you don't even know," he said, staring the thug down.

"But I do know her," the guy retorted.

"And you call her Jelly?" Lila asked, trying to get around Sonny, only he stood firmly in place, not letting her. "That's still fucking rude."

"I don't know what you think it means, but—"

"I know what you meant," Ali interrupted him then she glanced at Gio, who was on his way back. She turned to Lila with a purpose. "It's not *at all* what you're thinking. I'll explain later."

She lowered her voice, but Sonny still heard her ask Lila to please go and that she'd handle it. "*Why* and how does he know you?"

"From the last time I was here," Ali said quickly, nudging both Lila and Sonny away.

"So, did you all get acquainted?" Gio asked as he reached them.

"Sort of," Ali said then turned to Lila. "I'll call you as soon as I'm done. I promise."

That last part was mouthed as she shooed them away with her hand then turned back to Gio and the two guys. Lila finally grudgingly walked away.

"Unbelievable." Lila huffed as they walked out into the parking lot. "What else could the idiot have meant?"

"Ali seemed to be okay with it," Sonny reminded her. "So, we'll just have to wait until she calls and explains. I don't think he'd have been that ballsy if he really meant what we were all thinking."

"Well, he has done time. The fucktard can't be the brightest."

Sonny laughed, opening the passenger side door for her, then leaned in and kissed her. "God, I love my feisty girl."

It wasn't until he'd closed the door and started around the car that he realized he'd just dropped the L word on her so nonchalantly. His heart thudded and *he* felt like the *fucktard* now. Not sure if he should address it and wondering if she'd even caught it, he took a deep breath before opening the driver's side door.

The whole drive back to his place, Sonny was a mess. He couldn't tell if Lila was being weird or if he was just being paranoid. They still spoke of the thugs and Ali, but she didn't seem nearly as mad as she'd been about it earlier.

Sonny could barely concentrate on everything she was saying as he tried to wrap his brain around what he'd just done. It felt so natural, and he hadn't meant it in an *I love pizza* type a way. At the moment, he'd really meant it. While he knew Lila hated how easily she could lose it like she'd begun to do with that guy, Sonny loved how protective she was of her sister. As well she should be. Had it been one of his sisters, he would've been just as quick to snap at the asshole.

So, it'd been a heartfelt statement, one he'd never given much thought to as to how he'd go about ever saying it to someone for the first time. Now he'd just blurted it out and neither had addressed it. He had to fix this. This committed and serious relationship thing may be new to him, but he was certain the moment you declare your love for someone should be more memorable and far more romantic than this.

There was probably a relationship fail list somewhere he'd just topped.

Deciding he'd deal with his blunder head on, Sonny thought it'd be best if he waited until they got back to his place. He could use the subject to get Lila's mind off Ali and the whole Jelly incident that still had her riled up. But his plans were derailed when they got to the top of his driveway.

"Whose car is that?" Lila asked, sitting up straight as they came around the circular driveway and parked behind the silver Lincoln Town car.

Sonny refrained from groaning but did let out an exasperated breath. "Guess you'll be meeting my mom tonight."

"What?" She turned to him, wide-eyed. "Your mom? Why didn't you warn—?"

"I didn't know," he explained before she could get too worked up. "She does this every now and again. Shows up unannounced. I spoke to her the other day and your name came up. I told her I was seeing someone now—like seriously so—and she said she looked forward to meeting you. But we didn't make plans to do so." Shaking his head, he let it fall back on the headrest with a chuckle. "I should've known that woman wouldn't wait on me."

Without waiting for Lila to react, he got out of the car and came around Lila's side. She was making her way out but slower than normal. "Sonny, I don't think I'm ready for this."

"For what? Meeting her? It's no big deal. She probably made dinner. It's what she normally does when she shows up like this. We'll eat, chat, and then she'll be on her way. The woman is nonstop. She has a million things always going on."

Lila eyed him, still looking unsure. Sonny could only hope his mom would be in and out; he had other more pressing things he wanted to get to before this night was over.

They walked in the house hand in hand. Sonny winced when they heard more than one voice coming from the kitchen and some giggling. Lila turned to him, even more wide-eyed now. Sonny squeezed her hand in reassurance. "My sisters," he said in a lowered voice. "I should've known they'd wanna meet you too. I mentioned to my mom that I've been having you over after work lately."

"Santino, is that you?" his mother called from the kitchen.

His sister Millie walked out into the front room where he and Lila were. "Sonny," she said with a big smile and headed to them.

Madge and his mom followed, both going straight to him. As expected, his mom blew into the room and took over. Sonny didn't even get a chance to do the introductions. She introduced herself and his sisters, and within minutes, they were all in the dining room, chatting and eating his mom's homemade tequila-lime shrimp fajitas. "Rose Marie, these are delicious," Lila said after wiping her mouth then sipping her water.

"Thank you, *chiquita*," his mom said then quickly went into the spiel on how easy it was to prepare the shrimp.

Lila and Sonny exchanged glances throughout the dinner as his sisters and mom very quickly and quite skillfully interrogated them but made it sound like a regular conversation. Mostly Sonny could tell they were digging to see just how serious Sonny was about Lila. He was certain they were skeptical that he was taking this any more seriously than all the other times he'd begun to see someone. And here all Sonny could think of was the conversation he'd be having with Lila the moment he got the chance.

"Santino has never called me specifically to tell me about a girl."

"Mom," Sonny said, hoping to derail where this was going. "She doesn't wanna hear about that."

Lila and his sisters laughed. "Yes, I do," she said, touching his hand.

"I'm not gonna embarrass you, *Mijo*," his mom said, waving him off. "He didn't say he was calling to tell me about you, but a few minutes into the conversation, it just came out of the blue. 'I met someone.' It's when I knew. *This is different*. In all the years he's been traveling around for his baseball and calling me to tell me about life, work, his endorsements, and television appearances, not once has my Santino ever talked about who he's dating. Not without much reluctance and complete vagueness, and that was only when *I* brought it up. This time *he* brought it up, and he *wanted* to tell me about you. I gotta tell you it made me nervous."

Lila and Sonny exchanged glances again, and he could see she was touched by this. "You really didn't know who he was?" Millie asked, shaking her head.

Crinkling her nose and looking a little embarrassed, Lila shook her head. "I had no idea. I've never followed sports. I know it sounds stupid with me being a boxer now, but I just didn't. Before I did a little research on him and his teammates, I honestly couldn't name a single player on the team, much less recognize any of them, including him."

"I believe you," his mother said a little too loudly. "I believe you, *chiquita*." She reached out across the table and squeezed Lila's hand. "Before tonight, I wasn't so sure." His mother fell back in her chair as if completely relieved. "Now I'll sleep better."

"*Mom*," Madge said as surprised by her reaction as Sonny felt.

"What?" his mom said, sitting up. "Don't tell me you didn't have your doubts when I told you he said she'd never heard of him. A girl from Los Angeles."

His sisters admitted to being a little doubtful too, but also said they were convinced now and very happy for them. By the time his mother and sisters blew out just as fast they'd blown in and judging by his mother's relieved reaction,

Sonny knew she'd had one goal tonight: to make sure Lila was the real deal and not just some gold digger playing him. She and his sisters likely planned the whole thing the night he told her about Lila. They'd even called in Evangelina, his regular cleaning lady, to come in tonight to help clean up the mess they'd made in the kitchen. His mom tipped her very generously before once again giving Lila and Sonny crushing hugs and assuring them she'd be back soon.

"Treat her like a princess always, okay?" Sonny nodded with a smile and his mother turned to Lila. "Just don't break his heart. I honestly don't think he'd have the first clue how to handle that. I'm telling you—"

"Alright, alright," Sonny said, nudging his mom off.

His sisters laughed while Lila seemed to blush. Once they were gone, Lila and Sonny headed to his bedroom. He knew she was anxious to shower since she didn't get a chance to first thing as she normally did when they got to his place.

They stood in his master bathroom, cuddling and giggling about his mom's comments. They were now undressing each other as they waited for the shower water to warm, when her phone rang in the other room. "Oh, that might be Ali," she said, rushing out in just her bra and spandex bottoms.

Sonny followed her to the door and waited. She nodded when she picked up her phone and answered, "So, how'd it go?"

That cute brow lifted as she listened silently. "Hmm," Lila said, not sounding the least bit satisfied with whatever it was her sister was saying. "And *why* does this excite you, Allison?"

Already chuckling, Sonny thought back to when Lila had told him about Ali teasing her about thinking the tatted-up bad boys were sexy. Ali being attracted to this guy wouldn't be unheard of.

"Yes, for sure. I won't be home too late tonight, so if you're still up, I wanna know *everything*."

Once she was off the phone, she turned to Sonny with a smirk. "Well, he wasn't insinuating her booty shakes like jelly," she explained, putting down her phone, and started back to the bathroom.

Sonny laughed as he took in her sculpted abs. "Yeah, ex-con or not, I didn't think he'd be *that* stupid."

Lila told her about her sister having mentioned one of those guys looking at her funny when she was there before. "I guess she was eating a donut that day, and she'd forgotten how utterly consumed she'd been with devouring the thing. She said it was a jelly donut and that's what he was talking about. Like you and Gio, he was just surprised she was the same girl as the one he saw that first time because she looked so different. But she sounded a little too giddy about his remembering her. Though she claims it's not excitement; she was just *surprised*. I swear that girl better not be getting any ideas. I haven't spent my whole life, trying to keep her safe, only for her to end up with the likes of someone like him."

That made Sonny laugh again, and he reached out and hugged her as soon as she was close enough. "Relax. She just interviewed the guy. Let's not go marrying her off just yet."

Lila pulled back and looked up at him. "You laugh, but I told you she's already admitted that she thinks all those tats on a bad boy like that guy are sexy."

"Okay," Sonny said, kissing her nose to mollify her a little. "Maybe she thinks he's sexy, but he's way too old for someone Ali's age, and just like I didn't think him stupid enough to mean anything bad by 'jelly,' I doubt he's stupid enough to mess with Ali. I'm sure Gio explained to him whose sister she is. The guy's gotta know he'd be playing with fire if he even *thought* about so much as flirting with her."

Finally, Lila's expression eased up a bit. "He better know." She smirked then leaned her face against Sonny's chest, taking a deep breath and exhaling.

Sonny held her for a moment, keeping to himself what his first thoughts were when Lila mentioned Ali and the donut. It'd been a while since Lila mentioned Ali going into 5th Street the first time. Only way this guy would remember something like that was if watching her *devour* her donut had been *that* distracting it stayed on his mind all this time. And what would be more distracting than watching a girl suck the *jelly* out of a donut then lick her lips clean. If that was the case, his referring to her as jelly first thing when he saw her again, in a subtle way, had already been a form of flirting.

But he wasn't opening that can of worms, not when something more important was still gnawing at him. Bringing his hands up from her back, he cradled her face, and now that he had her undivided attention, he went for it. "Did you hear what I said to you earlier?"

Her brows pinched. "When?"

"Just before you got in my car tonight."

She thought about it but didn't seem to remember, and that made him smile. He'd worried for nothing. "I think you were too worked up still." He swallowed hard before going on. "I didn't even realize it until it slipped today that I love my feisty girl."

Her brows lifted as if she remembered now. Her expression changed when understanding set in. She seemed surprised—a bit stunned. But Sonny nodded. "I know now it's why I felt compelled to call my mom the other day and tell her about you. For the first time in my life, I'm in love, and it feels damn good. I love you, Lila."

He kissed her softly and was surprised to see how emotional she'd gotten so quickly when he pulled away. "I love you too, Sonny," she whispered back.

"You don't have to say it just because—"

"No." She shook her head vehemently. "I've been thinking it ever since the day I saw Marcelo after all these years. How maybe I'd mistaken ever being in love with him, because I felt nothing for him that day but annoyance. I'd always thought, if I ever saw him again, I might feel *something*. He *was* my first everything. Then I got to thinking that same night . . ." She paused for a moment as her face tinged with color. "After what I did to you and then us making love, I don't think I'd ever felt the profound happiness I feel from just one of your kisses. The deep emotion I feel in my heart when we make love." She glanced around as if searching for something. "Happiness is not a strong enough word. It's kind of scary what I'm feeling. For years, Ali's been the most important thing in my life, the only person who had my heart no matter what. But you're there now too. Only I *know* I've never felt something this all-consuming when it comes to *anyone*." She placed her hand over Sonny's against her face and smiled sweetly. "I've completely fallen in love with you, *Santino*. It's the one thing I'm certain of. I'd been feeling it for some time now. I just wasn't brave enough to admit it out loud. Hearing you say it just gave me the courage."

Feeling more than an enormous relief that he wasn't alone in this madness he'd been feeling for weeks now, he kissed her again. "I'm completely, utterly, and *madly* in love with you, Lila."

Sonny was done talking. He pulled her sports bra over her head and kissed her ravenously, surprised when she pulled away. "No way are you doing anything until I've at least rinsed." She moved over to the steaming shower door. "I feel icky."

With a tug to her spandex pants, she was naked in an instant, and Sonny raced to remove his clothes. Lila had gotten into the shower a few moments before he did. By the time he got in with her, she was thoroughly soaked. "Good enough," he said, lifting her up against the wall, laughing when she yelped.

In the next second, he was inside her with a grunt, and she wrapped those firm legs around his waist. "Fuck, I love you!" he said, burying himself *deep* in her.

# Lila

Even though it had crossed Lila's mind that the subject might come up eventually, she was still surprised when Sonny brought it up this soon. They were just a few exits away from her place when he brought her hand to his mouth and kissed it.

"I hate having to take you home," he said, staring straight ahead. "I know it's soon, but you're going to have to start thinking about getting another place soon anyway. You'd be surprised how fast you'll get well-known these days. With the Internet now, it's fucking overnight, and there are way too many weirdos out there that get easily fixated on celebrities. Doesn't matter what field and how small. You heard what happened to that young girl from *The Voice*, right? And she wasn't even the winner. Just a runner up."

He shook his head with a frown. "Fucking tragic. It's why I have so much security at my place. You never can be too cautious. I've had my share of weirdos I've had to get restraining orders on." He turned to her as they came to a stop in traffic. "So, I was thinking . . ." He smiled, kissing her hand again. "Now that you both have cars, why don't you and Ali move in with me? It's not that far a commute from 5th Street or her school, and I have plenty of room."

Admittedly, the thought that he might suggest something like that had crossed Lila's mind already. But it was such a scary one. Things had been as close to perfect as they could get, but this was so soon. What if things weren't always so perfect? Things could sour. Then what? She'd be scrambling to find her and Ali a new place to stay. She thought back to the day she'd found out about who Sonny really was. How livid she'd been and how *horrible* it would've been to not have anywhere to go but back to *his* place.

This time *she* kissed his hand and decided to stay positive. "That's sweet of you to offer, Sonny. And I'm in full agreement; now that I've made some money from the endorsement deal, and will be making more soon, thoughts of moving somewhere safer have been on my mind. But doing so and especially taking such a leap as to move me and my sister in with my boyfriend should be well thought out and a decision I can't make alone."

"So, just give it some thought. While I had hoped it would be, the move wouldn't even *have* to be a permanent one. I know your independence means a lot to you. But I'm telling you, once those commercials start airing and now that you've signed to fight for the title, it's just a matter of time before you can't walk out your front door without being mobbed. You may have to move sooner than you think. Just know that the invitation to move in with me, even if only temporarily, until you can figure something out, is there."

They reached her apartment, and Lila promised to seriously give it some thought and run it by Ali to see what she thought. Their kiss good-bye was longer—sweeter—and felt more heartfelt somehow than before.

"I love you, baby," Sonny whispered before Lila could pull away. "Miss you already."

"Me too." She smiled, feeling all warm and fuzzy. "And I love you too. I'll call you before I go to bed tonight, just so it's your voice I hear last."

They exchanged a few more kisses before Lila finally got out, her body tingling in all the familiar places.

Thoughts of their talk of moving in together were quickly squashed when she walked into her apartment and was met with her sister's big cheesy smile. Instantly, she was back to wondering just why her sister was so giddy after today's happenings.

"Okay," she said, putting her purse down on the sofa. "So, what else did this man say to you that has you all smiles?"

"Nothing," Ali said but failed to wipe the smile off her face completely. "And who says I'm still smiling about that?"

"So, you admit you were smiling about that earlier?"

"Look." Ali sat down at the table in their small eating area where her laptop was. "I know for you it's the norm to be noticed by hot guys—"

"Now he's *hot*?"

Ali gave her a challenging look. "Are you really gonna argue that he's not? I mean, yes, he's riddled with tattoos but that body . . . Come on? And you have to admit, despite what you may think of him, he is good-looking, just like that editor down at school. As annoying as he can be, I can admit that he's hot too."

Lila would give her that. That guy today wasn't bad looking—at all. It's what he represented that Lila didn't like about him. Danger. "I sincerely hope you're not even considering doing anything with this guy—"

Ali laughed before Lila could even finish. "I interviewed him about the program, and it was interesting to hear their back stories: what they were in jail for and what not. But I'd hardly say that constitutes us getting friendly. It was strictly business and I handled it just so. It was just surprising that he remembered me. You have to understand this is completely new for me. Unlike you, I'm not used to guys noticing and remembering me, much less guys like him."

Lila rolled her eyes, taking a seat at the sofa that faced Ali. "Ex-cons, you mean? So, what *did* they do time for?"

"The other guy, Rodney, was in for grand theft auto. His second time, though he claims it's his last ever. But get this. *Beast* did time for fighting in an underground fighting ring. It got raided, and he and a bunch of other fighters and organizers were all hauled in."

Staring at her sister, Lila could hardly believe this excited Ali. "Underground fighting? And his name is *Beast*?"

"It's what he was labeled after he really put a beat down on a few of his first opponents."

Ali went on to explain that, on top of it all, apparently when this guy flew into a rage, he went batshit crazy, hence the nickname.

"He goes by Beast. But like you," she added, sounding a bit cautious because Lila was already raising her brow, "he's now going to put all that anger and energy into boxing. He'll still be doing what he's so good at, only he'll be doing it in a controlled, *legal* environment with gloves on, not nearly beating someone to death with his bare hands. He also admitted to being involved in a lot of other shady things in his past, but now he's looking to straighten out."

Ali had already told Lila after her interview with Gio that they were, in fact, very stringent about who they let in the program: no sex offenders, no habitual offenders, and no one convicted of violent crimes.

So, she had to ask. "How did he get in the program when he openly admits to being a wild beast?"

"He wasn't convicted for assault or anything. He was arrested for being part of the illegal fighting ring, which personally"—Ali huffed— "I think is as dumb as convicting people for prostitution and solicitation. If two grown-ass people want to exchange money for sex, that's on them. If two grown-ass people wanna fight for the sake of entertainment and have other *adults* bet on them, then so be it. These laws are all about the government wetting its beak. Think about it. What he was doing, aside from the nearly killing someone, is no different from what you'll be doing soon. Only with you, the government gets to dig its claws into any earnings made from your fights. *So,* chicken shit."

Lila stood up, eyeing Ali as she walked into the kitchen. Ali was being entirely too defensive of this guy. "But you're done with this now, right? I mean you got your interview with Gio and now these two guys. You've got your story, and there's no need for you to keep in touch with this Beast guy, right?"

Continuing to type away on her laptop, Ali lifted a brow with an evil little smirk and stared straight into her screen. "Perhaps."

"No perhaps, Ali. I'm serious. If you've got everything you need for your story, then I don't want you staying in touch with this *man*."

Lila emphasized that last word because Sonny had been right. The guy was way too old for Ali to even be considering so much as a playful flirtation with. Thinking of what Sonny had said, reminded her of something else. So, before Ali could retort, she changed the subject—for now.

"Listen," she said, leaning nervously on the bar that separated the kitchen from the small front room. "We're probably going to have to start thinking about moving soon. Now that I've made some big money and will continue to, we can afford a better area. And with both of us having cars now, it doesn't even matter if we move a little farther away from my job and your school."

"Really?"

Nodding, Lila chewed her bottom lip before adding the next part. Ali's expression already looked as surprised as Lila had expected. "Sonny's offered to let us move in with him. His place is huge, so there's plenty of room, and I'm not sure how much I'll have to pay for rent, but knowing Sonny, he'll likely not want me to pay anything. Only that's not happening. Still, I'm sure it'll be a lot less than anywhere else." She crinkled her nose. "As nice as that sounds, Ali, I'm not sure that's a good idea."

"Why not? I thought you really liked him. And he seems to be *really* into you."

Lila smiled, feeling her insides warm all over again. "I do," she admitted. "And he is. In fact, he told me he's in love with me just today." Ali's eyes brightened as if pleasantly surprised. "I'm in love with him too. This just scares the hell out of me. Everything's happened so fast. You know I don't handle things well when I get angry. Already I've come across a few things online that have pissed me off to no end: photos of him with other girls. I know they're old, but I still can't help feeling so disgusted when I see them. I'm bracing myself for seeing something current."

"Well, that's silly. Why would you go looking?" Ali asked, sounding a little exasperated. "You've never been the type to follow gossip articles. Why start now if it gets you so worked up?"

"But what if it doesn't work out? I mean isn't this a little too good to be true? And I haven't known him that long? Suppose we have a falling out? Or even a little argument. I'd be stuck in the same house with him."

This time Ali laughed. "It's not too good to be true. Of course he's in love with you. What's not to love?"

Her sister smiled adoringly. But as much as Lila could appreciate the sentiment, she knew there were plenty of things about her that could be difficult to *love*. Her quick temper and foul mouth were just the starters. She could be difficult and Ali had to know this. Lila could already see it in her flattening smile that Ali knew what Lila was thinking.

"You need to start thinking more positively. The guy just professed his love for you, Li. Have some faith." Her eyes went wide suddenly. "You said his house is like a mansion, right? The neighbors will probably think we're the help when we roll in, in our cars."

Now Lila was laughing, albeit a bit nervously. From the sound of it, Ali would be all for it. Ever since she'd been seeing Sonny almost daily, Lila had been falling harder for him each day. This made her even more nervous. Once she was living with him, she could only imagine how much more profound her feelings for him would be getting.

"Don't get ahead of yourself," she said, breathing in deeper and trying not to sound as freaked out as she was beginning to feel about this. "I am trying to think positive, but this is a huge decision, so I won't be making any decisions just yet. I just wanted to run it past you to see if it's even something you'd be okay with."

When Ali's phone buzzed on the table, Lila walked away from the counter to make herself some tea before calling it a night. Her body was more than relaxed enough, so she'd pass out good and well, but her mind was still wired with the idea of moving in with Sonny this soon. So, she'd need a little of her trusty lavender tea to help her sleep.

Hearing Ali giggle under her breath had Lila glancing back at her sister curiously. Ali was chewing the corner of her lip and looking a bit giddy as she read whatever was on her phone screen. It was an all too familiar expression Lila had seen on her sister very recently. Like when she'd walked into the apartment today.

"What are you giggling about?" Lila asked, peering at her sister.

Ali's smile flattened when she realized Lila had caught her giddiness. She shrugged, tapping something into her phone. "He texted me earlier with some info he didn't have on him that I needed for the story. I thought I responded—"

"He who?" Lila asked, already dreading the answer.

"Beast," Ali said simply as if every hair on Lila's body wasn't already at attention.

"*He's* who you're texting with?"

Ali glanced up at her and tilted her with what looked too much like defiance. "It's not really texting. I just could swear I'd responded to his earlier text with the info he sent me, but I guess I never hit send. So, he was asking if I got the text."

"What else did he say that has you giggling, *Allison*?"

That made her sister smile big. "He's still referring to me as Jelly. And I already told you it has nothing to do with what you thought he meant by that. It just made me giggle to see it written out."

Lila took a deep breath. She *did not* want to be that kind of big nagging sister. Ali wasn't stupid, just young and impressionable still, especially given how much she seemed to be enjoying the new-found attention of "hot guys."

Before Lila could even try a subtler approach to her nagging, Ali put her phone down and stood up. "I have to get this story written, at least the first draft so I can run it past my editor tomorrow." She closed her laptop and picked it up. "But I'm gonna finish up in my room." Lifting her phone as she walked past Lila, she smiled. "See that's all he wanted: to confirm I got his text. I'm not texting with the guy, so don't worry. Aside from his *jelly* remark, he was actually very professional. Used some big words too. In fact, he came across as pretty smart. He's not as loathsome as I know you're thinking, Li. But again, you have nothing to worry about. This is probably the last I'll hear from him."

The tea kettle went off, interrupting any attempt to respond to her sister's comments, so Lila let it go. If Ali was really done with her story, then there'd be no more reason for her to keep in touch with the guy. She'd spare her sister any further nagging and just let her enjoy the little attention the guy had given her. It was nice to see her sister so giddy for once.

Ali stopped before going into her bedroom and turned back to Lila with a smile. "Let me know when we move into that mansion." She winked at Lila. "Stop overthinking everything, Sissy. I think you and Sonny are perfect for each other, and I'm telling you there's no denying he's crazy about you. I don't think you have anything to worry about, no matter how fast this is happening."

Lila smiled nervously, taking a deep breath, but shrugged. "I'll give it a few days before I decide. But I'll let you know as soon as I do."

She knew her sister was right. Lila was overthinking it. Worst case scenario, if anything that bad occurred and she needed to get away from him, she already had some money put away from her endorsement deal, and she had more coming. Maybe she'd just wait a little longer until she had more put away. This way, if something did go wrong, she'd have her first and last for another place ready to go and still have enough left for Ali's school.

# Sonny

It hadn't even been two weeks since the day Lila told Sonny she wanted to hold off on moving just yet. From the sound of it, she was hoping to give it at least a few more weeks, maybe even wait until after her first fight to make the move. Unfortunately for her but fortunately for Sonny, she found out less than two weeks later that what Sonny had warned her of was all too real. After the announcement of her fight was made, the buzz was on, especially because of her next opponent's large following.

The media was all over it, and Lila's face and the promotional photos were everywhere. As he'd warned, it'd been just a matter of time before someone got wind of where she lived, and one morning she woke to several reporters and photographers just outside her apartment building. She'd been more annoyed by it than spooked. But all it took was for one of those reporters to harass Ali, and the next thing Lila and Sonny were discussing was getting their things moved into his place ASAP.

That was weeks ago, and now Lila's first major fight was just a few days away. She and Ali were now Sonny's roommates, and he couldn't be happier. It'd help knowing she was sleeping in his bed when he had to leave for spring training next year. He couldn't be more grateful for the timing. Sonny had always known a relationship on his busy schedule would be a challenge. But busy schedule or not, nothing was keeping him from doing this now. It just helped that this was happening during his off-season. By the time spring training started up, they should have things figured out.

Sonny had figured living with Lila would be heaven, but he didn't expect for things to feel so normal as fast as they had, especially given Lila's initial unease about things moving so quickly. But as the days and weeks quickly passed with each day proving this was meant to be, Lila's misgivings were now gone.

It was slow and subtle, but the transformation Sonny was seeing in Lila was inspirational to say the least. She'd gone from the girl with the impenetrable walls to opening up and accepting that she deserved to be happy. This wasn't a fluke that was going to slip through her hands as swiftly as it appeared.

She'd even made strides in the ability to control her temper. Though every now and again the blaze was there just simmering under the surface. While she was making progress, she did have a few slips here and there. The "Jelly" incident with the tatted guy was a perfect example. She may've previously admitted to Sonny the work-release guys were scary-looking, but the moment she thought one of them might be insulting her sister, scary or not, there'd been zero hesitation to prepare to lunge if she had to. The girl was a force to be reckoned with, and while Sonny encouraged her efforts to maintain control, he reminded her often how her passion was part of what he loved so much about her.

The moment he walked in the house and met Lila's beautiful eyes, he saw it. She was on her phone, and there was no hiding the concern in her eyes. She lifted a finger before he could ask her what was going on.

"Yes, can you do that please? It's just not like her to not respond to my calls and texts."

Sonny put his bag down, already feeling concerned, and waited until she was off the phone. "Ali," she confirmed what Sonny knew could be the reason for such concern in her face. "Last text I have from her was from early this afternoon when she said she was driving to downtown for a breaking story. Downtown can be dangerous, and it's been a while since I asked her about the drug-dealing story she got chased for, so this makes me nervous. I didn't read the text until I was off today. I tried calling her, but she didn't answer. I didn't think too much of it. I lost track of her schedule, but I was sure she either had school or work in the evening. Then I got home and looked on the calendar. She doesn't have either today. I've been trying for over an hour now, but she still hasn't responded to my texts—"

Her phone rang and she answered it immediately. "Did you get a hold of her?"

She was quiet for a moment, and Sonny glanced down at his phone, on the off chance that maybe Ali had tried him. His thoughts were derailed when he heard Lila address her caller by name—Marcelo. He jerked his head up and away from his phone, and their eyes met immediately. But he waited until she hung up.

"That was Marcelo?"

She was already dialing someone else. "Yes, when neither Ali or Jen were returning my calls, I had no choice but to call him. I wasn't even sure if they'd be together. He said Jen was at work, which explained why she couldn't answer my call, but he agreed to call the store and see if he could find out where—" She stopped and held up a finger again. "Gio, can you do me a huge favor? I've been trying to get ahold of my sister, but she's not answering. Her friend said she's at the gym of all places. Can you please look around for her, and if you see her, just tell her to call me ASAP? Thank you so much."

She got off the phone with a frown. "She's still at the gym?" Sonny asked.

"It's what Jen told Marcelo. I forgot she'd mentioned she was going to start working out. She just hadn't mentioned when."

Pulling Lila's tense body to him, Sonny didn't even get the chance say anything when her phone rang and she pulled away immediately. She hit the screen the moment she saw who it was and brought it to her ear. "*Where* have you been? And why haven't you answered or responded to any of my calls?"

She was quiet as, apparently, Ali explained. Sonny watched closely, massaging Lila's back to try and relax her, since she was still so tense He kissed her temple as she continued to grill Ali. For a moment, he wondered if Ali's decision to start working out had anything to do with the *Beast* dude. Lila had since shared with Sonny her unease about her *baby* sister having given the guy her number. She'd also mentioned the fact that the guy was still referring to Ali as Jelly, something that felt too uncomfortably close to flirting.

But it'd been weeks and Lila hadn't mentioned anything more about him. She was already too riled up about this. No sense in bringing that up too.

"Okay, text me when you head home." She shook her head as she hung up. "She was working out. Left her phone in her gym bag in a locker.'

Sonny rubbed her back one more time before pulling her to him and leaned against the sofa back. "Did she mention what the story downtown was about?"

She nodded, her expression easing up. "Small fire at one of the school's extension campuses. But I'll ask her about that other story tonight."

"You see," he said, pecking her softly. "All that worrying for nothing."

She nodded, finally giving him a glimpse of that beautiful smile. "So, you're back now, but when do you do your next promo out of town?"

Sonny kissed her pouty lips. "At least a week. I made sure they didn't schedule me on or around the weekend of your fight. So, I'm sticking around for a while. But"—he paused, hoping she'd go for it— "since you're gonna get some time off from your training after this fight, I was hoping you'd come on my next trip with me." The second her brows jumped in reaction to that, Sonny spoke again before she could begin to make excuses. "It'll only be a week, and I'll get added security at my front gate that can help us track Ali down in case she ever doesn't answer your calls like today."

The corners of her lips slowly curved into a sweet smile. "I'm not that bad."

"Yeah, you are, but I like when you're bad."

The sweet smile morphed into a sexy one, and Sonny picked her up effortlessly, throwing her over his shoulder. "I'll take that as a yes to the trip, and now it's time to make up for the last two days."

Lila squirmed in his arms but was no match for his strength, despite all the muscle on her hard body. "Sonny, I haven't showered!"

"Sweetheart, I don't care."

"But I do. I feel gross!"

Sonny made a bee line to the bathroom in his master bedroom instead of the bed, already feeling his cock pressing against his jeans. "Then the shower it is. Wouldn't be our first time, and I'm sure it won't be our last."

# Lila

Just as her trainers and Sonny had assured her, her fight against the reigning champ was still an undercard fight, therefore, nowhere as big as she'd first thought. When she'd heard the phrases "reigning champ" and "Olympic gold medalist," they also reminded her that, sadly for women, the excitement in the sport still wasn't quite there. So, even though her fight had been for the title, just as they'd predicted, the stands had been mostly empty. After her fight, there were still several fights scheduled before the main event. All of them men.

Lila wasn't sure whether she should feel flattered or annoyed that all her trainers had seemed so surprised—almost let down—that she hadn't been able to knock the champ out. It's like they'd forgotten this was Lila's *first* fight against a real contender, and while she'd given the gal a run for her money, she hadn't been able to do it. But at least she hadn't lost. They'd gone the full ten rounds. Unlike any of her other fights and sparring matches where Lila had barely been winded, this had been beyond intense. She'd gone toe to toe with the champ, a few times having her in the corner or on the ropes fighting, and everyone in her corner had gone wild.

It ended in a stunning split decision, and *now* suddenly, people were interested. Apparently, not only was Mannering a former Olympian and the champ, she was undefeated, a fact Lila's trainers and manager had all curiously failed to mention. They'd showed her footage of Mannering taking a loss, but it had been before she'd gone professional. Lila hadn't bothered doing much more homework on her own, since she assumed her trainers had done it and they'd tell her anything she needed to know.

"You were already so worked up when I told you she was the champ," Preston said with an annoying smirk when she'd demanded to know why he hadn't told her.

"Yeah," Gio had been quick to back him up. "And we've talked about what a huge part of this sport is mental stamina. Remember? It's not about the size of the dog in the fight, but the size of the fight in the dog. Clearly, your fight is bigger, but if you'd gone in there with the mentality that she's the bigger dog, it would've affected your fight. Only reason you didn't beat her ass is because of the size of her *experience*. It's the *only* advantage she has over you. But you're a natural, Lila. You don't need all the experience she has. You nearly took the title tonight."

Of course, Preston had thought far enough ahead to make sure to get it in the contract that should the fight end in a draw—something he said he'd been sure Mannering's people must've chuckled at—there'd be an instant rematch. He'd also left the amount Lila would be asking for a rematch open. The promoters had been as confident as Mannering's people that nothing of the sort would happen, so they agreed.

Now that buzz of the little nobody who nearly took the champ was turning into a roar, Preston held off negotiating Lila's percentage of the take. Sports magazines suddenly wanted her on their covers. TV, cable, Internet, and radio talk shows all wanted the exclusive Cinderella story.

After the fight, Lila agreed to accompany Sonny on more of his promotional travels. At first, she dreaded it. She wasn't sure what to expect. But now that she'd be doing her own promoting, she was glad for the heads-up, not just for what promoting would be like, but for getting a taste of what it was like to be recognized with someone who was so used to it.

Their first official night out together was in Vegas. Sonny had sweetly remembered her saying she'd never been. So, before he had to be in Chicago that following week, they left a day early and stopped over in Vegas first. Being in his home and riding in his luxury cars had given Lila a taste of the lavish life. She thought she'd seen enough movies and Netflix shows about the rich to have an idea of what a day in the life of the filthy rich was like.

From the first-class seats on the plane to the instant VIP treatment both at the departing and arriving airports, it almost felt unfair. How could some people like Sonny, who seemed very used to it all, have this as their regular lifestyle? When people like Lila and her sister may've never experienced anything like it, had it not been for the unusual circumstances that had Lila here now.

The suite they checked into at the Palms resort was just ridiculous. While Lila wasn't by any means complaining, it just felt so over the top. It brought back memories of Sonny and their first FaceTime date, which felt like a lifetime ago now, of his sitting in his room with a grand piano just behind him. Again, the room was bigger than the apartment she and Ali had moved out of. *Much* bigger with every luxury imaginable, things Lila wasn't even aware existed in hotel rooms, such as the steam showers and fog-resistant mirrors.

When she'd been handed the iPad at check in, Lila had turned to Sonny at a loss.

Sonny smiled, thanking the lady behind the desk, and winked at Lila. He later explained it was the hotel's virtual concierge. "It's how we'll access any hotel info or services," he'd explained on the ride up in the elevator. "Which reminds me," he said, pointing at the screen. "Press the service button."

Lila had glanced down at the different icons on the screen. Within seconds, Sonny had walked her through scheduling a couple's massage in their suite for later that day before their night out.

It wasn't her first massage. Sonny had insisted on having a masseuse come out the day after her fight the week prior, when she'd been far more sore than she'd expected to be. But the couple's massage felt more special, and just like the first time, it'd been heaven.

The night out included dinner at a swanky steak and seafood house. Even all the times she and Sonny had gone out in Los Angeles had never been this fancy. It was always more about trying to keep things on the down low. Lila enjoyed her alone time with him, buying take out for the most part and eating back at his place versus the times they'd dined out and were inevitably interrupted. She hated having to pretend not to see people blatantly gawking at them too. It was awkward as hell.

That night, heads had turned as they'd been walked to their table, and by the time they were done with dinner, there'd been photographers outside. Sonny had warned her there might be. Vegas knew its boxing since the city *was* the boxing capital of the world. The restaurant was known to be frequented by celebrities. As much as restaurants like the one they'd dined at did their best to give their celebrity guests as much privacy as necessary, he said they all had moles, workers on the paparazzi's payroll.

It'd been a bit surreal when they'd walked out and the handful of photographers had called her name, not just *Sabian's* like in Los Angeles. In Los Angeles, most questions asked of Sonny were playful, things like if he was getting Los Angeles a much-needed championship. But with Sonny being one of MLB's most eligible bachelors, there were some nosey questions as well.

Seeing him walking out of whatever restaurant or coffee shop, holding Lila's hand *before* her fight, brought on nosier more private questions—about his relationship with this *beautiful young girl*. They *begged* for her name and if they were exclusive. But they were nowhere as pressing as the questions they asked in Vegas. They immediately recognized her as the "Cinderella" who nearly dethroned the champ.

Of course, like the first times they'd been out in public, Sonny had once again coached her on how to handle them. He told her to just smile politely. "I usually answer generic questions about the game and how I'm feeling. You know, go along with the fun banter when I get a wiseass trying to bust my balls. But I never give them anything when they get personal, especially about who I'm dating and shit. Some can get a little aggressive and annoying when they get too close. But for the most part, I've never had any issues with them."

As playful and charming as she witnessed his behavior with the paparazzi in Los Angeles, Lila thought she picked up on a harder demeanor that evening in Vegas. From the moment they started calling out to her by name, he seemed tense. Sonny was faster to rush away from them than usual. And his normal playful banter was noticeably absent.

By the time they got to Chicago for his promotional appearances on a few television and radio talk shows, speculation of their "rumored" relationship was all the buzz in the tabloids. Most were wondering if it wasn't just a publicity stunt for Sonny or both of them. No better way to keep their names in the headlines now that both seemed to be the biggest stories in sports for the Los Angeles area.

"If it gets to be too much, just say so," Sonny had said when they arrived at the airport and were followed the whole way from their plane to their awaiting car.

The photographers had been relentless and far more intrusive than Lila had ever witnessed. They pressed for clarification of their relationship. Were they exclusive? Was this serious? And most annoying, "Is there any truth to this being just a publicity stunt?"

"We can lay low for a while if you prefer," Sonny said once in the car behind closed doors. "Order room service or just have dinner at one of the restaurants in the hotels where the photographers are not allowed." He glanced out the window where the photographers were still huddled around the car just waiting for another glimpse of them. "Because those damn photographers are already annoying as fuck. But I can already feel it. This is only the beginning."

Both had ignored all the questions, as they walked quickly through the airport. He'd yet to comment on the publicity-stunt speculations, but Lila got the distinct feeling it's what really annoyed him.

"I can deal with it," Lila said honestly. "Maybe if we just clarified, they'd stop making rude assumptions—"

"I don't give a shit what they say or think," Sonny was quick to explain. "I just don't want *you* feeling overwhelmed by it all. This is all new to you. It's one thing to ease into being in the public eye, but for it to start like *this* for you . . ." He motioned out the window as the car pulled away. "It just doesn't seem fair, and I know it's all my fault."

"Fault?" she asked, touching his cheek with the back of her hand, and smiled, tilting her head. "Because my boyfriend is a superstar athlete they can't get enough of?"

Sonny took her hand away from his cheek and kissed it. "They know enough about me, Lila. It's *you* they're fascinated with. They know nothing about you, and the fact that you're dating someone famous only intrigues them further. And I'd never confirm anything to paparazzi.

They're bad enough as it is. If I start answering their pushy questions, it'll only open the floodgates to more. But I was gonna talk to you about that."

"About what?" Lila asked, leaning in and sprinkling kisses around the corner of his lips. He seemed so tense, and it was her way of calming him a little.

"After our night out in Vegas, my publicist has been getting nonstop inquiries about us."

Lila's insides fluttered even as she kissed the corner of his lip again and gazed into his eyes, breathing in deeply. Despite everything that'd happened between them, her living with him now and his declaring his love for her, it was still hard to fully wrap her head around the outrageousness of it all. This man, not just the superstar athlete, because, obviously, that's not what had been the draw, but this beautiful man who so easily stole her heart was actually in love with her too. So, hearing him speak in terms of *us* still made her heart flutter.

"Patrick Walker, the host of *Sports Thunder*, the show I'll be on today, is a buddy of mine," he said, squeezing her hand. "We go way back, and I know the question about *us* is inevitable. So, rather than give any confirming statements to the inquiring media, I thought maybe I should just give him the exclusive. It's the top-rated sports talk show in the nation right now, and confirming this on his show would pretty much make this official, publicly anyway. He's a good guy and called me this morning to ask if this was something I'd even want to discuss; otherwise, he wouldn't bring it up. That's a big deal."

"It is?" she asked, her heart speeding up as the enormity of this really sunk in.

Their relationship was *that* big a deal, that the host of the top-rated sports show in the nation would call him to ask him.

"Oh yeah," Sonny said with a nod. "It's all about ratings with these guys. You saw how hungry those photographers were for the answer to the latest craze in the tabloids. Here he could ask me about it, live—make teaser promos about it to get more viewers to tune in—and he's willing to pass on it because he's a good friend. And," he said, tilting his head with a smirk, "I'm pretty sure he might be a little pissed if his bosses are pushing for him to ask about it, get the story. He's a professional through and through, and I'm sure he thinks it's bullshit that they'd be insisting he discuss my romantic life on his *sports* show."

"So, what did you tell him?"

"I told him I wouldn't have an issue discussing it briefly, keeping it vague, but that I'd wanna run it by you first."

Lila glanced down at her phone. She had a voicemail from Preston she still hadn't listened to. But she'd read his text asking her to call him when she got the chance. It didn't sound urgent. Only now she was certain it had to be about this. If Sonny's people were getting calls inquiring about their relationship, Preston likely was too.

"I don't have a problem with it," Lila said, squeezing Sonny's hand.

"Good," he said, giving her a peck. "I'll send him a text giving him the go-ahead. And like I said, I'll keep it vague. Hopefully, once I confirm that, yes, we're a couple, the damn photographers will back off and move on to the next story."

## Sonny

"You're too damn close." Sonny snarled at the photographer walking backwards in front of him and Lila as they made their way back to the car at Hollenbeck Park.

The days of him and Lila being able to enjoy a stroll in the park even in the evening were over. Sonny wasn't the only one that had to worry about being recognized anymore. He'd been absurdly mistaken about the outcome of his public confirmation months ago of their relationship. Instead of interest dying down, it created a frenzy. Photos of the two were apparently in even higher demand now.

The buzz of the rematch had grown considerably, since any talk of it now inevitably included a mention of him. Unlike in the beginning, her manager, Styles, was now all for them being publicly affectionate. He'd even suggested they do a few appearances together. That maybe sometime up the road they'd even consider doing a reality show.

"Unlike other sports that garner plenty of women fans, boxing isn't up there with them," Styles had argued when Sonny had staunchly balked at the ideas. "You're not promoting her or the fight. Without doing anything but openly dating Lila, you're promoting the *sport*. Just the simple fact that you two are an item is intriguing enough to your hordes of female fans who wanna know more about her—about women's boxing. There's a real curious interest. How in the world did this virtual unknown land the most eligible bachelor in the MLB? Sure, she's beautiful with a killer body, but it's not like you didn't already have access to plenty of beautiful women. Already Gio said there's been a significant jump in the bag and shadow-boxing workouts down at the gym."

Sonny still hadn't been comfortable with the idea of them making appearances together. They were two different athletes in two completely different sports. The media was already making this out to be a team effort, but for what? To gain Lila a bigger following? Lila was her own person with her own accomplishments. But the couple had even been dubbed *Slyla* by the press now. It was fucking ridiculous.

Judging by the amount of paparazzi on their asses all the time now, most of the fans were highly embracing the union, but the speculation that this was nothing more than a publicity stunt was still out there. Sonny didn't even care what they said about him, but he'd be damned if he'd be adding fuel to the storm fire of infuriating comments about Lila not having earned the success she was seeing so soon on her own merit. That all the endorsement deals she'd landed ever since her first big fight had come from the popularity of their super couple status. Fuck that. His fans got to see and hear enough about them already, the way they were hounded. Appearances together were not necessary.

One positive thing that had come from Sonny's annoyance about the whole situation was that he was irritated enough for the both of them. All this time, Lila had been the one known for her explosive temper. She'd done enough in-depth interviews now, both on television and in magazines, where they covered everything the world wanted to know about her. Where did she come from and why had she been hiding all these years?

Lila had told them about her upbringing, her mother and grandfather being fighters as well, and her life in foster care when her mom died. She'd also explained how and why she'd ended up at 5th Street then inevitably in the ring when her whole life she'd sworn she'd never fight. So, the world knew about her struggle with controlling her temper, as well as her unyielding protectiveness of her sister. As private as Lila was, Style's had convinced her that her fans would appreciate her honesty and it might even help some who might be struggling with the same issues. He said her success would signal to the many kids out there in the foster care system that there was hope for them too.

Ironically, because Sonny fucking *hated* what a circus her life had become—because of him—they'd traded places when it came to who the calm one was about this. Lila did her best to assure him she was fine with it all. That she knew it wouldn't last forever. Like with everything else in the tabloids, as soon as the next big story happened, they'd be old news.

Sonny shielded Lila as their driver held the door open for her to get in. "Back the fuck off!" Sonny barked at one photographer who leaned in too close to take his shot of Lila.

Lila tugged on Sonny's hand to pull him into the backseat with her. "Unbelievable," Sonny said after the door closed and let his head fall back onto the seat.

As was the case lately, Lila rubbed his leg in a soothing motion. Even more unbelievably, he heard her giggle.

Lifting his head, he turned to her. "Are you laughing at me again?"

"Again?" she asked, looking confused, but still smirked.

"Yeah, like you did that first night when I dripped ketchup on my shirt."

She laughed even more now. "I'm not laughing *at* you," she said between chuckles then leaned in and kissed him.

Gazing at him, she stopped laughing but chewed her lip as if she needed to stifle any further giggles. "I just think it's funny that's you *ever* thought you could hang out at a park—in East LA no less—and not be recognized, but especially now that things have gotten so crazy."

"We did that first night," he reminded her. "And a few more times after."

"Only because it was dark and there was no one tailing us." She rubbed his still furrowed brow gently. "I enjoy a nice walk in the park as much as you do, especially one where we shared our first kiss. I just think it's time to concede that it may not be so easy to do that anymore without the photographers catching wind of it and showing up. But we can find other places to take romantic walks, places where they wouldn't be allowed."

Sonny pulled her to him. "All the way," he said as he tugged at her leg. She obliged by shifting in her seat enough that he could pull one of her legs over him then straddled him. "I've been meaning to tell you I'm so proud of you. You've come a long way with your ability to keep your cool." He pulled her hair behind her ears on both sides, indulging in that beautiful smile before going on. "These fuckers have had me this close to wanting to strangle them with their own camera straps."

Lila laughed again. "I know and I guess this is still too new for me because it doesn't bother me as much as it does you. Either that or I'm more worried about you doing something just like that, than about them being so intrusive. I've been more focused on just getting through it and getting you away from them than anything else. But it's nice to not be the one losing it for once."

Since he really was proud of her and she had made strides with her temper in the past several months, he'd keep to himself that he still saw the fury anytime Ali mentioned being hounded by them. But he supposed when it came to her sister that would never change.

That reminded him of something. "Your sister gonna be late again tonight?"

Lila nodded, already smiling. "She's got some lab hours she needs to get in before the end of the week, so she said she wouldn't be home until after ten."

"Well, since our romantic walk was ruined," Sonny said, slipping his hands inside the back of her jeans, "maybe we can take a dip in the Jacuzzi tonight and take in the stars that way."

"Sounds good to me," she said, swaying her hips against him as she kissed him deeply, making him groan with anticipation.

Not that they couldn't sit in the Jacuzzi if Ali was home, or even get sneaky under the water if they so well pleased— and they *always* did—but the last time they'd been out there and knew Ali wouldn't be home anytime soon, he'd enjoyed having Lila completely naked. Even took her from behind as she leaned over the side. Just thinking about it now had him tugging down her pants.

Before he even got the chance to, Lila leaned over and hit the button to raise the center partition for some privacy. Sonny groaned again. The first time they'd done this in the car, Lila had been nervous and embarrassed about the driver hearing and even knowing what they'd been up to. But this was something else she'd clearly come a long way about.

Pressing the button to the speaker up front, Sonny spoke into it as Lila pulled a leg out of her pants. "Take the long way home."

"Got it" was all the response he got.

His driver, Craig, knew the deal. Sonny unzipped his pants, and Lila wasted no time pulling him out then stroking him. But instead of straddling him again as he thought she would, she spun around and sat on him. He easily slipped deep into her hot wetness. "Oh *fuck*," he muttered with a guttural gasp, and he knew why now she'd spun around.

Doing it the other way wouldn't have allowed for such deep access. Lila took him in as deep as possible then wiggled her ass as a moan escaped her.

"Don't," Sonny warned, holding her ass a little tighter. "I wanna go a little longer, and if you do that . . ."

He let his head fall back without finishing because she started sliding up and down and it felt *so fucking* good. Each time she'd push down as far as she could, wanting him as deep in her as possible, and he loved it.

They moved slowly at first, both wanting it to last for as long as possible, but as good as it felt, Sonny knew he wouldn't last too long. He brought his hands around her front and played with her clit, feeling her entire body begin to slowly come undone. The more she trembled and panted, the faster they went. Each time she sank onto him, taking him as deep as possible, but even then, Sonny lifted his hips to fuck her as hard and profoundly as he possibly could.

Breathlessly and frantically, she bounced on him, faster and faster until Sonny could feel the familiar tightening around his cock as her pussy began to spasm, making him a goner. Burying himself one last time as he pushed her down onto him, he came as hard as he'd anticipated. Between the tension he'd built up the moment they spotted the photographers in the parking lot of the park, realizing their night out was over, and having to push past them, he needed this release more than ever.

The more incidents like today happened, the more Sonny worried that Lila might eventually get sick of this immense change in her lifestyle.

Lila let her head fall back against him. Sonny kissed her neck softly and wrapped his arms around her waist. "God, I love you, baby."

She laughed softly, still trying to catch her breath. "Guess those photographers chasing us into the car wasn't such a bad thing after all."

"Guess not," he said, forcing his smile, despite the feeling of pure ecstasy his body was still enjoying. "I'm sorry they get so crazy, but I promise you I'll find a way to fix this. Get more security or something."

Lila turned to face him better and ran her fingers through his hair. "Stop apologizing, Sonny. It's not your fault, and it really doesn't bother me as much as it does you. And you know what else? You were right earlier. Before the fight, before the media knew anything about me, it was never this crazy. You were actually nice to the photographers back in LA the few times they saw us out in public." She nudged him with her elbow. "The night we met you were even able to hang out at a club, amongst a bunch of non-celebrities, and not get mobbed. Preston was right too," she added, nearly ruining the little speech that'd begun to make him feel a little better. "Your fans are just curious to see who the great Double S Sabian might be setting his sights on."

"You mean who I'm fucking crazy about," he said, wrapping his arms around her even tighter. "Who brought me to my knees and who I have every intention of making my wife someday."

She went still suddenly, but Sonny didn't miss a beat. He kissed her cheek. "*Someday*," he reiterated. "Didn't mean to scare you there, but it's happening, Lila. I know your career is just getting started, and right now we both have a million things going on, but you're it for me, babe. There's no doubt in my mind that I wanna spend the rest of my life with you. You may not be there yet—"

"I am," she said, turning to him even more. "And you didn't scare me, just caught me by surprise. I agree right now is not a good time, but one thing I know for sure is I've never been happier than since I met you."

Feeling his heart swell, Sonny smiled, lifting his brows, exaggerating his surprise to her comment. "Even with all the paparazzi bullshit you've had to deal with?"

Lila smiled even as her eyes glistened. "Sonny, you've changed my life—*me*—for the better in so many ways. I never thought I'd say this to any man, but aside from anything that might upset my sister, there's nothing I wouldn't sacrifice to be with you." She leaned in and kissed him softly then pulled away and smiled. "So, yeah, *bullshit* paparazzi issues are a very small sacrifice I'll gladly make. I'll take you any day. I love you."

"I love you more," Sonny whispered, kissing her back, then squeezed her even tighter, feeling a dread he hadn't felt since the day he walked into that training room with Tatiana hanging all over him.

To have lost her back then would've been bad enough; he was so hung up on her already. But to lose her now for any reason he knew he'd never get over it—over her. He was only glad she seemed to be as far gone as he was, because as much as he'd tried to play it down, this relationship was anything but a normal one. *Anything* could complicate things real fast.

## 24

## Lila

Oh, the irony was rich. As worried as they'd both been that maybe the media frenzy would eventually be a cause of contention between them, it'd done just the opposite. Lila was as floored by the whole *Slyla* madness as Sonny was annoyed by it. But because of the insanity of it, there was no way anyone could deny how crazy they were about each other now. Nor could they doubt their utter devotion to one another. The paparazzi caught every adoring gaze, every kiss and sweet moment they could, and these images were all over the Internet and tabloid covers.

With so many of Lila's campaigns and advertisements featuring her now signature badass glare, the press was quick to point out what a polar opposite she was when around Sonny. More than once now they'd even caught her annoyance when she'd been seen around other men who were clearly trying to hit on her. As much as those photos pleased Sonny, he'd made no secret of the fact that it pissed him off.

"The asshole would have to be stuck under a fucking rock for the last few months not to know you're spoken for."

Thankfully, in each of the incidents, it'd been an unknown crew member of whatever commercial or promo she'd been on the set of. If it had been another celebrity or even athlete, the media would've had a field day with it. And that was the kind of issues they'd dreaded.

There were no paparazzi allowed on the sets, but just like some of the restaurants they'd frequented, there were moles in the crew itself, trying to make a quick buck on any photos they could sneak. So, these photos had obviously been leaked.

In any case, what Lila had been so worried about way back—that she'd screw this up somehow with her temper—didn't appear to be the case, not when it came to seeing photos or reading stories about Sonny with other women. So far, everything had been perfect. The rematch was just weeks away now. Other than the fact that she wasn't as free to fly off with Sonny on a whim anymore because of her training, life couldn't be more wonderful.

Sonny still had to go out of town for his promos. But even then, without Lila ever suggesting it, he made every effort to get back that same day, even if it meant sitting on two long flights in the same day. To Lila, that spoke volumes and gave her a little relief that she wasn't the only one so completely sprung. She heard and saw the sincerity in his eyes whenever he couldn't get back in just one day. Like this last trip he'd taken. He had no choice but to be gone for two days, and he hadn't been a happy camper. He had every opportunity to be out there living the glamorous life, jetting all over, since technically this was still the off-season for him. Yet, all he could think of was getting back to her.

The very thought made her smile as she finished washing her hands for lunch. She still hadn't checked her phone and was anxious too, but she'd needed to use the ladies' room first and wash up a little since she'd been covered in sweat and felt gross.

Rushing out of the employee bathroom, she went straight to her locker, hoping not to get stopped. She'd gotten better about being friendlier when it came to signing autographs. But like the photographers, some fans could be pushy. It wasn't enough for her to sign one thing. Some of them had several photos, magazine covers, and even gloves they wanted her to stop and sign, even when she was clearly in a hurry.

Once at her locker her heart fluttered as it still did every time she knew she was that close to hearing from Sonny. It'd only been two days that he'd been gone, and already she could hardly wait to see him later that day when he got back.

The instant smile was on her face the moment she saw she had two emails from him. But because she knew his emails could get long sometimes, she decided to check the text from Ali first. She usually only texted when she needed to tell Lila something significant.

> **Call Jen. I'M FINE. So, don't Frank out! I just can't talk right now and it's too long to explain.**

The obvious auto-correct typo didn't garner so much as a smirk from Lila like it normally would. She immediately checked the time it was sent, even as her previously fluttering heart was now beginning to pound nervously. It had been sent twenty minutes ago. It was only then that she noticed the missed call she had from Jen less than five minutes ago. Clicking on it, she hit send. "Don't freak out?" she whispered under her breath. "Is she kidding me?"

"Lila," Jen answered.

"Jen, what's going on?"

"I'm not sure. I just got here."

"Got where?"

"The hospital."

"*Hospital?*" Grabbing her bag out of the locker, Lila slammed it shut with her heart at her throat. "Why are you at the hospital?"

"Ali's in the ER, but I don't know a whole lot more, except she wanted to talk to me first so I could explain it to you."

Already in a sprint, Lila headed out to the parking lot, glad to see her driver outside chatting with the driver of another town car. Motioning to him that she had to go, he rushed to open the back of the car and opened the door before she was even close. "Was she in an accident?"

"I don't know the details."

"Well, did she tell you *anything*?"

"Umm . . . hold on."

Someone was talking to Jen in the background, and as much as Lila strained to hear what they were saying, she couldn't make anything out.

"They're letting me in now. I'll know more in a second."

Lila got the hospital info and relayed it to the driver before sliding in. "Quickly please," she said before he could close the door. "My sister's in the hospital." The moment he closed the door she went back to grilling Jen. "And you don't know anything else? She just told you she was in the ER?"

"Well, no . . ." Jen paused as she thanked someone for something, but if Lila didn't know any better, Jen was purposely avoiding telling her more.

"*Jennifer*," she said, losing her patience now as the car pulled past the photographers at the gate. "What did she tell you?"

Clearing her throat, she heard Jen take in a breath. "She was in a fight, Lila. But I don't know the details. All she said was she thinks she broke her hand."

That familiar red haze of fury Lila had been blinded with so often throughout her life, threatened to do her in now. But she gripped the phone, taking in a deep breath herself. She

was better than that now. It was a fight. She wasn't attacked.
"A fight? With who?"

"I don't know. Some girl at school. But if she broke her hand, then I'm guessing the other girl can't be in too great a shape either. Just get here and she'll tell us both the rest. I'm going into the ER now, but I can't be on my phone in there. Drive careful, Lila. She said she's fine."

Lila let her know she wasn't driving but that she was already on her way. As her heart pummeled away, she reminded herself of her sister's text. *I'M FINE.*

It was just a fight. God knew Lila had been in plenty, and she could see how easy it'd be to break her hand. She winced, remembering the girl's wrist she'd broken the night she met Sonny and how much pain she'd been in.

To distract herself before she drove herself crazy, she texted Gio to let him know why she'd skipped out on lunch and wouldn't be back today. Of course, traffic would be the pits, and it felt like an eternity before they got there.

Remembering how easily she was recognized these days, she pulled out the light jacket with a hoodie and the dark glasses she always carried now and put them on.

The moment the car slowed at the ER entrance, Lila didn't even wait for the driver to come around and get the door. One of the more relentless photographers pulled up alongside of her town car, but Lila didn't have time to worry about him. He wouldn't be let in the ER anyway.

She rushed through the crowded emergency waiting room, trying to remain calm. *It was just a fight,* she kept reminding herself. She's well enough to make phone calls and send texts.

When she was finally let into the busy ER, she spotted Jen standing by the bed in the corner where Ali was sitting up talking to her. Lila's eyes zoomed in on her sister's scratched face, and she swallowed hard, taking even deeper breaths as she got closer. For a second, Ali moved the icepack away from her head and Lila saw the huge lump. Ali covered it as soon as she spotted Lila walking toward them. A guy in scrubs was at her bedside now with a wheel chair and began helping her into it.

"You can't walk?" Lila asked, feeling her adrenaline spike and her heart drop.

"I can," Ali explained. "But I have a bruised rib, so it hurts to stand. They don't want me getting further injured, so it's just procedure."

"What happened?" Lila asked, pulling her sunglasses off as the attendant continued to help Ali into the chair.

Lila didn't miss the exchanged glance between Ali and a very nervous-looking Jen. "Some ghetto girl, who already had a black eye, confronted me about me trying to get with her boyfriend. It was stupid. I told her I didn't know what she was talking about. But when I tried to get in my car, she pulled my hair, and I had to defend myself. She ran when she heard the sirens, but the police did take a report with her full description."

Shaking her head, Lila let that sink in before asking. "Do you even know her boyfriend?"

Again with the exchanged glances, and now Lila could really feel her patience thinning. The moment the attendant recognized her, his eyes widened, distracting her momentarily from her thoughts. "Hey, you're—"

Lila immediately lifted her finger over her lips then pulled the hoodie over her head, glancing around in hopes that no one else recognized her. "Where are they taking you?"

"X-rays," the attendant answered for Ali, still looking a little star struck. "That and an MRI to rule out a concussion. But the doc ordered lots of X-rays since she's banged up in more than just one place, so this may be a while."

"It's just my ribs and hand," Ali said, sounding a little annoyed. "Mostly just my hand."

"And your head," Lila said then ground her teeth, frustrated that she'd have to wait to get more info from Ali.

Then she remembered the exchanged glances between her sister and Jen. The ride there took a while, and Jen was already there before Lila left the 5th Street parking lot. She had to know more.

"Okay, let's have it, Jen. What really happened?"

Jen's eyes widened. "What she said—"

"No." Lila shook her head, taking a step closer to Jen. "You know more. Who is this guy? Is Ali really seeing another girl's boyfriend?"

"No." Jen shook her head adamantly. "I think she knows him and maybe talks to him, but she's not seeing him."

Lila tugged Jen along with her to one of the empty corridors just outside the ER so they could have some privacy. "Who is he? What's his name?"

Jen shook her head, her eyes going wide. "Oh, my God, she told me when I got here, but I can't remember his name. I've never met him, so I don't know him. I think she met him when she interviewed him once for a story, so he's an acquaintance but not even a real friend."

Lila peered at Jen, wondering if maybe she was trying to cover up for Ali. Then something hit her. "Ali said the girl was ghetto. Does this have anything to do with the drug-dealing story you two were following?"

That sparked something in Jen's nervous eyes, and Lila knew she had her. "No." She shook her head, but it was hardly convincing.

"Jen?"

"It doesn't."

"*Jennifer,* you're lying to me and this is about Ali, my sister, being hurt or in danger. You know what that does to me, so I'm gonna ask you one last time. How is this related to those drug dealers? Did *they* rough her up? Is this jealous-girlfriend story bullshit?"

"No." Jen shook her head again. "It isn't. A girl and her friend really did confront Ali about her flirting with her boyfriend. But—"

"And her friend?" Lila asked, trying desperately to keep her cool. "So, there was more than one? Another girl or one of the drug dealers?"

Jen exhaled a bit loudly. "No, it was two girls, but the other girl didn't touch Ali; it was all this girl that claimed she has a boyfriend Ali was throwing herself at."

"Claimed, what do you mean claimed?"

"It's a long story and Ali made me promise—"

"I have time, and I don't give a shit what Ali made you promise. You really think I'm gonna just let this go? My sister's in there with a head injury and broken bones for fuck's sake. This is over, Jennifer. Whatever you two were keeping from me ends now. I wanna know everything."

"Okay, okay." Jen held her hand up. "It might have to do with that story we were trying to get. But we don't know for sure."

Lila did her best to listen without interrupting as Jen told her everything. Jen explained that, even after Ali had promised they wouldn't actively go out investigating the drug dealing story, they had. Only soon afterward, they found out that Marcelo knew the guy from his days of dealing back when. Jen said her brother only knew the guy's street name—Scar—but that he was still in touch with some of their mutual acquaintances in the neighborhood.

Marcelo confirmed what Lila had thought when she first heard about this—that Scar and his friends were, in fact, just small-potatoes drug dealers. As far as Marcelo knew from those acquaintances he kept in touch with, Scar was still a nothing but a pusher in the drug dealing world.

Ali said Scar had made it a point to let them know he knew who Ali and Jen were, by addressing them once by their first and last names. But because they lost interest in the story after what Marcelo told them, nothing ever became of it. That had been *months* ago.

"We stopped investigating altogether, and the guy never bothered us again," Jen insisted.

"So why do you think this is related?"

"A few weeks after Scar had made it a point to address us by name, he and his buddies were busted. Or so we heard. Marcelo heard about it and asked us if we'd had anything to do with it, but we didn't know anything about it until he told us."

Apparently, Scar got pinched and was put away months ago. Jen said they hadn't seen him or his buddies around since. She admitted that she and Ali were nervous that maybe he'd thought the same thing Marcelo had. That they'd had something to do with his getting busted. But they figured with him locked up they had nothing to worry about.

"Earlier this week, he was back," Jen said, and that made every hair on Lila's body stand at attention. "He didn't say anything to us, but Ali mentioned a couple of days ago that twice she'd caught him watching her as she'd walked to her car. She'd gotten the strange feeling he was following her. But she said she'd play it by ear since he hadn't done anything, and since Sonny's place was like Fort Knox lately, she felt safe enough. But"—she paused, unnerving Lila to no end— "Ali said he was there today."

"With the girl?" Lila asked, feeling ready to kill.

"No," Jen said quickly and obviously getting more nervous by the moment as Lila's attempts to stay calm wore thinner and thinner with every word Jen said. "She said she'd just seen him a few minutes prior to the girl approaching her by her car. It made her especially nervous because she saw him exchange glances with one of his buddies across the parking lot. It almost felt like they were waiting for her, so she'd hurried up. And that's when the girl approached her."

"What exactly did this bitch say to Ali?" Lila didn't even try to mask her anger anymore.

"She didn't finish telling me, but she did say the other girl with the girl with the supposed boyfriend had referred to her as Eva. Ali had me call Marcelo to ask if he knew her, and he said he's heard of her."

"Why do you keep saying *supposed* boyfriend?"

"Because Marcelo said last he heard Eva was married with kids."

"Wait. So, Marcelo might actually know how to track the bitch down? Get him on the phone," she said before Jen could even answer her first question.

Lila knew hunting Eva down was a bad idea. But there was no way, *no fucking way,* she wasn't going to. She'd do her best not to lose it completely if she did get a hold of her, but at the very least she was making sure this bitch got arrested.

## 25

## Sonny

As usual, the first thing Sonny did the moment his plane touched down in Los Angeles was check his phone for any possible messages or calls he might've gotten from Lila during his landing. She still hadn't responded to his emails, but he figured she must still be in training.

As unrelenting as the paparazzi still were, Sonny was sure they'd picked up on the fact that he was less likely to snap when he was alone as opposed to when Lila was with him. Lila had pointed out more than once now that maybe they should be grateful for their nonstop coverage. The publicity did help gain them fans and at the same time made it clear to any naysayers looking to cause problems that they were in fact crazy for each other.

"Sabian, what's the rush?" one photographer yelled out as Sonny dashed through the airport, anxious to get to his awaiting car. "You in a hurry to get back to Lila?"

For the first time in months, Sonny cracked a smile at one of them. "Yeah," he said, chuckling under his breath. "Actually, I am. Two days has been too long."

Too damn long. This was insanity. He'd been beyond annoyed with Banks when he'd told him he had two back-to-back promos out of town. With him living in Tinseltown, Sonny didn't understand why his agent couldn't just book all his promos in town.

Surprised that he'd responded to the photographers' inquiry and taking advantage of his obvious good mood, the paparazzi started more questions flying. Sonny didn't want to regret encouraging them the next time he was mobbed with Lila by his side, so he only answered one more of their questions, the one that had him smiling from ear to ear again.

"Are you in love?"

"*Absolutely*."

Since he had no new calls or messages from Lila when he landed, he didn't bother with his phone again until he was in the car. He scrolled through a couple from the numbers he recognized and then clicked on the text from a number he didn't. It'd been sent over an hour ago, but like most of the calls and messages from unknown numbers, he hadn't bothered with it when he saw it on the plane. The moment he clicked on it, he went numb.

**Sonny, this is Jen, Ali's friend. Something's happened. Call me ASAP please!**

He'd barely finished reading it when his finger hit the call button. "What happened?" he asked the second Jen picked up then caught himself before she could answer. "Wait. Are Lila and Ali okay?"

"Yes," she said quickly then added, "Lila is. Ali's in the hospital, but she's going to be okay."

After getting the name of the hospital, Sonny instructed his driver to head there instead of home then got back to Jenny, his heart already pumping hard. "Okay, so what happened?"

"Ali was attacked in the school parking lot."

Sonny listened with bated breath to the whole story. When she finally got to the part about Lila asking Jen for her keys so she could sneak past the photographers outside and then storming out of there in a rage, Sonny nearly lost it. "*What?* Where'd she go?"

"I guess Marcelo told her the general area where Eva could be found. He's meeting Lila, and they're gonna try to find her."

Normally the thought of Lila meeting up with Marcelo would irritate the fuck out of him. Now he prayed Marcelo would have the sense to calm her. At least she wouldn't be out there by herself running around like the mad woman he was sure she was feeling like.

"And you're sure Ali wasn't really seeing this girl's boyfriend?"

Sonny wasn't sure about their theory. Just because last Marcelo heard this girl was married with kids didn't mean anything. The guy had been gone for years. She could be divorced and now had a new boyfriend. Sonny had a bad feeling there was more to this.

From the injuries Jenny described, this girl must've been *pissed*. Jenny assured him that, as far as she knew, Ali wasn't seeing the guy. "*Maybe* she had a crush on him, but that's as much as she's ever let on to me."

"And she didn't know he had a girlfriend?"

"We didn't get a chance to talk for too long. Since we knew Marcelo knew the guys we'd been investigating from way back, we were busy on the phone with Marcelo for a while. Then Lila got here and then Ali was taken away for tests and X-rays. She's still not back; they're taking forever."

She explained how the nurse did warn them it might be a while. As soon as he was off the phone with Jenny, he tried Lila. No surprise she didn't answer, so he sent her a text.

**Take a deep breath and think this through before you do anything rash. You're better than this now, Lila. We both know this. Call me ASAP.**

He sent it, praying she'd come to her senses and just call him. He knew, if he could just talk to her, he might be able to talk her down.

They reached the hospital, and he rushed to the ER. Even with his generic ball cap and dark sunglasses on, heads turned, and an instant buzz filled the waiting room. Luckily, he was let into see Ali. "She was just brought back to her bed," the starry-eyed attendant said as she let him in.

Sonny rushed over to where he'd been directed, immediately spotting a very worried-looking Ali. "You have to go find her, Sonny," Ali said as soon as he was close enough.

"I will, but first I need to know more."

Seeing all the gawking faces as he made it through the crowded ER had Sonny closing the curtain around Ali's bed. The last thing he needed was to be interrupted right then. As soon as he had it all the way around her bed, he turned to Ali again. "Who's this guy the girl was talking about?"

The uneasy exchanged glance between the two girls only confirmed Sonny's initial gut feeling. There was more to this. "I'm not even sure if it's the same guy she's talking about," Ali said anxiously. "The only Leo I know is someone I interviewed for a story a while back and still keep in touch with occasionally, but there's never been anything remotely romantic between us. And unless he lied because it did come up once—as part of the interview . . ." she added, lifting her chin. "He said he didn't have time for a social life." She paused again to roll her eyes, almost annoyed. "He called women poison."

"Well, if this is someone he's been involved with," Sonny said as he pulled out his phone to see if Lila had responded at all but frowned when there was nothing, "then I can see why he'd think that."

"Oh, that reminds me," Ali said, reaching for her purse with her good hand. "I did text Leo to ask him about Eva earlier, but I hadn't heard back from him."

She fumbled with her purse, looking for what Sonny assumed was her phone. He turned to Jenny, who stood on the other side of the bed. "Jenny, call your brother. Find out what Lila's up to and if they found Eva yet."

"I can't call in here, but I've been sneaking texts," she said, pulling out her phone.

"Leo says he doesn't know an Eva," Ali said, staring at her phone screen. "That he's never done the girlfriend thing." She frowned as she finished reading his text. "Again, with the women are poison crap."

"Then who the hell is this Eva chick? You think maybe she mistook you for—"

"She's Scar's girl," Jenny said, looking down at her own phone. "Marcelo just confirmed it with one of his friends."

"Scar's girl?" Sonny asked.

"So, this *was* retaliation?" Ali asked, her mouth dropping open. "He must really think I had something to do with him getting busted."

Sonny shook his head as a mixture of confusion and alarm overwhelmed him. If Lila knew this now, she was sure to be thinking the same thing and probably ready to do some violent retaliating herself. He turned to Jenny again. "Does Lila know?"

"Yeah, and she's livid."

"Damn it," Sonny muttered. Did this guy not have a brain? Why would he tell her? "Tell him not to give Lila any more info. Tell him to lie if he has to—say he doesn't know anything else."

"My car was low on gas, so he's stalling by stopping at the gas station," Jen said, still reading her text. "He said he's gonna put air in my tires too."

"Good, 'cause something's not right here. This doesn't make sense."

"It makes perfect sense," Ali said. "Scar sent his girlfriend or maybe he didn't even have to. Maybe she was just waiting to get her hands on me."

"If that's the case, why the lie?" Sonny peered at her. "Why not just say that's what this was? Retaliation? It'd make more sense. If they really thought you'd ratted him out or something, this would at least be a warning to keep your nose out of his business from here on. What exactly did she say to you?"

Ali seemed to ponder it for a moment as if trying to remember. "Gosh, it happened so fast. I was rushing to my car, because of Scar and his friend. I had this strange feeling they were gonna come after me. Then out of nowhere, I hear 'Hey, bitch, you need to stay away from my man.' I didn't even realize she was talking to me until she got in my face."

Ali explained she said she didn't know what the girl was talking about then tried to get in her car when the girl pulled her hair.

Sonny winced at the visual. "That's when she started beating on you?"

"Hell no," Ali said with a smug smile. "I'm sure that's what she thought she was gonna do."

Ali explained exactly how everything went down. That's when something dawned on Sonny that had every muscle in his body going taut. "Why would they just come after you? Why not go after Jenny too? She's the one they saw taking the pictures, right?"

Before Ali could respond, he turned back to Jenny, who was busy tapping away at her phone screen. Sonny chose his words cautiously. "Who's your brother getting all this info from?"

Jenny glanced up from her phone and shrugged. "He has lots of friends on the street." She frowned before looking back down at her phone again. "Lots of connections for all the illegal stuff he's still into." She stopped talking and read something on her phone screen again then looked up at Sonny, eyes wide. "He says he knows exactly where Eva is at right now, where they can find her hanging out, but he hasn't told Lila."

"Tell him not to," Sonny said, hitting speed dial and ignoring the "no cell phones" sign on the wall.

The call to Lila went straight to voicemail. *Fuck*! Sonny was now convinced his gut had been right. Something about this smelled bad, only he couldn't be sure how much, if at all, Marcelo was involved in this.

"Marcelo's friends know you're his sister, right?" Jenny nodded, staring at Sonny quizzically. "And they know you and Ali are good friends?" Again, she nodded but said nothing else. "It's probably how Scar knew your full names and exactly who Ali was. Who her sister is." He didn't wait for her to respond this time. Instead, he started to walk out, stopping just outside the curtain. "Text me Marcelo's number and tell him to do whatever he has to keep Lila put."

Sonny rushed out to his waiting car in the parking lot. The moment the text with Marcelo's number came through Sonny called it.

"Hello?"

"This is Sonny—Sly Sabian—Lila's boyfriend. Listen to me. If you care at all about Lila, you won't tell her you know where Eva is."

"Dude!"

When Sonny heard Lila's angry voice demanding Marcelo tell her where Eva was, he knew he'd just blown it. Marcelo's phone was connected to the car's blue tooth and she'd heard him.

"Lila!" Sonny pleaded. "Don't do this. Just tell me where you're at and stay there. I'm coming to get you. This isn't what you think."

"Bullshit! Did you see what that bitch did to my sister?"

"But she didn't," Sonny started to say when the line clicked. "Fuck!" he roared, banging his fist on the seat.

# Lila

It was only a handful of the fabric around Marcelo's crotch area, but it'd been grabbed with enough fury to send the message. Lila wasn't bluffing. If he didn't tell her where that cunt was, she'd be reaching deeper and squeezing until he was screaming for mercy like a little bitch.

"She's at the park."

"What park?" Lila asked, squeezing the fabric a little tighter.

"Hollenbeck," he said, trying to pull her hand off his crotch. "Fuck, Lila! There, I told you. Get off me!"

She did only because she needed to start the car. "I will for now," she said through her teeth. "But if you're lying, my hand and your crotch *will* meet again. And this time, I'll grab a lot more."

Marcelo chuckled, tapping something into his phone. "I remember liking your hand there."

If Lila didn't still need him, she would've thrown his ass out of the car the moment he told her where this bitch was. But she did. She had no idea what this Eva girl looked like. She was trying to save herself from having to walk up to every group of people hanging at the park and asking if one of them was Eva. Ignoring the comment, Lila skidded out of the gas station. "And you're sure she's there, right?"

"It's what my contact told me. Said her whole little crowd is down there right now, which is another reason why this is a bad idea. I know you've always been able to defend yourself and you're trained to fight now to boot, but this is a *crowd* you're taking on, Lila. A crowd of thugs. Street-fighting thugs. They might even have guns on them. Think about it."

"I have," Lila said, motioning to his phone. "Call the police. Not the emergency line, just the police department."

"What for?"

"Just do it."

Marcelo stared at her for a moment, not saying anything. "Call them!"

With a huff, he started tapping at his phone screen again. "What do I say?"

"Nothing. It'll be on the speakers, right? I'll do the talking."

The ringing started through the speakers. When the woman answered on the other end, Lila calmly explained who she was and where she was headed: to Hollenbeck Park to talk to the girl who'd put her sister in the hospital after attacking her earlier that day. She told the lady there'd been a report made of the attack on the college campus parking lot, but the girl had gotten away, and this was their chance to nab her.

"Her boyfriend is a known felon, and clearly, she's no law-abiding citizen either. I suggest you get someone out there ASAP because I don't want to, but if I have to, I *will* take justice into my own hands."

The lady took a little more info from Lila, but couldn't give her an ETA on when she could get a patrol car out there. In no mood to argue, Lila hung up. They'd been warned.

"Are you out of your fucking mind?" Marcelo asked the moment she hung up. "You just called the cops on yourself, Lila. We both know you won't be doing much *talking*."

"You don't know that."

Marcelo scoffed, sitting back in his seat. "Bullshit. You're gonna tear that girl up, and the cops are gonna get there right when you're doing it. *God,* you're stupid."

"Fuck you, Marcelo! You don't know shit about my life anymore. Just 'cause *you* never will doesn't mean people *can't* change and I've grown."

She shook her head, deciding he wasn't worth her breath. Instead, she took a deep breath to try and calm herself, but instinctively she was already fisting and relaxing her hand. Lila *had* thought this through as Sonny's text asked her to. And she *had* grown, damn it. But this was Ali they'd fucked with. The visual of her sister's injuries, her holding her side in such pain, was too much to endure.

Lila had every intention of at least *trying* to stay in control. Only just as she had in high school when she beat the last girl who'd messed with her sister on school grounds, Marcelo hadn't been completely off in saying she'd called the cops on herself. She'd had ulterior reasons for it, aside from telling them where they could find their suspect at large. If she'd been afraid of killing that girl back in high school, had she done it somewhere where she would've had more time to beat her, she had even more reason to fear she might murder someone today. As calm as she was trying to remain, one smartass remark from the girl who attacked her sister so viciously, and crowd or not, she was certain today's beating might turn deadly—*if* the cops didn't arrive in time to save her.

Even before they turned onto the street alongside of Hollenbeck, Lila's adrenaline was already pumping. "This is *so* stupid," Marcelo said as they drove slowly looking for the girl.

"You sure you'll recognize her?"

"If I don't, I'll recognize her crowd," Marcelo said, taking in one of the groups they passed. "I know several of the guys Scar hangs with. This isn't them."

He shook his head again, exhaling loudly, driving home his point of this being stupid without having to say more.

"I'm doing this for Jen, too, you know. If they did this to Ali, then Jen must be next. Doesn't that worry you, asshole?"

"Jen's not the one flirting with this girl's man."

Lila turned to him, feeling completely exasperated, not to mention disgusted. "Are you fucking retarded? You still think this has anything to do with Ali flirting with this girl's man? Her man is who Ali and Jen were investigating. His ass got busted, thrown in jail, and they're blaming Ali and Jen for it."

"So, why did she say this was about Ali hitting on her man?"

"Because, you idiot, she probably meant to blindside Ali. She did come up to her from behind."

It amazed Lila how *infinitely* different her relationship with Sonny was compared to how it had *ever* been with Marcelo. She'd never dream of disrespecting Sonny like she so easily did this dumb ass. And Sonny would never dare speak to or treat her the way Marcelo did. But Marcelo just brought out the worst in her—always had. That she'd stayed with Marcelo for as long as she had was beyond belief now. One thing was for sure. Sonny had forever spoiled her for other guys. She'd never again allow any guy to treat her or make her feel any less special than Sonny did. But then again, she didn't think anyone would ever come close to making her feel what Sonny did.

"I don't know," Marcelo continued to argue. "Jen *did* say she thought Ali had a crush on the dude."

Lila's stomach dropped a little but quickly reminded herself this was Marcelo. "Didn't she just text you to tell you the guy this girl mentioned was Leo?"

"Yeah, but we don't know what Scar's real name is. Scar's just his street name, remember?"

Lila hadn't even thought of that. There was no way Ali would be crushing on some drug-dealing thug. That made no sense. She shook her head. No matter what the reason, even if, by some infinitesimal chance, Ali had developed a crush on Scar, that was still no reason for that bitch to do what she had to her sister.

"I don't know," Marcelo continued as only his stubborn ass could. "Maybe like she kept from you the fact that she was still investigating Scar, she's kept more from you, Lila. I mean look at you. You're out here ready to give someone a beat down even if it may get you locked up. She knows what a crazy ass you are. I'm not saying you two aren't tight enough. But maybe she keeps stuff from you to save you from yourself. Ever thought of that?"

Glaring straight ahead because she didn't even want to look at him right then, Lila tried to hide what his words did to her. As much as what he'd just said pissed her off, it also stung because she knew it was true. She hated the thought that Ali felt she had to keep anything from her because she was such a *crazy ass*. Sonny was right; she was better than this now. She had grown. At least she thought she had until she'd seen Ali's injuries. Someone else had done this to her baby sister and purposely! How the *fuck* was she supposed to *ever* control her rage over something like this?

"That's them," Marcelo said, pointing in the direction of a crowd huddled around a car in one of the parking lots. "I recognize that car."

"Do you see her?"

Marcelo was quiet, peering at the small crowd as they turned into the parking lot. The group of about ten turned, taking in the car as they got closer. Lila slowed just as they reached them, stopping in the middle of the parking lot. They all took her in now, and Lila saw the instant recognition in their eyes.

"I think that's her," Marcelo said in a lowered voice. "The one in the black, holding something to her eye."

Just the sight of the bitch ignited something inside Lila. "Are you Eva?"

"Who wants to know?" the girl asked, moving the hanky or whatever it was she held against her eye.

To Lila's surprise, it was swollen shut. It almost made Lila smile. She had scratches all over her face as well and a fat lip. She looked worse than Ali. Had *Ali* done all this? The visual of the huge lump on Ali's head assaulted her, squashing any desire to smile.

She yanked the keys out of the ignition and got out. "I'm the sister of the girl Eva beat earlier today," she said, slamming the car door shut with a purpose.

The idiot next to Eva with a big scar across his cheek smiled big. While Eva attempted to smile smugly, Lila saw it, the same fear she'd seen all her life in the eyes of anyone who knew they were about to feel her wrath.

"Yeah, she's Eva," the guy with the scar said. "What are you gonna do about it?"

"You need to turn yourself in," Lila said, taking a deep breath. "My sister was assaulted today, and someone *will* be held accountable."

Scarface laughed even while Eva remained quiet, the forced smile on her face gone now. "Yeah, I'll bet she's in the hospital. You should've seen the beating she took." He nudged Eva. "Go ahead, Eva. Tell this bitch to get the fuck out of here before you put her in the hospital too."

Though they attempted to be discreet, a girl and a guy behind the car were obviously videotaping the confrontation with their phones. The only thing keeping Lila from reaching out and grabbing the girl by her shirt to tell her one last time she needed to turn herself in, was the fact that she seemed hesitant to step forward.

The second time the guy nudged her, she jerked her arm away. "Stop it, *pendejo!*"

"My sister do this to you?" Lila asked, motioning to the girl's face.

When Eva didn't confirm nor deny it, Lila almost smiled in strange relief. Maybe Ali hadn't just stood there and taken a beating. But the urge to smile waned when she saw the exchange between Eva and Scar. That's when Lila remembered what Ali had said. The girl who attacked her already had a black eye when she'd approached her.

Glancing at Scar with all the stupid gang tattoos on his neck and the teardrop tattoo just under his eye brought back memories. For too long, Lila had allowed Marcelo to disrespect her, and while he'd never hit her because he knew she'd go batshit crazy on his ass, she knew too many girls in the neighborhood who did allow their boyfriends to slap them around.

Her eyes locked with Eva's, who didn't seem nearly as aggressive as her douche-bag boyfriend. "I could make that eye worse, Eva. *So* much worse."

For the first time in her life at a moment like this, Lila felt something other than rage. A strange calm came over her because she knew, if she unleashed her fury on this girl, she could seriously hurt her—or worse. Only as angry as she'd been earlier, she wasn't anymore.

Not only could this ruin her life, something told her she was missing something. Shaking away thoughts of her sister sitting in the ER in pain, she continued. "That's not why I came here. All I'm asking is that you turn yourself in."

"Nah, fuck that," *Pendejo* said, moving forward and once again nudging Eva. "She *fucked* up your skanky sister, made her squeal in agony like a filthy pig, and she'll do the same to you. No one's turning themselves in, you stupid bitch."

The buzzing in Lila's ears had started before the asshole finished talking. Just like that, everything she'd worked so hard to keep under control gave way. All the fury she'd felt from the moment Jen said Ali had been in a fight erupted. The visuals Lila had when she stormed out of the ER, visuals of going for the jugular and holding on for dear life until there was nothing but a lifeless body left inundated her, and she did just that. With a guttural roar, she went straight for the jugular.

# 27

# Sonny

Hollenbeck Park. It was the final confirmation Sonny needed. Both he and Lila had done enough interviews, dodging endless intimate questions about their relationship by giving vague answers. One of the ones they'd indulged the prying media with was their account of the night they met and their first kiss. Both had mentioned the park being near and dear to them. Of course, these assholes had chosen this place to reel Lila in.

"Pull in here!" Sonny instructed his driver. "That crowd over there. Take me there!"

Sonny's heart nearly pummeled through his chest when he saw the scuffle in progress, and then he saw it. It was a mess of people, shoving and holding others back, but as they got closer, what was really happening became clearer. Right there in the middle of what he'd first thought was a guy holding Lila back—maybe Marcelo—was Lila and a guy going at each other. There was one other guy trying to get in between them, but Lila looked enraged. Worse yet, the guy she was trying to hit was reaching out menacingly for her too.

The car had barely slowed when Sonny opened the door and jumped out. "Lila!"

His yelling didn't have much of an effect on the still-scuffling crowd. As soon as he was close enough, he grabbed the guy by the shirt with both hands and slammed him on the hood of the car but lost hold of him when the guy nearly slid off.

Scrambling, the guy moved off the car hood but stayed close enough. Sonny could grab him again if need be. Not surprising, not only did Sonny have the crowd's attention now, most held their phones up and he could already hear his name being murmured among them.

"That crazy bitch came at me, *puto!*" the guy yelled, tugging down his rumpled shirt, then turned to Lila. "I'm not the one who fucked up your prissy sister. She did, but then that's what happens when a skanky whore moves in on someone else's man!"

The girl he pointed at was one Sonny hadn't even noticed standing off to the side. To Sonny's surprise, Lila didn't react the way he thought she might to the guy's insult of Ali. She didn't even appear as enraged as she'd been when he arrived moments ago. Instead of responding to the guy, she was looking at Eva.

"Did he make you hurt my sister?" Lila asked Eva, quieting the buzz in the crowd.

When Eva didn't say anything, the guy started to. "What are you talking about—?"

"Shut up!" Sonny said, grabbing him by the shirt again.

"Did he?" Lila asked again in a voice so calm Sonny could hardly believe she'd gone from raging to this in such a short time.

Eva glanced in Scar's direction. "Don't look at him," Lila said calmly again. "Is he why you had a black eye before the fight? He put you up to doing this?"

Scar started to protest again, but Sonny shook him, still holding on to his shirt roughly. He was floored that it appeared Lila had figured this out without him having to explain it.

Eva shook her head but turned away when her one good eye began to glisten. Lila took a step toward her when the short but loud siren got their attention. Two squad cars with their lights on pulled up to them in a hurry. The crowd began to disperse.

"Everyone stay where you are," the cop said through the car's speaker. They all did as they were asked; then the cop got out of the car. "Who's Lila?"

"I am," Lila said, lifting her hand.

Scar, who'd tensed up considerably when Eva had turned away looking emotional, tried coming loose from Sonny's hold, but Sonny only held on tighter.

Eva and another girl appeared to be arguing about something. Their voices were hushed but just loud enough that Sonny could make out a few of the words like, "You have to" and "Don't be scared."

". . . she's in the hospital right now," Lila continued to explain to the officer. "But a report was taken and Eva's boyfriend admits she's the one who attacked her."

"He made me do it," Eva finally spoke up.

"You lying bitch!" Scar yelled as Sonny held onto him even more roughly now.

"She's not lying," the girl with Eva said. "I was there when he slapped her around and threatened that it'd be worse if she didn't do what he was asking."

"That's bullshit!" Scar muttered, shaking his head.

"It was supposed to be just a slap." Eva turned to Lila. "He said it'd be all it'd take to piss you off. But your sister got all crazy and shit."

"And then what?" Lila asked, turning to Scar, looking as disgusted as only she could. "You'd get me here somehow, egg me on, and then *she'd* take the beating, you fucking coward? For what?"

"Money, of course," Sonny said, grabbing Scar by the arm when he tried to pull away.

"I got this," the other cop said, taking Scar by the other arm and pushing him down on the hood of the car. "Hands behind your back."

"This is bullshit. Why am I being arrested?"

"He's on probation," Eva said quickly. "And he's been drinking and doing weed. Check the car. His stash is in there."

"Eva, you bi—"!

The cop didn't let him finish because he pulled him up by his cuffed hands then slammed him back down.

"Everybody else take a seat on that curb," the cop talking to Lila ordered. "Hands where I can see them. Not you," he said, motioning to Sonny with a smirk. "I know you're good."

"What about me?" the guy Sonny had seen trying to separate Lila and Scar asked.

"Especially you, Marcelo," the cop said. "Can't I go one week without having to detain you or one of your damn friends?"

"These aren't my friends!"

"Sit down!" the cop said, raising his voice.

Sonny eyed Marcelo, who glared at Lila but was smart enough to shut up and walked away to sit with the others. The cop holding Scar walked him to the back of his squad car then proceeded to search his car as Lila continued to give her statement to the other officer.

He called over Eva, who explained Scar's inane plan. It might've worked if they hadn't been so ridiculously obvious about it. Eva said, when Scar realized Ali was Lila's sister and that Lila was dating Sonny, he hatched a scheme to try and extort money out of them. He did his homework, reading every article about Lila and even had someone stake out 5th Street to see if he couldn't gain more insight on her. Because they knew Marcelo's sister was so close to Ali, he'd been unwittingly used to pass the word along to Lila about who Eva was and where she could be found.

Eva turned to Lila with pleading eyes. "It was just supposed to be going up to her and maybe push her or slap her. Scar didn't want her to know it had anything to do with him, so we came up with the idea that I'd tell her to stay away from my man. I chickened out last minute. This was supposed to have happened the other day, but I told him I wasn't doing it."

"So, he beat you?" Lila asked again in that almost foreign-for-Lila calm tone. Though it was laced with plenty of disgust.

This time the tears escaped the corner of Eva's eye, but she nodded.

"Did he do this to you?" the officer asked, motioning to her face.

"Yes and no—"

"You don't have to lie for him anymore," Lila said, reaching out to touch Eva's arm.

"No, I mean he did, but it wasn't this bad. Your sister head butted me today in the eye, and I had some other bruises already, but like I said, she got really crazy." She touched her eye gently. "I wanted to go to the emergency room, but he didn't let me. He said he didn't want you to miss me when you came looking for me because he was so sure you would."

The utter rage that Lila had rid herself of earlier was back in her eyes as she glanced at the car where Scar was sitting. Sonny slipped his hand in hers and squeezed. He didn't blame her. Even Sonny wished he'd get a few minutes alone with the asshole.

"I hope he's getting arrested," Lila said, turning to the cop.

"Yeah, he's going right back in, and he'll be in for a lot longer this time." He turned to Eva. "But I gotta arrest you too, sweetheart."

Eva nodded as if she'd already known it. Although the officer did say they'd be making a stop at the ER.

The ride home was a quiet one. Sonny could tell Lila had mixed feelings about the whole thing now. He understood why because so did he. They left Jenny's car with Marcelo and drove away in the town car. Sonny reached for Lila's hand and brought it to his lips. He kissed it softly. "I knew you'd come a long way, but you blew me away today."

Lila smiled, but he could see it was a bittersweet smile. She leaned her head against Sonny's shoulder, and he kissed the top of her head. "Just sucks that she'll have to pay for something that monster forced her to do."

"You know," Sonny said cautiously. "Looks and sounds like she got more of a beating than Ali did. Ali *could* drop the charges if she really wanted to."

Instantly, Lila lifted her face to look at him. "I feel bad for her, Sonny, but it doesn't take from the fact that she attacked my sister. Ali's hand—"

"Is broken in three places because of how hard she beat Eva." Sonny couldn't help but smirk despite the topic. "I knew your timid little sister was a spitfire the day I met her, but I didn't know she had all that in her. You should've seen the proud look on her face when she talked about having picked up a few things from you over the years. That knot on her head is from head-butting Eva so hard it swelled up Eva's eye as bad as it did. Said she learned the move in the self-defense class you insisted she take. And you heard Eva. Even she said your sister got all crazy." The bewildered expression on Lila's face made him smile. "I thought it from the moment she first grilled me, but now I'm sure of it. You two are definitely cut from the same cloth, baby. I'd say big sis did a damn good job of teaching Ali how to defend herself. I wouldn't worry too much about Ali taking care of herself anymore. Sounds to me like she enjoyed being the badass for once."

Lila began to smile then frowned. "She broke her hand in three places?"

"And she's proud of it, babe." Sonny chuckled.

The tug at the corners of her lips gave way to the disapproving frown she tried to give him. "Well, I don't want her turning into me either."

Sonny laughed. "Why? That's not a bad thing. She would've been proud of how you handled things today. And it's not like *she* went out looking to beat someone's ass." He kissed her when her brow lifted at the jab. "She was just defending herself. It's what you're supposed to do. Granted, breaking your hand in three places because you're beating on someone that hard is maybe going a little overboard. But hey, just like those girls at the club who came at you, it's the chance you take when you decide to attack someone. Sucks that it seems Eva didn't have much of a choice."

"Some would argue she did," Lila said with a solemn frown. "I'm sure it's not the first time he hit her, and unless she gets her shit together and does the smart thing—runs while he's in jail and has the chance—it probably won't be the last."

"Might not get that chance if she's locked up too."

Their eyes met, and for a moment, Sonny saw it again, that same foreign tenderness he only ever saw in Lila's eyes when she spoke of her sister and when she was she was gazing at him. "I'll talk to Ali when we get home. It's entirely up to her."

"Of course," Sonny said, kissing her softly. "I'm proud of you, baby. I didn't doubt for a minute that you had it in you to do the right thing. I just wasn't sure how goading she might be, especially once I figured out this was all a setup. I figured they'd say whatever they had to, to piss you off."

"Yeah, well that asshole finally did make me lose it. Not for a second did I think of lunging at her, not after I realized what he was doing."

"Can't blame you for that. I would've wanted to beat his ass too. Still," he said, leaning his forehead against hers. "You were amazing today."

"Thank you," she whispered. "And thank you for showing up when you did. He was bigger and stronger than I was, so I was this close to trying to gouge his eyes out."

Sonny laughed. "Just one more reason not to piss my babe off. Ouch!"

She kissed him softly then a little deeper until she had Sonny moaning. When she finally came up for air, Sonny stared at her, licking his lips. "*Damn.* What was that about?"

Sinking her teeth into her bottom lip, she gazed at him adoringly. "I didn't think I could feel any luckier than I already do to have you in my life. But after having to spend time with Marcelo today, there's no doubt about it anymore. I'm the luckiest girl alive."

Smiling big, Sonny's eyes went from her lips to her eyes. "That bad, huh?"

She shook her head, squeezing her eyes shut with a groan. "He just brings out the worst in me. And you . . ." She paused and smiled. "Well, let's just say the moment you got there today I was reminded how far I've really come. How different I am from the girl I once was long ago. And so much of it is because of the love you've filled my heart with, a love I never in a million years thought I'd feel until I met you. I love you so much, Sonny."

"I love you too, baby."

# 28

## Lila

Like every other video and photo taken of Sonny and Lila, clips of the confrontation between Lila, Eva, and then Sonny slamming Scar against the hood went viral. Fortunately, with Scar being such an asshole throughout the video, everyone agreed Lila had good reason to want to pull his tonsils through his throat. So, what Preston had feared, that she might lose sponsors, didn't happen. There'd been some talk of a lawsuit from Scar for his "injuries" from having been slammed onto the hood by Sonny. But with Scar's record and his probation violations piling up, the judge threw the case out and slapped the book at him. Ironically, the viral video helped. Sonny had only come to the defense of his girlfriend. He could've continued to pummel Scar once he had him on the hood. But he hadn't.

Lila couldn't imagine why Scar would be stupid enough to take such a chance just a week and a half after getting out of jail. Sonny said it's what greed did to people and he probably really thought he'd be getting a big payday out of this.

Even though Ali agreed to drop the charges after Lila explained everything to her, she didn't have to. Eva's defense was able to plea bargain. Because of the circumstances, Scar being a career criminal who was obviously violent, Eva had had good reason to fear for her life had she not complied with what he'd asked her to do. She also agreed to testify against him in the lawsuit Preston and her lawyers had *insisted* Lila file against Scar. On top of all the other probation violations and assault charges for hitting Eva, he was now also being charged with conspiracy to commit extortion.

Even though it'd only carry a misdemeanor punishment if he was convicted, they said it sent out a message to any other idiots who might get any funny ideas in the future. It also tacked on several more years to his already mounting sentence.

Just like before the whole Eva debacle, everything was back to perfect again. Lila went on to win the rematch against Mannering. There was no knock out again, and she'd won by decision, so there was already talk of another rematch.

They waited months before Preston gave the media a formal statement about Lila and Sonny's engagement. The whole world knew now. It still amazed Lila that the wives of 5th Street had called it so early on. Sonny and Lila or rather Slyla—which Sonny still hated the sound of—were dubbed US professional sports' royal couple.

Ali couldn't have been happier for Lila and Sonny. Lila was living on cloud nine. It was all too surreal. Her win had opened so many new avenues for her. Of course, Preston was quick to pounce on every lucrative endorsement deal possible, and she was high in demand as fitness *superstar* model as well.

Lila knew her career might've had the same outcome had she not met Sonny when she did, but her heart knew life wouldn't be as perfect as it felt now if she hadn't. She even wondered now if the outcome with Eva would've been so much different. Things could've ended a *lot* worse had her reaction been what it was back in high school. Seeing Ali hurt in the hospital like that would've had the pre-Sonny jaded Lila out for blood. What she told Sonny that day was true. If it weren't for him, she might not have had any sympathy for Eva. But she'd been there once herself, putting up with a disrespectful asshole and truly believing that's just what all men were like. Maybe someday Eva would meet someone who might make her see how wonderful it could truly be.

Ali and Lila walked in the front door together. To her utter surprise, Sonny was there and something smelled heavenly. Seeing him, even if it'd only been a couple days since they were together last, had her choking up.

She rushed to him, and he lifted her in his arms, kissing the side of her face as she buried it in his neck, chuckling. "I missed you too," he whispered in her ear.

Lila pulled away, wiping tears and feeling silly. "Why are you home early?"

"Today was my actual travel day. I just didn't tell you because I wanted to surprise you."

If she smiled any bigger, her face was going to hurt later. "What smells so good?"

"My mom stopped by earlier to drop off a special order I put in: tortilla soup and some *chile rellenos* with all the fixings. When I told her they were two of her *chiquita's* favorites, she freaked because they're two of her specialties. She's been waiting for the day she could make them for you. I was just warming everything up."

Sonny set the table, and they all sat and devoured the heavenly meal his mom made. Just as Lila sat back, stuffed, and patted her full belly, Ali got a text. It wasn't unusual that she'd be engrossed in her phone while they were trying to enjoy a meal together. She was your typical twenty-year-old. But Lila noticed the troubled expression.

"Something wrong?" Lila asked, sitting up.

Ali glanced up from her phone at Lila. "No, just a developing story Jen had some updates on." Ali got up, taking her plate, and excused herself to make a call.

As was the case lately, as much as she wanted to have been her usual sex-kitten self tonight, Lila felt exhausted. After taking months off her training, she'd gotten back in the gym this past week, and it was kicking her butt. No sooner had she leaned against Sonny in bed than she felt herself dozing off. "Sorry, I'm so tired," she murmured.

Feeling Sonny wrap his big arms around her and pull her to him tightly made her smile and inhale his masculine scent blissfully. "It's okay," he whispered against the top of her head then kissed it. "You get some sleep. We have the rest of our lives for everything else."

Lila smiled, cuddling up next to him. "Mmm, the rest of our lives. I love the sound of that."

*Earlier that same evening . . .*

## Allison

As much as Allison tried to concentrate and enjoy the delicious dinner Sonny's mom had prepared, it was *impossible* not to think of Beast. She felt so damn responsible for his having to hide out now. She was only glad Marcelo's friend had been willing to put him up for a few days until the coast was clear enough for him to leave town.

Nearly choking on her food when she read the text, she attempted not to look as panicked as this made her. So, she avoided making eye contact with either Lila or Sonny by keeping her eyes on the screen, and read the text again.

**Marcelo's friend was arrested tonight for possession with intent to distribute. He's in jail now, and while it might be okay for Leo to stay at his place still, Marcelo said there's a possibility his place may get searched for more drugs.**

"Something wrong?" Lila asked.

Allison glanced up at Lila as casually as she could and let her know it was just a developing story. But she couldn't sit still any longer. Grabbing her near empty plate, she excused herself to make a call.

For the millionth time, she thanked God there'd been too much going on at the time, and Lila had all but forgotten the name Eva used as the supposed boyfriend Ali was trying to move in on. On top of everything else Lila had, had to deal with, the last thing she needed was to know Ali was still in touch with Beast.

Jen explained again about Marcelo's friend Ron getting arrested. "Marcelo's not sure they'll search Ron's apartment, but if they do, that could be very bad for Leo, right? I mean didn't he already miss checking in with his probation officer?"

"Yes, he did. He had no choice. He *has* to lay low."

"Maybe you should call him and at least warn him. Let *him* decide."

"But he can't be seen on the streets, and I know he'll refuse my helping him sneak out."

"So, what are you gonna do?"

"How long ago did this happen?"

"Just now," Jen said anxiously. "Marcelo walked out of the 7-Eleven where Ron was being arrested. Ron's friends were let go, but they told Marcelo why they'd arrested Ron, and Marcelo called me."

"Good."

Remembering the stories Beast had told her about being arrested, Allison knew she had time before Ron got processed. She'd wait a few hours until Lila, who slept like the dead lately, was out for the night.

Allison didn't even consider calling Beast. He'd leave before she could get to him. He'd want no part of her helping him. It'd been hard enough to convince him to take her help when she offered to sneak him into Ron's apartment. But it was the least she could do. If it hadn't been for her telling him about Eva using his name when she'd attacked her, this may've never happened.

He'd been convinced it was no coincidence as Allison had begun to think. Eva assured her it was just a random name Scar had told her to use. But Beast hadn't bought it for a minute. With Scar so recently out of jail, he'd been sure there was more to it. Maybe someone was sending him a message.

Rushing around in her room putting together a small bag of her things, Allison shook her head. *God,* she could kick herself now for ever having mentioned it at all. He'd been livid because he thought maybe someone might've mistaken her for his girl—or just someone he cared about—and maybe that's why she'd been targeted. As if he hadn't already been so standoffish and reluctant to get any friendlier than their strictly business interviews. She'd tried to assure him it was all a setup for the sake of baiting Lila. That even Eva had testified that it had been. Still, he hadn't been able to just sit still and let it go.

Allison waited until almost midnight when she was sure Lila and Sonny were knocked out. Then she waited until she was just outside Ron's apartment to send the text she knew would worry Lila regardless, but she had to at least give her this. It might be days before this was taken care of. Rereading it one last time with a wince, she took a deep breath.

I had to leave very last minute and didn't want to wake you. It's that developing story I mentioned. I got a lead I have to follow up on. I may be gone a few days but DON'T WORRY. I'm fine. I'll check in often and be home before you know it.
Kiss, kiss, I love my sis!

With her heart at her throat, she hit send, got out of her car and hurried to the apartment, glad it was on the first floor. She lifted her hand, hesitating for just a moment before knocking on the door. Her heart pounded even harder when she heard noise on the other side of the door then saw the curtain on the side window move. "Beast?" she whispered.

The door opened, and there he was in all his glory in nothing but his boxer briefs with every tattoo on his bulging body exposed. His intense eyes devoured her from top to bottom just like they always did, making her heart spike further. Before she had a chance to say anything, he pulled her in and closed the door. Spinning her around in the dark room, he pinned her to the wall and pressed his hard body against hers. His snarled words against her ears both alarmed and aroused her. "What the hell part of 'you need to stay away from me' do you not understand, Jel?"

## Beast

### (Boyle Heights 2)

### Coming in 2017!

# What's next?

*Read an excerpt of Elizabeth Reyes's next release right here!*

## Girl in The Mirror

### By

### Elizabeth Reyes

***Chapter 1***

The beeping sound and the feel of someone's hand in mine was the only proof I had that I was alive. I couldn't feel or move any other part of my body and I couldn't see anything. I had no idea where I was, but something told me I was safe. I was being taken care of and then it dawned on me. *Who* was I?

A wave of terror swept over me. I felt my eyelids flutter in response to the overwhelming emotion. I don't know how, but I managed to control it and attempted to open my eyes, but I couldn't. The fluttering was erratic; then I heard a gasp.

"Maggie," a woman's voice, who I didn't recognize, whispered anxiously. "Maggie, can you hear me?"

*Maggie?* Was that me? I felt my throat constrict because I hadn't the slightest idea who Maggie was. I fluttered my eyelids again, feeling the warmth underneath them.

"Maggie," the woman said again; then I felt her hand on my cheek. "It's Mama. I'm right here, baby. Don't cry.

You're gonna be okay." I heard her sniffle as her words became more emotional. "Can you hear me, darling? Squeeze my hand if you can."

I did and she gasped again "Thank you, Jesus!" she said, and then she was crying.

I fluttered my eyelids until I started seeing specks of light come in and out. But I couldn't make anything out.

"Did you call for a nurse?" I heard another woman's voice ask.

'Yes!" the woman who said she was my mama cried out. "She's waking." She squeezed my hand. "And look. She's crying."

I heard more voices and beeping sounds, and then I started to feel more of my body as other parts were touched in different places. A big blur neared my face and spoke softly. "Maggie, this is Deandra. I'm your nurse. Squeeze your mother's hand if you can hear me."

I squeezed the hand holding mine again.

"Yes!" the woman said again still sounding very emotional.

"Are you in any pain?" Deandra asked. "Squeeze once for yes and twice for no."

I squeezed twice. How could I be in any pain when I couldn't feel anything? I wondered if maybe I was paralyzed. My eyelids fluttered nonstop in panic now. I needed answers.

"Do you know where you are?" Deandra asked, and I could shake my head but just barely.

"Do you remember the accident?" I shook my head again and this time managed to open one eye.

A petite blond woman with sunken tired eyes, leaning over me, held her shaky hand to her mouth as her face crumbled. "Hi, baby," she said through trembling lips.

It was all too much to take, and then I realized I could feel my face now too. Because like her I felt my face crumble, and my lips were also trembling. "Oh, baby don't cry," she said, wiping tears from my cheeks.

A tall dark-haired woman stood on the other side of the bed. "Do you know where you are?"

The warm tears streamed down my cheeks as I attempted to shake my head again despite the pain of doing just that. "Don't try to move," Deandra said quickly and I stopped. "Just squeeze your mama's hand."

I did twice. "She said no," the petite woman said.

"Do you know your name?"

Even though the other woman had called me Maggie, I still wasn't sure if that was really my name, so I squeezed twice.

Deandra nodded at the other woman as she brought her other hand to her mouth. "That's normal," she said in a reassuring voice then turned to me and smiled. "It's normal, sweetie. You've had some head trauma. Do you have any idea how long you've been out?"

Again, I squeezed twice, feeling more panicked with each question. She nodded again with a smile. "All normal. You've been through a lot. Sometimes it's better that you don't remember right away. Are you able to speak?"

I tried in vain to move my mouth, but I had so little strength I couldn't, much less muster the words from within me. So, I squeezed twice again.

The woman trying to hold it together, holding my hand, shook her head. "It's okay," Deandra said. "Don't exert yourself. It's still early. But tell me. Do you know who this is?" She motioned to the woman holding my hand. My eyes were on the woman who was supposed to be my mama, but I didn't recognize her. I squeezed twice, feeling the tear slide down my cheek again.

Deandra wrote something down on the clipboard she'd lifted from somewhere to the left of me. "It's okay," she said even as she continued to write then check her watch. "You're gonna be fine. You suffered a major head injury, but the doctors do believe with time and the right therapy you'll make a full recovery."

She said something else about swelling in the brain and then me being in a medically induced coma for weeks. All I could think about was I didn't recognize my mama in the least. And I couldn't remember a single thing about myself or my life.

After filling the complete blank in my head about who I was, I found out a few more things before succumbing to my exhaustion. I was just shy of nineteen years old. It was the summer just after my high-school graduation, and my ability to speak and the memories would come with time. I just had to be patient. Before I knew it, everything I worked so hard to do was gone when the exhaustion overcame me and everything went black.

~~~

Each time I woke, I stayed awake a little longer. And each time I made more progress. I was opening both eyes now, but I still couldn't talk. I could listen and understand everything my mama told me. I'd been in a car accident where I was thrown from the car. Aside from the head injury, I had a few broken bones, but otherwise, the doctors were calling it a miracle that it wasn't worse. Only, unlike previously when I couldn't feel anything, the pain was alive and well now—everywhere.

The day I was given a mirror so I could see what I looked like, I cried. I knew now my mother's name was Loretta. Since it was still so hard for me to see this stranger as my mom, she'd become Loretta to me in my head. It felt less weird than thinking of her as mom.

Loretta assured me I was still banged up and didn't normally look this pale with such sunken eyes. But that's not why I was crying. I cried because I hoped the day I looked in the mirror it would jolt a memory of some kind, but it didn't. I'd never seen the girl in the mirror. Just like with my mother, I didn't recognize *anything* about myself.

I could nod now and point and even sit up with the help of the adjustable bed. I could feed myself and even walk to the bathroom with the help of the nurses and my mom. I was still in a world of pain, but I was grateful for the progress, even though it didn't sound like it with all the moaning and groaning I did with every tiny movement. I had broken ribs, a broken collar bone, and a pelvic fracture that I was told was much worse in the beginning. I could walk now, but it still hurt like hell. My broken foot was in a cast, but I was able walk on crutches; though I still got dizzy a lot. But I still couldn't talk and I had *so* many questions. I got frustrated some days and cried often. They all kept telling me to be patient—that my progress was coming along better and faster than they'd anticipated.

As the days passed and Loretta sat and talked to me, I began to get the distinct feeling that she wasn't telling me everything. Was I alone in the car? Was anyone else hurt? As somber as she seemed sometimes, I had the ugly gut feeling someone had died.

She stared at me strangely sometimes. I didn't know if she was trying to evaluate me or what, but I was certain she knew something I didn't. Maybe my injuries were worse than the doctors were letting on. Maybe the doctors had told her to keep a close eye on something specific about me. But *what?*

While I'd managed to feed myself, I still didn't have full command of my hands and fingers. The therapist came every day, and we'd do exercises to strengthen my grasp. I was humming now too. I did it a lot because I wanted my voice back. My physical therapy for my hands and my humming and trying to figure out how to get the words to my mouth were my main objectives. Whichever came first would get me what I wanted—*communication*—whether by writing or talking.

One night I woke in the middle of the night. A feeling of utter dread consumed me. I didn't know what to make of it, only that something was very wrong. I'd begun to hum days prior. It'd been the closest I'd come to being able to talk. I was now beginning to make other noises besides just humming.

Humming again, I moved my mouth out of sheer frustration. "Muuuah!" The sudden sound out of my mouth startled me, and I brought my fingers to my mouth. "Muuuuuaaaah."

The excitement drowned out the dread, and I did it over and over. Soon the noise coming from my mouth started to sound like words. "Tah . . . taah . . . taahk . . . talk."

It took me a moment to figure out the foreign feeling in my face was a smile. I glanced around and saw it was only two in the morning, but I couldn't sleep now. I continued to practice speaking. I didn't do it in front of the nurses because I still couldn't form sentences, and I feared they'd insist I not exert myself. By the time Loretta arrived that morning just after eight, I was completely exhausted and ready to just pass out. But I'd finally been able to string a few words together, so I knew I wouldn't pass out. I couldn't. I had too many questions.

"I . . . can . . . talk," I said as soon as she put her things down.

Loretta froze, staring at me, then brought her hands to her mouth. Her eyes welled up, and she smiled, even as her brows pinched together in undeniable emotion. She rushed over and hugged me gently, mindful not to hurt me. "Oh, baby, I knew you would. I told you to just be patient."

"Mom," I said because it felt rude calling her Loretta even if in my head that's who this stranger was to me—Loretta. "I . . . don't . . . rem . . . member."

I felt her go tense, but she squeezed me one last time before pulling away. "It was a bad accident, Maggie. You sustained a significant head injury that the doctors assure me you'll recover from. But, of course, things are still going to be fuzzy. The doctors said it would take some time."

I shook my head as she smiled at me sympathetically. "I . . . don't . . . rem . . . member any . . . thing," I said, frustrated that the words came so slow. "Not . . . fuz. . . zy." Her eyes widened as what I just said seemed to sink in. "I . . . don't . . . rem . . . member . . . me. At all."

I felt the emotion overwhelm me because, for as much as I'd said it in my head, hearing the words made it so much more real. I brought my hands over my face but pulled them away just as quickly. I couldn't waste time crying. I could feel the exhaustion pulling me under, and I still had so many questions.

Her hands were at her mouth again, and she shook her head, staring at me wide-eyed. "You really don't remember *anything?*"

"*Nothing.*"

"Don't panic, okay?" I could see her trying to stay calm, but her eyes looked as anxious as I felt. "I'm sure this is just temporary. It was a pretty nasty injury you got."

"Was . . . I . . . alone?"

The horror in her eyes was my answer. I wasn't. There were others. Who? And how were they doing? Was it family? Because except for when she'd gone home to sleep at night, she'd been here with me every day. So, does that mean that they . . . ?

Something started beeping on one of the monitors. Loretta turned to it, looking worried.

"Who . . . else . . . was . . ." I shook my head even as I felt my heart thumping, when another beeping sound started and distracted me, throwing my wording off.

The nurse on duty today, Keisha, rushed in. "Ms. Maggie, what's going on?"

"It's her blood pressure, I think," Loretta said, anxiously staring at one of the machines.

"Sure is," Keisha said, frowning at the machine, then rushed to pull something out of a drawer. "Not good."

"Who . . . else?"

Keisha froze mid-stride and stared at me. "You're talking."

I nodded but turned back to Loretta. "Who?"

"She's doesn't remember anything," Loretta informed her. "Not me, not the accident, not even who she is."

Keisha continued to administer something into my I.V., turning back to my mom then to me.

"She's asking about the accident," Loretta added, her words full of apprehension.

Keisha's eyes went a little wide and she shook her head. "I don't think—"

"Who . . . Mom?"

I don't even know why I was crying or why I needed to know so badly. Just like the strangers Loretta said were friends and neighbors who came by on occasion to visit me—the ones with their faces etched in pity—whoever else had been in the accident with me I'd likely not remember anyway. I could only conclude that my getting so upset and worked up was because of my lack of sleep. My exerting myself to talk wasn't helping because I could barely keep my eyelids open. Then Keisha clarified why I was suddenly so tired.

"I gave you something to sedate you a bit. It'll help bring your blood pressure down and . . ."


## Chapter 2

"What day is it?"

Loretta glanced up from the tablet she was reading on. "Still Wednesday. Only it's evening now. You're talking faster now."

I thought about it for a minute then smiled. Only it was fleeting. The recollection of what we'd spoken of last came to me.

"Maggie, before you start." She set the tablet down on the chair next to her. "The accident you were in was a bad one. The details of it will be very upsetting to you, and the doctor said telling you about the accident needs to be done with much care and with a therapist present but later. Your brain is still in a very fragile state. Think of how far you've come. You don't want any setbacks, do you?"

As bad as I wanted to know, the last thing I wanted was to go back to the frustration of not being able to move or talk. Grudgingly, I nodded. "I have other questions."

She stared at me, her eyes full of apprehension again. "If it's anything that will upset you—"

"I don't think it should." I shook my head, even though I wasn't entirely sure about that. "Do I have a father? Siblings?"

She pressed her lips together and nodded as if she was willing to give me this one. "We're all alone, honey. Just you and me. It's why I've been so terrified you might not be okay. I've been a single mom since you were born. Your dad has never been around. My parents are both gone. My dad died when I was just a little girl and grandma passed a few years ago. The only sibling I have, I haven't seen in years. Her husband is in the military, and they move about the world all the time. Right now, he's stationed in Okinawa. She has small children and can't make the trip, but she's been in touch via the Internet."

So, it was just Loretta and I? "What about friends?" The friends who'd come by to see me didn't feel intimate at all. "Don't I have close friends?"

She nodded. "We'll talk about that when you're better."

My heart thudded. That was a clue. Maybe my friends were in the car with me. Maybe they were dead, and that's why they couldn't come see me. I nodded back to show I understood.

"What do I do? Go to school? Do I have a job?"

Loretta took a deep breath then smiled. I didn't know this woman very well, but I'd seen her be emotional on more than one occasion: from happy, worried, and deeply poignant. At the moment, I couldn't quite make out the emotion in her eyes. It was cautious or something. I could only imagine it had to be hard for her only daughter to not know anything about herself. "You just finished high school, and you've been in the process of touring different nursing schools that you were supposed to attend this fall."

"Nursing?"

I glanced around at the equipment in the room. All the equipment seemed so sterile and complicated.

"Yes. You've been talking about becoming a nurse ever since I can remember."

She told me a little more about myself. I was a very good student, pulled almost all A's in my high-school honors classes and I loved animals. I was an avid reader and even enjoyed writing. "When you're better, we'll go through photo albums and see if that doesn't help you remember stuff."

I hadn't even thought of that. I could hardly wait now. "Listen, honey," she said, sounding a bit more serious. "Tomorrow there will be an officer coming in here to question you about the accident. He's already been instructed not to tell you any of the details because of your delicate condition. He knows you don't remember anything, so all you have to tell him is just that. That you don't remember. You weren't even the one driving, so it's just a formality, but I wanted to give you a heads up."

"Is someone in trouble?" I asked, *hating* how devoid of any memories my mind was.

"No one's in trouble, darling. It's just that because of the nature of the accident they did need to investigate. But again, we'll talk about all that later when you're better."

~~~

The interview with the officer was probably one of the fastest in the history of police interviews. He asked if I remembered anything about the accident. I told him I didn't even remember anything about myself. That I had zero recollection about anything at all from my past. He wrote something down in his notebook and asked that if I did remember anything at any time to please give him a call. I agreed, he wished me a speedy recovery, and he left.

Several weeks after that, when it was determined there was no more risk of swelling in my brain and most of my fractures were near healing, therefore no more need for me to be monitored day and night, I was told I'd be released in a couple of days. But not before a psychiatrist I'd already spoken to a few times came in to see me first.

I still didn't remember anything about my life. Dr. Esh, my neurologist, hesitated to make a solid diagnosis because he said it was too early to tell. But it appeared I had a form of retrograde amnesia. I cried when I looked further into it because it was the worst kind. While there was the possibility of regaining some or all of my memories, I read stories of many who never had.

The doctor explained to my mother and me about PTBIS, post-traumatic brain-injury syndrome. He warned that there *would* be symptoms and I could experience them for weeks, months, years, or even for the rest of my life. It was daunting to hear the many different symptoms I might experience.

Many of what he called more common symptoms didn't seem too bad, such as difficulty with focusing, mood swings, inability to control certain impulses and urges, and emotional liability. But there were others that felt more alarming, like seizures, behavioral outbursts similar to Tourette's syndrome, and other stuff I didn't even know what they meant. Tinnitus, for example, which he explained is ringing or buzzing in the ears, was actually quite common after a traumatic head injury.

He gave us paperwork on PTBIS with links to websites that go over all the many other symptoms I might want to look up if I experience any. He explained there is no treatment for PTBIS itself, but that some of the symptoms could be treated or controlled.

The day the psychiatrist came to see me, I was surprised Dr. Esh said he needed to be there as well as a nurse. But I was even more surprised when he asked Loretta to leave the room.

"What's going on?" I asked, feeling nervous as she willingly walked out.

The psychiatrist, Dr. Patel, nodded as Dr. Esh began. "I wanted Dr. Patel here when I explained the details of the accident to you. I think you're well enough to know the traumatic and difficult details and agreed to be the one to tell you because it's still too hard for your mother to relive. She will also require therapy and is already getting some to help her deal with what she witnessed that day. Something no parent should ever have to."

This was news to me. My heart sped up. "She was in the accident too?"

"No." He shook his head. "But she was one of the first to arrive at the horrific scene and was forced to identify the bodies for the authorities."

"Bodies?" I asked as my insides went cold.

"Yes," he nodded, glancing at the only monitor I was still hooked up to: the one that tracked my heart beat and blood pressure. When it didn't show anything irregular, he went on. "There were two other passengers in the car with you who lost their lives: your best friend Shelby and . . . your sister, Madeline."

I couldn't breathe. I couldn't speak. Tears burned my eyes until I was crying and I was handed a box of tissue. How could I possibly feel grief over people I didn't even remember, but my heart ached despite that.

Even as they gently told me the rest, I continued to cry through it all. The doctor went on to explain my sister's convertible Volkswagen Bug had gone off the side of an embankment. None of us had been wearing seatbelts, and we'd all been thrown from the car. My sister's and Shelby's bodies had been badly mangled, and they were pronounced dead at the scene. I'd barely been clinging to life when I was found, and they said there was so much loss of blood it was a horrendous sight. It's why Loretta still couldn't even talk about it without falling apart and why she'd asked to not be there when I was told. It was simply too soon for her to stomach reliving the memories.

Dr. Patel said, even though I hadn't been driving, survivors' guilt was perfectly normal. I should expect to feel unwarranted guilt over having been the only one to survive, but there were many ways of coping with it. He encouraged me to talk about what I was feeling now there with him or any time later with my mother or in my therapy sessions. I should never hold it in. He warned that there would be a lot I'd be dealing emotionally in the weeks to come when it all sunk in and I got to see photos of my sister and best friend and learned more about them. I was given a list of websites and even local support groups for others going through something similar, not just dealing with amnesia but survivors' guilt, and he encouraged me to attend some of the meetings.

Dr. Esh said the *session* had gone well. It was the beginning of a long recovery, both physically and emotionally, but he was confident I'd do well with both. I was completely numb and couldn't even fathom the nightmare Loretta had had to live through. What she was *still* living through and would be for a long time. At least I didn't remember anything. How in the world had she done it all on her own?

She walked into the room after the doctors left, her eyes red and teary. "So, you know now?"

I nodded, still feeling too numb to say anything except, "I'm so sorry."

She rushed over and hugged me. "I am too, baby," she said, her voice breaking. "I just praise God he spared at least one of my girls."

We cried for a little together, holding on to each other until she pulled away, wiping her tears. "We'll be strong together and get through this. We've already gotten past the hardest part. Dr. Esh said he's releasing you tomorrow."

I didn't even get the chance to try and regain some of my past by going back to the home in Huntsville, the town I grew up in, because Loretta informed me that, just when the accident happened, we'd been in the process of moving. She'd gotten a promotion, but the position was in Denton, a city over three hours away from Huntsville. But she assured me she'd take me back to visit and see the schools I attended and my old neighborhood once she could. Only she'd already taken so much time off from work to be with me in the hospital, so it might be a while.

While it was disappointing to not get to go back and at least see if anything struck a memory, I was almost positive it wouldn't. Loretta did point out buildings and such that I should've remembered, such as the Little Caesar's pizza where I worked last summer, my very first job and the water park just outside our town that she said I had season passes to, so I must've spent a lot of time there. None of it sounded the least bit familiar. As we drove farther out of town, she pointed out places we'd stopped at when driving in and out of town. It was terrifying to not remember *anything*.

Weeks after I'd been out of the hospital, we got the okay from my new doctor in the new city we lived in for Loretta to tell me the rest of what I still didn't know about my sister. I thought I'd prepared myself. But nothing could've prepared me for what she still had in store for me.

## Coming This Spring!!!

## Add to your GoodReads shelf now!

Stay tuned for the cover reveal, more teasers, and release date!

Also, be sure to visit my website for more updates on what else to expect this year!

Elizabeth Reyes debuted her first novel under her pen name **Amanda Wylde** in 2016 Remi's Choice. Read more about her alter ego and the entire first chapter of **Remi's Choice** at http://elizabethreyes.com/alter-ego-amanda-wylde/

# Also by Elizabeth Reyes

There's a difference between whom we love, whom we settle for, and whom we're meant for.

Things sizzle when these fighters meet their romantic matches outside the ring.

If there's one thing I learned my whole life, time and age are but an illusion.

"Maybe he was just a friend," Sarah suggested.

Angel smiled, shaking his head. "No such thing as guys and girls being *just* friends."

# ACKNOWLEDGMENTS

First and foremost, I'd like to thank God for getting through 2016. It was an especially trying year for my family, and we're not out of the woods, but we can at least see the light at the end of the tunnel. Without my faith in the Lord that this, too, would one day be just an unpleasant memory, I don't know how I would've made it through the year.

With that said, I'd like to thank my readers for your patience and sticking with me even while this has been the longest I've gone since the beginning of my writing career without publishing an ER title. I know you've all been waiting for so long for this one, and I appreciate your patience and love. You, too, are who got me through this past year. I love you and thank you all SO much!

As always, thank you Mark my "assistant," my everything. Without your love and support, I KNOW I would've thrown my hands in the air as I felt like doing so many times. Thank you for the optimism when it was SO hard to find. I love you.

Thanks to my two grown "babies" for continuing to believe and encourage me not to give up on my dream "job," despite the uncertainties of self-publishing these days.

I'd like to thank my longtime and loyal bloggers, who after all these years have stuck with me It's hard to believe I'm going on year seven of this incredible journey! You guys have been a HUGE part of my continued success, and I thank every single one of you from the bottom of my heart!

I lost a few beta readers this year because life happens. But I'd like to thank my longtime STILL WITH ME beta readers: Emily Lamphear, Theresa Wegand, and last but CERTAINLY not least, Amanda Clark. Hootie, your humor was especially appreciated this year. Thank you, my friend!

A VERY special thank you to my "critique partner," JB Salsbury! Your input has been invaluable to me. Not to harp on the year I had, but for so much of it, I felt totally out of it. Like I'd even lost my writing mojo. Your words of wisdom helped to put everything into perspective. It felt like magic after reading your feedback; it was like a light bulb each time. Your very honest and helpful suggestions were PERFECT and I CANNOT thank you enough!

Thank you to Theresa (Eagle Eyes) Wegand, my one-stop superhero, beta reader/editor/formatter, listener to all my whiny rants/vents and obsessive worrying. This time around they were THICK.=/ As always, your work is impeccable, and I can't say enough about it. I hope to be working with you for years to come! And thank you for sticking with me, too, even with everything that's changed.

Thank you to Amanda Simpson of Pixel Mischief Design for my cover art. You're an amazing talent and awesome to work with. 2017 is looking promising already, and I can hardly wait to see what masterpieces you come up with for me next!

Shout out to my street team "Team Reyes!" To my admins, Leslie Cary, Jenn DaSilva, Delashawne Acevedo, Sarah Mannering. I'm so happy to have had the pleasure of meeting you finally. Dela, it's gonna happen, I promise! It's ridiculous that you live the closest to me, yet you're the only one I haven't met in person! >.< I will make up for that VERY soon. I promise!

Lastly, *gracias a mi "par de consentidas"* for making me laugh so much and ALL your love! I'm truly blessed to have readers like you two and all my other royal sisters!

# ABOUT THE AUTHOR

USA Today Bestselling Author Elizabeth Reyes was born and raised in southern California where she lives with her husband, Mark and their two adult children, Mark & Megan, a Great Dane named Dexter, and one big fat cat named Tyson.

She spends most her time in front of her computer, writing and keeping up with all the social media, and loves it. She says that there is nothing better than doing what you absolutely love for a living, and she eats, sleeps, and breathes these stories, which are constantly begging to be written.

**Representation:** Jane Dystel of Dystel & Goderich now handles all questions regarding subsidiary rights for any of Ms. Reyes' work. Please direct inquiries regarding foreign translation and film rights availability to her.

For more information on her upcoming projects and to connect with her--she loves hearing from you all—here are a few places you can find her:

Website: www.ElizabethReyes.com
Facebook fan page:http://www.facebook.com/pages/Elizabeth-Reyes/278724885527554
Instagram
Twitter: @AuthorElizabeth
Amazon Author page
Email EliReyesbooks@yahoo.com

Add her books to your Good Reads shelf

Join her FB Street Team for exclusive giveaways, excerpts, read alongs, book chats and much much more!

She enjoys hearing your feedback and looks forward to reading your reviews and comments on her website and fan page!

Made in the USA
Middletown, DE
04 June 2020